FROM SLAVERY TO SEGREGATION

FROM SLAVERY TO SEGREGATION

RECKONING
WITH
WHITE SUPREMACY
IN THE
AMERICAN SOUTH

———

KEITH M. FINLEY

LOUISIANA STATE UNIVERSITY PRESS
BATON ROUGE

Published by Louisiana State University Press
lsupress.org

Copyright © 2024 by Louisiana State University Press
All rights reserved. Except in the case of brief quotations used in articles or reviews, no part of this publication may be reproduced or transmitted in any format or by any means without written permission of Louisiana State University Press.

Designer: Kaelin Chappell Broaddus
Typefaces: Miller Text Roman, text; Alternate Gothic Compressed Black, display

Library of Congress Cataloging-in-Publication Data

Names: Finley, Keith M., 1973– author.
Title: From slavery to segregation : reckoning with White supremacy in the American South / Keith M. Finley.
Description: Baton Rouge : Louisiana State University Press, [2024] | Includes bibliographical references and index.
Identifiers: LCCN 2024012720 (print) | LCCN 2024012721 (ebook) | ISBN 978-0-8071-8133-1 (cloth) | ISBN 978-0-8071-8336-6 (epub) | ISBN 978-0-8071-8337-3 (pdf)
Subjects: LCSH: Southern States—Race relations. | White supremacy movements—Southern States—History. | Racism—Southern States—History. | Slavery—Southern States—History. | Southern States—Politics and government.
Classification: LCC F220.A1 F56 2024 (print) | LCC F220.A1 (ebook) | DDC 305.800975—dc23/eng/20240710
LC record available at https://lccn.loc.gov/2024012720
LC ebook record available at https://lccn.loc.gov/2024012721

This book is dedicated to my beautiful wife, Jessica, who, despite my shortcomings, remains my best friend, zealous supporter, and moral compass.

CONTENTS

Acknowledgments ix

Introduction 1

1. Forged in Conflict: The Origins of Defense 17

2. The Essential Mythology 48

3. The Link and the Albatross 80

4. The Connecting Thread 112

5. The Difference This Time 145

Conclusion 177

Notes 187

Bibliography 213

Index 243

ACKNOWLEDGMENTS

Many people have either directly or indirectly assisted in this book's production. Friends and colleagues at Southeastern Louisiana University have made my twenty-year stint there a pleasure. In particular, Samuel C. Hyde Jr., has done more to advance my career than anyone. I owe him a debt of gratitude that I can never fully repay. Mr. and Mrs. Jack Gautier graciously endowed the C. Howard Nichols Professorship, which I held for the previous three years. This award proved of immeasurable assistance throughout the writing process. Likewise, I extend recognition to my many students, both undergraduate and graduate, who have inspired me to seek a narrative of the past that is relevant in the present.

Rand Dotson at LSU Press warrants special recognition. He believed in the book even when the author had doubts. Similarly, the outside readers of the manuscript went above and beyond the norm in offering suggestions and recommending much-needed revisions. Because of them, this is a much better book. My copy editor, Dabian Witherspoon, also warrants special recognition for his careful scrutiny of this manuscript. His attention to detail saved me from several embarrassing errors. He has been a pleasure to work with.

Several members of my family also deserve special recognition. My parents remain steadfast supporters of all of my endeavors. My boys, Joseph and Joshua, have grown into fine young men and have started families of their own. I could not be prouder. To my granddaughter, Camille, welcome to the family! The exuberance and curiosity of my daughter, Grace, fills my heart with joy. She remains a blessing and a source of constant amusement. Thanks to her, the Christmas tree in the Finley home makes its annual appearance before the end of October! Finally, my wife, Jessica, to whom this book is dedicated, deserves special attention. From the first time we met, she has been my tireless companion and helpmate. My life has been immeasurably enhanced by her presence in it. Words of gratitude fail to account for the manifold ways she has lightened my load and uplifted my spirits. Whenever in doubt, I turn to her for reassurance and support. She has never failed me.

FROM SLAVERY
TO
SEGREGATION

Introduction

As the American people sheltered at home during the coronavirus pandemic in May 2020, a video of a white Minneapolis, Minnesota, police officer with his knee on the neck of a lifeless Black man, George Floyd, went viral. Floyd's death sparked waves of protests across the nation and raised a number of unsettling questions regarding the state of race relations in America. Although the exact sequence of events that led to his death remains uncertain, the indelible image of the deceased Floyd in a law enforcement submission hold remains the salient feature of the incident. For those who viewed the election of President Barack Obama in 2009 as the harbinger of a post-racial America, it was a sobering reality check. The summer of 2020 became a watershed moment in American history as the nation experienced a profound racial reckoning that followed not only Floyd's death but that of other African Americans, including Breonna Taylor and Ahmaud Arbery, at the hands of whites. Americans, who previously had given little thought to the problem of racism, were awakened to the reality of ongoing injustice. Many came to realize that white supremacy was not just a relic of the past, but a problem in the present. In the years following that fateful summer, a contentious debate over the dark forces that shaped America's history has consumed the country, and terms such as "systemic racism," once largely confined to the academic universe, have entered public discourse. This book unravels the history of white supremacy found in the American South and offers insights into the malleability and longevity of this insidious ideology. Indeed, there is no better time than the present to assess the historical roots of white supremacy in the South and, by extension, the United States as a whole.

Scholarly interest in all aspects of southern history remains considerable. Today, students of the region can learn about the South in books that grapple with the history of the region from the top down as well as from the bottom up and from an array of perspectives including that of groups once neglected by scholars. Indeed, the number of monographs that address some aspect of southern history is dizzying, providing a daunting challenge to both scholars and their graduate students who crave insight into the region. Whether one is interested in the piney woods of southeast Louisiana and upcountry South Carolina before the Civil War or the cities of Atlanta and Charlotte following the landmark *Brown v. Board* verdict, a book or several books are likely available to whet his or her appetite.[1] Historiography in all fields of southern history is vibrant and constantly opens new vistas for exploration by challenging convention. Researchers are now examining the South within a larger national and even international framework rather than as a discrete entity. Similarly, historians are pushing back the boundaries of the comfortable chronology that once dominated regional studies and are uncovering truths about the South that were formerly obscured owing to the narrow strictures imposed by previous scholarship. No longer wedded to the confining periodization established by their predecessors, contemporary historians are exploring the long duration of the threads that shaped the region. History, after all, is best understood as a continuum not a series of isolated events that fall neatly into a preordained timeframe. By exploding widely accepted "eras" in southern history, today's scholars are successfully tracking themes in regional development from germination to mature form that often overlap periods previously viewed in a myopic manner. For example, Reconstruction historians, who once worked primarily in the 1865–1877 framework, have pushed the margins of the period outward to 1862 on one end and the start of the twentieth century on the other. In doing so, they have enriched our understanding of the South while challenging conventional interpretational models. Likewise, civil rights scholars have adopted a "long" narrative by finding the origins of that fight much earlier in the twentieth century than previously considered.[2] Despite these important developments in historiography and the ongoing dialogue regarding the threat of white supremacy, comparatively less attention has been given to the broad sweep of ideas that informed the racial orders constructed by white southerners. Michael Perman's *Pursuit of Unity*, which spans both the Old and the New Souths, demonstrates the value of adopting a meta-level approach to this issue and casts light on the nuances that many scholars have demonstrated on an infra level in their more narrowly defined research projects. Perman's work underscores the presence of common threads that unite different eras of the region's political history, including the one-party and filibuster traditions.[3] A deeper analysis of the ideas that shaped the threads divined by Perman is needed.

This study provides an analysis of the key features shaping white southern identity over the expanse of the nineteenth and twentieth centuries as explained in the region's proslavery and pro-segregation arguments. It treats the South's two racial systems as part of the same whole rather than as discrete entities rooted in different time periods. Scholars reading this book will likely enumerate legions of individuals and events left unaddressed in its pages. The intention here is not to account for everything, only to engage the most salient and oft-repeated themes used in defense of the South's race-based social orders. These frequently touted arguments reveal the main elements of southern culture precisely because of their repetition across time and space. These beliefs, in turn, became fixtures in regional life for generations and continue to echo in the present. White defenses of slavery were naturally different from the defenses of segregation because the nature of the two institutions deviated in clear ways. Nonetheless, the arguments favoring these institutions shared an array of common traits that are a primary focus of this book. This work offers an analysis of mainstream white southern thought in the nineteenth and twentieth centuries while also shedding light on the larger American struggle with racial injustice which, although most pronounced in the South, impacted the entire nation. It captures the essence of white attitudes across two centuries, highlighting the evolution of regional thought concerning race and politics as well as the themes that tied disparate eras in southern history together and that in many ways still influence the South today. Likewise, it underscores the intense passion and often emotional nature of white attitudes regarding race which made them exceedingly difficult to discard. Southern whites grew up in a world in which race was woven into the cultural fabric; its ideology reinforced at all life stages and its precepts evident in both public and private institutions. Ultimately, an examination of the long history of white supremacist rule sheds much light on America's contemporary racial reckoning.

Over the past six decades, historians have uncovered many truths regarding southern history but none as important as the primacy of the African American community in bringing about the changes addressed in this book by adapting to and ultimately thriving in the face of racial oppression that spanned generations. Prior to the 1960s, scholars tended to depict the enslaved and those victimized by Jim Crow, especially prior to WWII, as passive participants in the swirl of events around them. Today, historians link the efforts of the Black community to changes once believed to have originated from other sources. For example, the Emancipation Proclamation once conceptualized as both a shrewd and ethical endeavor undertaken by President Abraham Lincoln is currently viewed as something that was initiated, in part, by the enslaved themselves. As northern armies headed South, they became lightning rods for those in bondage who recognized that Yankee soldiers represented freedom, even if at the time the sole purpose of those troopers remained to preserve the Union. Army commanders were forced to manage the wave of runaways who entered their ranks on the fly. Naturally, they looked to Washington for guidance on how to address the situation. Compelled to provide battlefield commanders with a plan, Lincoln issued his Emancipation Proclamation, which transformed the role of federal troopers from conquerors to liberators.

The twentieth-century grassroots civil rights movement is similarly understood as a central factor in prompting federal action to address the egregious racial injustice evident in the South. Part of a larger Black liberation fight that was international in scope, the American civil rights movement played a pivotal role in toppling Jim Crow segregation by providing the impetus for political change. The literature makes clear that African Americans throughout the twentieth century challenged the evils of segregation in both overt and covert ways. Whether those challenges took the form of communist-inspired workers' cooperatives among Black Belt farmers in Alabama or the pushback against Jim Crow separation on public transportation networks undertaken by service members returning from World War II, Black southerners were an integral part of the drive for racial justice in the twentieth century and were the single most important force behind civil rights advances.[4] This book seeks not to challenge the centrality of the Black experience in the age of slavery and Jim Crow; instead it aims to understand the worldview of white southerners who witnessed the challenges to their racial order all around them yet chose to define those challenges as the product of external forces. The white South's willingness to deceive itself is a crucial aspect of the region's development. Insulated in thought and devoted to the notion of a docile Black underclass, most white southerners simply failed to grasp the revolutionary democratic movement for change that developed, in part, because generational prejudices prevented them from seeing what was so plainly manifested around them.

Resistance to integration as well as to emancipation took multiple forms—many of them the same, many of them different. An analysis of the struggles for both racial orders reveals evidence of how much segregation's defenders looked to the region's past, just as it underscores the lessons the region learned from the devastating Civil War. In the end, the history of the twentieth-century South is irreparably linked to the centuries before it. One cannot understand the ferocity of resistance to *Brown* without having an awareness of not only how the South emerged after the Civil War but also of the ideas that paved the road to disunion in the first place. Segregation had its origins in the institution of slavery. The fate of African Americans in the first half of the twentieth century was in many ways sealed by emancipation. In America, segregation without slavery was unthinkable since the Civil War that freed the slaves and the Reconstruction period that attempted to define the rights of the freedmen were a part of the same whole. True, there exists ample evidence of discontinuity in southern history. No one who came of age in the wake of C. Vann Woodward's career can think otherwise; discontinuity is, after all, a feature of this book.[5] But so is continuity in the form of a commonality of perception regarding race, in the sense of being assailed by outsiders, and in the similar appeals to the highest secular authority in the pantheon of regional and American beliefs, the Constitution. Revisiting the often odious writings and racial musings of the South's past is crucial to understanding the region's development and its current circumstances. The intellectual shackles that shaped the negative mandates birthed by the region's racial inheritance require an understanding of the threads that guided the region's development. A detailed analysis of the traditions that buttressed the South's racial order represents a crucial step on this path.

White preservers of the status quo in the nineteenth and twentieth centuries left behind a voluminous body of literature in their defense of regional racial customs and in what they perceived as the relationship of these institutions to the American political tradition. In its coverage of the antebellum period, this book explores the treatises composed by well-known proslavery thinkers who wrote extensively on the alleged need to maintain slavery. Pamphlets, articles, and essay compilations were widely produced in the first half of the nineteenth century to defend the institution of slavery, especially once abolitionist sentiment gained momentum. Many of these publications diverged widely in terms of the main contours of their arguments and the various theories they pulled together in making their case. These publications shed light on the broad constellation of ideas and shared intellectual heritage that bound the region's white inhabitants together. The public commentary of the region's antebellum political leaders is similarly explored for the insights provided concerning the outward face of the proslavery fight. In most cases, regional political leaders mirrored and often directly borrowed the ideas espoused in popular proslavery tracts, indicating the broad support for the basic assumptions contained therein. These ideas found expression in state houses, public squares, and newspapers. Politicians often served as the primary conveyors of southern ideas to the outside world. The antebellum white southern milieu was infused with a coterie of arguments and platitudes concerning race and politics that solidified into dogma as the Civil War approached. Popular regional ideology, in turn, faced a severe challenge owing to the failed secession effort and bitter Reconstruction period. This book traces these ideas as they were adjusted in this tumultuous period and follows their reinvention as the foundational doctrine of Jim Crow.

It has been said that the South learned nothing from the Civil War. This assertion certainly rings true when one considers the rapid return of a race-based social order following the Civil War and the resurrection of a conservative states' rights philosophy upon the removal of Reconstruction Era Republican governments. The New South that took shape following the war demonstrated its continued reliance on the intellectual tradition inherited from the Old South. At the same time, the conception of its place in the global arena had changed for good. Southerners in both the antebellum South and the Confederate States of America sought to project their will on the national and international stage by ensuring the perpetual expansion of their economic interests. After the war, southern aspirations were trimmed, focusing primarily on survival and isolationism, revealing a significant departure from the past. Despite efforts to afford the freedmen full legal and political equality during the period of federally sponsored Reconstruction, white southerners demonstrated they were as yet unprepared to accept their former bondsmen as equals. They would continue to resist the expansion of democracy in the region for decades to come while adopting a siege mentality that saw all external criticism against the South, along with concentrations of federal power, as grave threats.

Segregation's defenders adopted many of the same approaches as their antebellum forebears in championing the South's second racial order. The books, pamphlets, articles, and public musings of Jim Crow's champions are likewise examined in this work with special attention given to how many features of the proslavery worldview found expression in the twentieth century. When Jim Crow segregation emerged in the South, the region's civic leaders and public intellectuals forged a defense of the institution that solidified as time went on. The South of the twentieth century teemed with an array of commonly employed defenses for segregation that appeared in venues large and small by mid-century. Borrowing heavily from the intellectual threads found in the Old South, denizens of the New South ultimately crafted a racial order within the comfortable ideological confines that had long existed in the region. What emerged in the twentieth-century defense of segregation powerfully underscores how intellectual traditions, even discredited ones, mattered profoundly in shaping southern thought. At the same time, the avalanche of published and unpublished musings in defense of slavery and Jim Crow powerfully revealed the constant need in the region to buttress and defend the status quo, reinforcing in the minds of the region's white citizens that they lorded over a system that not only benefitted them but was also absolutely essential for peace and stability. These theories carefully framed the widely touted narrative of a distinctive and superior "southern way of life," which revolved around the presence of a race-based social order.

White southerners came to view their battles in defense of slavery by the mid-nineteenth century and segregation by the mid-twentieth century not strictly in regional terms, but increasingly in national ones. In both centuries, they argued that the actions of those opposed to the region's racial orders were using the South as a cudgel upon which to lay waste to the American political system. Because of this, their defense of regional racial customs attempted to transform themselves into crusaders for the heart and soul of the nation. Time and again, white southern apologists sought to reconfigure their fight into a larger national one that they claimed might focus on southern racial matters at that time but one day would threaten everyone's basic liberty. It is not difficult to discern in this rhetoric the causal chain that resulted in the infamous "southern strategy" popularized during Richard Nixon's 1968 presidential run. Indeed, white southerners had employed this messaging since the nineteenth century. Today, many scholars link the massive resistance fight of the mid-twentieth century to the rise of modern conservatism and its racially coded narrative of private property and individual liberty.[6] This book not only lends credence to this supposition, but it also points to the need to look back further in southern and American history to find the true origins of such conservative thought. Massive resistance proved an immediate precursor to many modern conservative ideas, but its basic intellectual threads derived from earlier generations. By joining the white intellectual world of the antebellum era to the age of Jim Crow, this work reveals an unbroken intellectual heritage that ultimately gave rise to later twentieth-century conservatism.

Understanding this story is essential to comprehending America's history and does much to shed light on contemporary politics and modern racial turmoil. Although the tactics utilized in defense of the region's racial orders changed with time, the ideas that buoyed these systems transcended generations and indelibly shaped the South's development.

Context is a critical element when sketching the broad contours of intellectual thought that shaped southern history. Chapter 1 offers an overview of the manifold historical forces that drove the region's development—or, at least, white perceptions of it. It provides a broad synthesis of the South's evolution from the early days of slavery in the colonial world to the unraveling of the Jim Crow order in the mid-twentieth century. By offering a glimpse of the main political chronology that shaped the white southern narrative of this period, the chapter provides a birds-eye view meant to contextualize the thematic approach found in subsequent chapters. Southerners in the early-nineteenth century embraced the federal constitution of 1787 and used its protections to launch an aggressive expansionist campaign westward, with an eye toward eventual overseas growth, resulting in a critical conflict to determine whether the North's or the South's imperialist impulse would control the west and define broader national policy.

Time favored the more populous North. As check after check on southern expansion brought about by growing northern control over Congress became evident, the South sought to safeguard the institution of slavery, along with its growth, amidst a mounting chorus demanding change. In both the nineteenth and twentieth centuries, the South found itself occupying a minority status while being assailed first by abolitionist forces and later by civil rights advocates.

Externally driven change, at least as conceptualized by those who dominated the political order, visited the South by way of the Civil War, compelling the region to reimagine itself along the comfortable lines provided by race in the ensuing years. Only a perceived second wave of external pressure drove the region away from its racially defined sense of normal and, in the process, put to rest the odious rule of white supremacy that had long shackled the region. Along the way, both small and large episodes of African American day-to-day grassroots resistance were summarily overlooked by white southerners who placed their own struggles in the context of a larger "us versus them" dichotomy with "them" in this instance representing external, typically northern, forces. In the process, terms such as "siege mentality" and "beleaguered" were increasingly used to describe the South and proved instrumental in shaping regional identity going forward. Whereas the Old South was boldly expansionist with an overtly imperialist outlook even as it began adopting a siege mentality prior to the secession drive, the New South was always intensely insular. Twentieth-century southerners sought not the formation of an integrated empire in the Americas as their forbears did; instead, they desired the continuation of their familiar racial order in a fast-changing world. There would be no exporting Jim Crow. In the 1900s, southerners were less the preservers of what they considered a superior socioeconomic order that slaveholders in the first half of the nineteenth century once believed in; they had been transformed into the "beleaguered" defenders of a system hoisted upon them by war and a biracial inheritance. By their reckoning, segregation still proved a superior system when contrasted with the teeming racial unrest found in the North; however, its presence proved more of a social necessity, owing to alleged Black lawlessness, rather than an economic imperative as once argued by white southerners in defense of slavery.[7]

Following the initial contextual chapter that offers a synthesis of the key social and political battles that shaped southern history across the two-hundred-year period addressed in this book, each subsequent chapter tracks a key theme found in southern thought across the nineteenth and twentieth centuries. The remaining chapters assume a basic chronological framework in which an idea central to white southern arguments in defense of the region's racial systems is analyzed from its point of origin in the antebellum era, through the period of dislocation and social change brought by the Civil War, to its reappearance in the age of Jim Crow. By adopting this approach, the work captures the evolution of several disparate strands in southern thinking and explains these iterations in the context of the swirl of events that influenced them from start to finish. Each chapter thus renders a complete picture of individual concepts that anchored defenses of slavery and segregation across a wide expanse of history by focusing on the words of the people who reflected and shaped southern thought in the past and who gave life to much of the political discourse found in the region today. In addition to tracing lines of continuity, the book also illustrates threads of discontinuity as they emerged over time. Ideas, concepts, and strategies formed in the antebellum age often did not reemerge intact after the Civil War. Shifts in emphasis or direction developed as the swirl of perceived challenges confronted by the region changed. This book investigates these evolutions as well.

Chapter 2 focuses on the essential mythology of the South. It examines the southern worldview by exploring the ideals espoused by the region's white citizens and assessing the values regional denizens held dear. By necessity, the musings of white southern influencers are taken at face value without excessively dwelling on the logical inconsistency found throughout their body of work. Understanding the past requires examining historical actors in the context of their times. As such, southern talk of paternalism in the antebellum order, for example, is accepted not from the modern perspective where it is dissected as an outright lie but as a facsimile of what white southerners believed existed around them at the time when they penned their ideas. By the same token, the myth of tranquil race relations that allegedly existed in the Jim Crow Era South is treated in the same manner as the alleged paternalism found in the antebellum period. Wedded to a racialist worldview in which skin color determined everything, southerners restored the rule of white supremacy by adopting a significantly modified paternalist narrative that dwelled on Black depravity instead of alleged white magnanimity—although the latter construct also remained a feature going forward. Looking at the mythology that permeated the South opens a window into how citizens in the region viewed themselves by illustrating what they aspired to be and how they desired to be perceived. Likewise, it points to a fundamental naiveté regarding the aspirations of the region's African Americans who proved anything but content with their situation, yet whose struggles scarcely found mention in white southern treatises. Both feared and reviled, African Americans found themselves victims of violence and discrimination while heroically struggling to carve out a niche in a region determined to hold them back.

Chapter 3 captures the most unsavory of all of the region's rhetoric—its vile ideals on race. Nothing exemplifies the thinking of the white South more than its compulsive effort to depict the world in racial terms. Racist beliefs dating back generations found full expression in the nineteenth- and twentieth-century South as the region defended its race-based social orders from external criticism. From the "school of civilization" model touted before the Civil War to the fears of Black retrogression and licentiousness stressed in the age of segregation, the South and race are inextricably entwined. A belief in a strict racial hierarchy with whites at the top of the social pyramid remained ever-present throughout the period covered in this book. Even as the racialist perspective that shaped the American worldview gave way to the concept of cultural relativism in the twentieth century, white southerners clung to racial beliefs that had long shaped the region's outlook. Wilbur Cash's "proto-Dorian convention" never went out of style in a region where race always mattered. The nature of the crude discourse which served to validate the inhuman racial orders the South defended is without question disturbing. Nonetheless, these race-infused arguments offer the clearest window into the "mind" of the South as it, in effect, influenced the entirety of the region's intellectual thought. The strictures established by race shaped political, social, and economic discourse in the region. Even when not directly referenced, race proved omnipresent. Its tentacles spread in all directions, giving voice to a myriad of beliefs regarding individual rights and freedoms that over time assumed a less racially charged form. To understand the meaning of race to the white South is to understand much of the region's history. Similarly, the echoes of past prejudices continue to shape ongoing racial discord in America. Before such thinking can be fully eradicated, its history must be grasped.[8]

Chapter 4 explores the region's rigid adherence to a narrow interpretation of the Constitution predicated on the inviolability of state rights in the face of federal prerogatives. Indeed, this conservative assessment of the Constitution rivals only race in terms of its importance in the region. Support for a strict interpretation of the Constitution is a clear thread informing southern arguments for generations. Southerners always claimed that their assertions regarding slavery, and later Jim Crow, derived from the Constitution. Written into the document were essential safeguards for the institution of slavery and in its Bill of Rights was included protection of private property in all forms including, southerners argued, human chattel. By carefully linking their fight to the very document that gave rise to the American government, southerners cast all efforts to alter the region's racial orders as not just assaults against the South but affronts to the legacy of the Founding Fathers, as well as harbingers for the destruction of the nation. Segregationists, in turn, embraced the same alarmist attitude and carefully highlighted a broad series of cascading calamities that would follow any and all efforts to alter the region's racial order. Far from perverters of the Constitution as often charged, white southerners depicted themselves as the true preservers of the document as the founders intended. Throughout the period, white southerners described their racial order in the same manner as their forebears did, labeling the Jim Crow edifice as both divinely and constitutionally sound. In the South, the U.S. Constitution was interpreted as protecting its race-based social order, providing it cover from charges of injustice. Outside of the region, of course, southern efforts in both the antebellum and Jim Crow eras to tie their fight to the Constitution and the Bible were often derided as illogical and immoral by those committed to racial change. Inside the South, the region's African American community—by peaceably asking for a seat at the table—served witness to the hypocrisy around them. Despite activist accusations, the region, according to southern spokesmen, represented an essential check against the forces bent on subverting the nation's inheritance. Combatting the drive toward unchecked political power and the trampling of state authority allegedly embodied in the abolitionist crusade and later the civil rights movement served as the publicly touted rationale for the fight to safeguard the South's racial institutions. When before a national audience, white southern politicians stressed their fight was neither about race nor selfish sectional interests. Instead, it was a battle for all Americans as their bedrock institutions were allegedly threatened by the nefarious forces calling for racial change. Whether it was South Carolinian John Calhoun demanding protection for the "concurrent majority" in the Old South or Georgian Richard Russell calling for a return to the founding principles of the republic in the modern South, white southerners supported an inviolate notion of the Constitution that remained fixed to an idealized understanding of the events of 1787. This emphasis on a static Constitution locked in the late eighteenth century still resonates with regional voters.

The final chapter explores the South's response to the "moments of truth" in the region as reflected in the period surrounding the raid on Harpers Ferry in 1859 and the election of Abraham Lincoln in 1860, as well as in the wake of the *Brown v. Board* decision in 1954 and the *Brown II* verdict in 1955. In the "moments of truth" selected in this study, signs of discontinuity were plainly evident even if the goal of preserving white rule remained the same. When slavery came under attack in the lead-up to secession, the southern states rallied together, worked together, and eventually left the Union together. The region coalesced around the need for uniformity of action against the many perceived threats rising against it. True, many southern politicians operating on the national level were long attuned to the fact that control over the process of territorial expansion was continually slipping away from the South, endangering the future of the region if it remained in the existing Union. It is one thing for a handful of politicians representing wealthy landholders to sound alarms at a distant threat; it is quite another thing when a series of sensationalized events appeared to usher in an era of outright hostility against the South. John Brown's Raid transformed often desultory commentary on abolitionist schemes into a tangible and immediate threat to southern survival. White southerners were now paying attention to the national political scene like never before, and they were frightened by what they saw. The failure of the northern populace to wholeheartedly condemn John Brown's raid on Harpers Ferry coupled with the election of Abraham Lincoln, whose Republican Party supported limiting the growth of slavery, represented the final straw. With northerners controlling both chambers of the national legislature and the executive branch, southerners saw no alternative save for leaving the Union to preserve their "way of life" before the increasingly hostile national government moved to destroy it. President-elect Abraham Lincoln did not directly assert his wish to destroy slavery, but to slaveholders, it was only a matter of time before he and the hated Republican Party made such a move. It was far better to strike from a position of strength than to suffer death by way of a thousand cuts, they rationalized.

Similar to the process that unfolded when slavery came under sustained attack in the nineteenth century, segregationist politicians in Washington recognized that the battle against Jim Crow would be ceaselessly waged against them long before the majority of the region's citizens awakened to the idea. As early as the New Deal, and certainly by the end of World War II, the region's leaders grew concerned about their ability to sustain segregation. Slow change over time might raise a few concerns, but something more impactful was required to spur public fears. In the Old South, the twin blows of the Brown Raid and the 1860 election served as the catalysts for widespread defiance; the modern South needed a similar looming threat to spur white resistance. The 1954 *Brown* decision provided an immediate challenge to the segregationists' "way of life." Integration was coming to the region. The only thing undecided was the exact moment. Paranoia quickly gripped the region, resulting in the mobilization of an array of campaigns designed to thwart the ruling. Southerners in the era embraced the concept of "massive resistance" to mitigate what the region's whites considered an affront against long-cherished social norms. Despite considerable discussion of concepts such as interposition, the white South responded in something other than a unified fashion. Rather than forge a united front, the region adopted a scattershot approach in which each state, and each town in many cases, chose what white stakeholders considered the best option for handling the dilemma posed by integration. Federal efforts to integrate rim South states were met with an array of resistance efforts—as had earlier assaults mounted against Jim Crow's periphery—that were steamrolled by the might of national power. Whereas in the antebellum era, southern U.S. senators and representatives decried the election of Lincoln and bid their chamber colleagues a peaceful farewell to go it alone outside of the Union, twentieth-century southern political leaders on the national level worked within the federal system for most of them understood that the only true recourse for the South to slow the advance of progress was to gum up the legislative process via filibusters and procedural maneuverings. With many national leaders taking a backseat, the South lurched into a period of general lawlessness in locales where racist demagogues stirred the faithful for a final act of defiance before succumbing to change. If the South was of one mind on the need to maintain white privilege by whatever means necessary, the remainder of the nation, certainly was not. Isolated and marginalized, southern leaders limped into the final fight to safeguard their racial order with an air of defeatism which never crossed the minds of the founders of the southern Confederacy—at least not in its early days. Pockets of chaos emerged in the region, but in the end, its leaders and citizens curtailed their resistance efforts and admitted defeat much like their forebears did against "overwhelming odds." Abandoning any notion of an apocalyptic battle to the last measure, the white South gave up the ghost of Jim Crow after failing to thwart what they labeled federal hegemony by trying to work within the system that allegedly created the region's problems. Indeed, the myth of the "Lost Cause" which provided solace to a defeated Southland after the Civil War perfectly framed the final days of Jim Crow. The effort to protect segregation from inside of the political system met with the same failure as southern efforts to preserve slavery outside of the federal union. In the end, white southerners in the twentieth century conceded the field and abandoned large sections of the cities and towns they once vigorously defended against even token integration in exchange for lily white suburbs farther afield where they could again lay claim to their individual rights and liberties as they believed their forebears once did.

The collapse of *de jure* segregation marked the end of an important intellectual link to the antebellum era that stressed the sanctity of a race-based social order. For almost two centuries, the American South carved out a position that placed it in the crosshairs of the larger union, first via its unbending adherence to slavery and then in its obsessive devotion to segregation. Neither race-based order withstood the onslaught of change forged by the march of modernity and the push for greater democracy. As the South dug in its heels in defense of race and a static interpretation of the Constitution, the remainder of the nation evolved, however slowly, to embrace a fluid interpretation of the document that adapted as the country grew. A nation founded on principles of natural rights could surely not remain a country that sanctioned slavery, just as it would not remain a power that permitted segregation to persist under its flag. Whereas the nation at large marched toward change within the purview allowed by larger cultural shifts, the South remained mired in a stagnant outlook that permitted little growth. As Jim Crow breathed its last fetid breath, the region's citizens began the process of picking up the pieces from the wreckage, but they did not abandon all of the themes that once flowed inexorably from the need to defend racial privilege. Indeed, still prevalent in the region following the end of segregation was a devotion to individual property rights, a distrust of outsiders and the might of the federal government, and a narrow construction of the Constitution that underscored the connection between the modern South and the centuries that preceded it. Despite their troubling origins in the southern defense of regional racial institutions, many foundational tropes of white resistance efforts still inform voting behavior and shape policy preferences among the nation's suburban electorate. Its influence and the satellite beliefs it gave life to did not merely vanish in the 1960s following the passage of sweeping federal civil rights laws. The constellation of ideas that emerged during the early nineteenth century became so ingrained among a large section of the electorate that they survived the deaths of slavery, the institution that gave them life, and segregation, the institution that sustained them. Overt appeals to race are increasingly viewed with abhorrence no matter where they are uttered, yet their vestigial remnants are not far removed from contemporary political discourse as America's current racial reckoning underscores. Race still shapes the contours of the region's, and the nation's, politics, albeit in a more coded form, at least when compared to previous centuries where overt and vile prejudice found full expression. Today's interracial electorate serves as the ultimate check against the resurrection of direct appeals to racial intolerance, rendering the states' rights conservatism of the present infinitely more colorblind than its previous manifestations. The South will no doubt continue to depart from its race-obsessed history with the sins of the past hopefully serving as guideposts to future generations of how easily an educated citizenry can go off the rails if ensnared in an echo chamber of narrow provincialism.

1

Forged in Conflict
The Origins of Defense

The American South remains a region with a rich and often violent history that shapes its present. Despite evident changes, such as the rise of megacities, the influx of immigrants, and a shift away from an economy rooted in agriculture, many still consider it different, a place shaped more by its past than anywhere else in America. Below the Mason-Dixon Line, one does not need to look far for the threads of continuity that tie the past to the present. Explorations in southern history reveal that both continuity and change often exist side by side. Evidence of discontinuity is equally balanced by examples of stasis. The defense of the "southern way of life" as manifested in the arguments for slavery and segregation illustrates change. At the same time, it reveals a transcendent ideology rooted in white supremacy. To unravel the nature of this peculiar region, one must start at the beginning.

The introduction and spread of staple crop agriculture in the region—first with tobacco in Virginia and later with cotton, thanks to the invention of the cotton gin—determined the South's destiny. Its future became linked with the whims of international market prices for its commodities. An economy of scale governs staple crop agriculture, making success in the pursuit incumbent upon acreage under plow. The white population in colonial America proved too small for large-scale farming while the use of indentured servants proved too fraught with potential difficulty. Episodes such as Virginia's 1676 Bacon's Rebellion underscored the pitfalls of relying on voluntary servitude. In the end, servants would go free, entering a world where good land was scarce and economic competition fierce. Marginalized young men pushed to the periphery of established settlements represented a volatile demographic. Governor William Berkeley and the ruling elite of colonial Virginia learned this lesson the hard way. Labor thus was at a premium in colonial America. Planters needed a permanent solution to their labor woes and found slavery the perfect fix.[1]

African slavery was nothing new in the European world. Indeed, the Spanish had employed it long before the British and became staggeringly wealthy in the process. The aggressive conquest of wealthy empires in the western hemisphere coupled with the use of a captive labor force made Spain a global superpower while offering others a blueprint for a similar pattern of exploitative relations. Profit-driven British merchants originally trafficked humans for others before they began supplying their own nationals with slaves. When they did, American colonists found the solution to their labor shortage. Although some in Anglo-America flirted with the notion of emancipating slaves in a manner similar to that employed with indentures, it became evident that African slaves promised the greatest economic reward when viewed as lifelong possessions. In short, freeing slaves represented a lost investment. Questions of morality rarely entered the capitalist dialogue. It simply did not make fiscal sense to invest in property only to relinquish it before maximizing profit. For large landholders, it was a win-win scenario. They now had a bountiful labor supply with no fear of losing a worker at the cessation of a contract. A slave's tenure was for life, terminated only by death. The same rule applied to a bondsman's progeny. Abolishing slavery after it had successfully provided a solution to the labor crunch struck many as unthinkable. Southern colonies with large numbers of slaves had already invested too much in the institution to concede to its dissolution. More than money governed attitudes toward manumission. In a colony like South Carolina, for example, the Black population was in the majority. Many feared that emancipation would unleash a political and social revolution leading to anarchy. The future of the region and its system of coerced servitude became entwined; separating one from the other could not be accomplished without bloodshed. Slavery thus remained an integral part of the region's identity and the very basis of its social order.[2]

As the American colonies formally severed their ties with England in 1776, the rhetoric of Revolution that resonated with words like "liberty" and "freedom" no doubt weighed on the minds of slaveholder and slave alike, and it prompted an important dialogue in a land where race-based slavery was openly practiced. What became apparent, at least for the colonies that relied on plantation agriculture, was that revolutionary zeal extended only toward colonial relations with the mother country, not to the slaves. Antislavery sentiment always existed in the United States and before it under British colonial rule. Moved by revolutionary fervor, a number of northern states eradicated the institution in their borders in what some call the First Emancipation. These locales took the Revolution's clarion call of freedom literally and gravitated either toward immediate or gradual emancipation as a result of the revolutionary experience. Regardless, in a region where slavery did not represent the lifeblood of the economy, such a step represented more symbol than substance. Ultimately, slavery was challenged in the fledgling nation almost from the start of its bid for independence. The issue would wax and wane in importance over the years but never go away. Each generation born into the slave system on either end of the whip represented another step removed from the early days of the institution in British North America when many considered African slavery akin to indentured servitude with a finite labor contract. Some most notably Benjamin Franklin wanted a final showdown over abolition as a means of securing the spirit of the Revolution. To do otherwise was to sacrifice principle for expediency. Most did not see it the same way as they considered preserving the fragile nation, forged in battle yet still rife with internal conflict, the most important objective and the surest way to secure the Revolution. Delaying legislative action on slavery until a later date emerged as the preferred method of dealing with the crisis. Too much was at stake to do otherwise. An examination of the U.S. Constitution that eclipsed the short-lived Articles of Confederation underscores that Franklin and his vision of the Revolution did not represent the majority opinion.[3]

The United States Constitution, the bedrock of the republic, further enmeshed slavery into the national order and made the long-term future of the institution inextricably linked with that of the nation as a whole. Vast fortunes resulted from slavery and vast fortunes would, in turn, disappear if the institution's demise came about by any means other than the absence of profitability. America's founders certainly felt uncomfortable putting the term "slave" in the Constitution; after all, most of them had participated in the revolutionary movement in which slavery represented the antithesis of the republican ideology they embraced. With the memory of the Revolution recent, it remained best in the eyes of the Philadelphia delegates to keep the name of the decidedly un-republican institution of slavery out of the document. Despite the use of euphemisms such as "all other persons" to describe the enslaved in the US, slavery found all the protection it needed in the Constitution. It was an essential part of the emerging American fabric and an issue that fell beyond the scope of the new government being created in Philadelphia. In perhaps the most widely quoted proslavery comment made at the Constitutional Convention, South Carolinian John Rutledge remarked that "religion and morality had nothing to do with this question . . ."[4] Often overlooked is the complicity of non-slaveholders in safeguarding the institution. For example, Oliver Ellsworth, who represented Connecticut in Philadelphia, echoed Rutledge's comments when he championed the notion that the federal government should stay out of the slavery debate altogether as "the morality or wisdom of slavery are considerations belonging to the states themselves."[5] With sentiments such as these finding expression in debate, the safeguards for slavery provided in the Constitution are not surprising.

Article I, Section 9 is often touted as a sign that some of the founders harbored deep reservations regarding slavery. In it, convention delegates observed that the transatlantic slave trade–euphemistically labeled "the migration or importation of such persons as any of the states now existing shall think proper to admit"—could be prohibited by Congress starting in 1808. If anything, this provision reflected reservations concerning the loss of life associated with the middle passage, not necessarily with slavery itself. This remained a subject that divided the framers. As a result, they obfuscated rather than confronted the institution directly or meaningfully in the document. Even more illustrative, the new government planned on profiting from the transatlantic trade. When one considers that all such "imported" persons were subject to federal taxation, the link between the new union and slavery becomes clear. In the end, slaveholders at the 1787 convention had little to fear from future prohibition as they knew that the natural domestic increase amongst their chattel would more than offset the loss from external sources. Important, too, came the realization that domestically raised slaves had distinct advantages over imported ones. They already knew the language, they were a generation removed from the "primitive" state, they were born and raised in a subservient environment that better ensured "docility," and they had already been acclimatized to the "new world" environment. In short, slaves purchased on the domestic market proved a much better bargain than those imported either from the volatile Caribbean or from distant Africa. With the life span of a typical southern slave eclipsing that found elsewhere in the western hemisphere, the slaveholding interest saw little reason to trifle over the future loss of the Atlantic slave market. They already had all that they needed at home.[6]

Although slaveholding representatives found their interests protected by the Constitution, it is evident in hindsight that the document also created a federal system that ensured regional conflict. Historian Peter Onuf has argued that sectionalism sprang directly from the nature of the Constitution. The document balanced the power of population with the number of states, a decision that made voting blocs whether regional, economic, or some other construct pivotal for the protection of minority interests. Clearly, the agrarian South with an economy predicated on plantation slavery possessed a population far below that of the mixed urban and rural economy developing in the North. Inevitably, the U.S. House of Representatives would become a stronghold of the increasingly slave-free North owing to its apportionment being determined by population. In the Senate, each state, regardless of population, had two delegates—which clearly benefitted the less populous slave states. In the short term, representatives from slaveholding states viewed the purpose of the national government as being limited to safeguarding southern interests by permitting territorial expansion and negotiating favorable treaties that opened global markets to the region's agricultural commodities. Slaveholders had every reason in the late eighteenth century to celebrate the new government, but they did as such based on the expectation that regional interests in the borderlands and overseas would be protected in perpetuity by a powerful federal presence. Over time, southern regional strength, which was predicated on national growth, came under increased stress as antislavery sentiment became enmeshed with the issue of territorial expansion. Once considered the bulwark of southern stability, westward expansion emerged as a battleground over regional interests that elevated concerns regarding the South's willingness to sacrifice its evolution for the sake of the Union.[7]

At issue was the balance of power in the Senate, in addition to a constellation of ideas that grounded southern loyalty to the new Constitution, especially the legal status of individual property rights. If too many non-slaveholding states joined the Union, then the slaveholding interest would be reduced to minority status in both the House and the Senate, thereby undermining the region's imperialist designs. Little wonder that subsequent additions to the American Union brought with them an intense debate over slavery. During the constitutional convention and ratification process, the implications of the new government infrastructure remained hidden or, at least, veiled behind the much-vaunted republican virtue that allegedly guided the actions of the convention. After all, if the good of the whole overrode one's narrow self-interest as republican ideology demanded, then the union would weather all storms. Slaveholders looked at the apparatus that was created and considered its dictates fully consistent with regional aspirations. Before long, the implications of the federal system became painfully apparent for southerners.

The controversy sparked by the debate over Missouri statehood in 1819 eventually cooled, but to no less astute an observer as Thomas Jefferson, the "death knell" of the union had revealed itself. The slow declension toward secession had commenced with all the alarm of a "fire bell in the night."[8] Before such a cataclysmic outcome could emerge, the Missouri Compromise, which established thirty-six degrees thirty minutes north latitude across the Louisiana Purchase territory as the northern boundary of the slaveocracy, brought a momentary lull in the debate over slavery. Despite the compromise, many southerners viewed the fierce debate surrounding federal interference in the territorial process with grave foreboding as it pointed to future limitations on slavery's expansion and an unexpected restriction on property rights. Speaking on the floor of the House of Representatives in the midst of the debate, Charles Pinckney of South Carolina remarked, "The alarm, given by this attempt to legislate on slavery, has led to the opinion, that the very foundations of that kind of property are shaken; that the establishment of the precedent is a measure of the most alarming nature; for, should succeeding Congresses continue to push it, there is no knowing to what length it may be carried."[9] Pinckney's assessment offered an ominous portent for the future by insinuating that one day the federal government could interfere with individual property rights beyond the enslaved. Politicians might have bought time in 1820 when it came to slavery, but the tone of the discussion underscored the contentious nature of the subject and the incredible significance southerners attributed to the issue. When the battle over the balance of power rejoined, it would be with a theretofore unseen ferocity. Before then a tenuous peace ruled.[10]

As Revolutionary criticism of slavery dissipated and the new nation fell into an uneasy calm on the subject, a consistent defense of the institution proved less necessary save for platitudes concerning the role it played in the South's and, by extension, the nation's economy. Throughout the region, slavery was accepted as a matter of course and warranted infrequent discussion save for the need to lampoon the occasional antislavery treatise that found its way into print. The appearance of such polemics, however, kept the South perpetually on the defensive, even if the immediate concerns over such treatises were short-lived. A series of unexpected developments in 1831 prompted southerners to re-examine the racial institution in their midst and to offer a far more organized and detailed explanation and justification for its existence. Although not directly linked, the precipitating events became joined in the minds of white southerners as they found their "way of life" assailed in a far more aggressive and concerted manner than before.

At the start of 1831, Massachusetts abolitionist William Lloyd Garrison began circulating the newspaper *The Liberator*. In it, he roundly condemned the practice of slavery and the people who perpetuated it. That Garrison opposed slavery at all was bad enough to the white South. That he did it with such vitriol proved especially frightening. Garrison was not alone as others were equally as trenchant in their criticism of the slaveholding South.[11] He differed in that he ceaselessly pressed the call for change week after week and year after year in his paper. He made very personal arguments that challenged everything white southerners believed about themselves. On one occasion, Garrison observed concerning slaveholders, "They are not Christians; and the higher they raise their professions of patriotism or piety, the stronger is my detestation of their hypocrisy. They are dishonest and cruel—and God, and the angels, and devils, and the universe know that they are without excuse."[12] An age of constant agitation over slavery was at hand. The slaveholding South grew troubled by the ferocity exhibited by this new breed of abolitionist. Things would only get worse as the cacophony of northern outrage expanded. Garrison's devotion to the cause proved both shocking and revolutionary in its day. Slavery, for Garrison, was an unforgivable sin that besmirched the nation's honor. It had to be destroyed. In issue after issue, his paper condemned the South, urging its denizens to give up the barbarous practice. Most historians recognize that Garrison's reach was never very wide and that his was always the minority opinion in the North, but his message did extend to the slaves, many of whom read, or at least had read to them, the pages of *The Liberator* reprinted in local newspapers. Southern papers printed the abolitionist screed to inform their readership of the "outrageous" slander being perpetrated against them. All it took was one or two literate slaves to spread throughout plantation districts the remarkable dialogue occurring up North that hinted at the prospect of liberation. The perception of sweeping Yankee activism proved sufficient to stir slave souls and to chill those of their captors, even if the actual reach of abolitionist sentiment proved modest. By itself, Garrison's efforts represented an ominous warning of troubled waters ahead. Couple the publication of *The Liberator* with a violent slave revolt and then a sinister regional plot crafted by abolitionist forces bent on destroying the South emerges.[13]

Following the initial publication of Garrison's newspaper came the Nat Turner slave rebellion in western Virginia in August 1831. Although eventually quelled, the rebels succeeded in killing several slaveholders and their families. The Turner rebellion evoked widespread fear in the white South as it challenged the placidity that many thought, or at least hoped, existed amongst those enslaved in the region. Some began wondering if perhaps the slaves were not as contented as once assumed. Still others feared that, if word of the revolt spread, copycat episodes would develop. What if a much larger and closely knit slave community in the heart of a plantation district was filled with the spirit of revolution? The mere thought of such an uprising or series of uprisings worried everyone in slave country. Death could come from the very people who handled your food or cared for your children. Paranoia spread. Slave insurrection perpetually remained in the back of white southern minds as something possible and based on what they had read from similar revolts elsewhere, such as San Domingue, something to be feared. Hostile Blacks setting on unsuspecting whites filled plantation districts with dread. Capturing the terror of his constituents, Virginia governor John Floyd in his December 1831 address to the state legislature, stressed, "I cannot fail to recommend to your early attention, the revision of all laws, intended to preserve in due subordination the slave population of our state" lest other communities fall prey to "the dagger of the murderer and midnight assassin."[14]

In the wake of the rebellion, Garrison's publication was perceived as a precursor to, and an influencer of, Turner's insurrection. Under attack like never before, the "southern way of life" needed greater protection. Outsiders were to be challenged and slave rights and freedoms limited further still to forestall another uprising. According to proslavery author Matthew Estes, at the time of the Turner Rebellion, "the abolitionist excitement was just then beginning in the North, and the South had no arguments to meet them; they had never pretended to defend slavery in the abstract, hence they were taken aback by the arguments of their opponents."[15] Then, the region's native sons set to work producing what they considered a reasoned defense of the institution that had come under intense scrutiny. Southern defenses of slavery invariably consisted of a component to reassure the region's denizens that they lorded over a necessary system, while also including an appeal to outsiders not hopelessly devoted to antislavery arguments to consider the implications of emancipation for both the South and the nation as a whole. Lacy Ford's pioneering work *Deliver Us From Evil* skillfully examines early proslavery arguments, many of which were crafted in the Revolutionary Era that ultimately sowed the seeds for the ideologically similar arguments advanced in Estes's time.[16] As Ford reveals, the defenders of regional racial norms had a well-worn constellation of proslavery arguments leveled by their forebears, from which they could pull together a systematic defense. The arguments they crafted reflected the region's heritage by encapsulating what it meant to be "southern" in the nineteenth century and shaping what it meant to be "southern" well into the next century. Ford pinpoints a clear line of continuity in southern thought spanning the eighteenth and early nineteenth centuries that is traced in this book into the twentieth century. Time would codify the nature of the slave system as it existed in the region, just as it would heighten the voices of protest against it. Unifying the white South became a crucial component of the proslavery fight as challenges to white rule intensified. White southerners cast every argument they could think of at the problem, hoping that something would take root in what appeared to them as a desperate race against time.

As the guidelines and customs governing what some have dubbed the "Second Slavery" tightened, a complex pattern of misuse emerged with profit maximization as its goal. Ruthless capitalist exploitation serving national and global demands for cotton resulted in the commodification of human life across the South.[17] Limited exceptions to this norm existed as seen in the case of elderly slaves who were emancipated after decades of hard work. Thus, freedom most often came when a slave had lost his or her profitability owing to infirmity. For the rest, years of exploitation remained. By the 1830s, plantation slavery was firmly enmeshed in southern life with its own set of rules and regulations. The vast majority of white southerners did not own slaves, but whether they did or not, slave ownership had become an essential status symbol in the South. The measure of a man's success in the region was quite often gauged by slave ownership. In an agricultural society, owning a large plantation meant stability and familial success. Slaves became an essential barometer of that wealth for only they could till the hundreds of acres planted in cotton, tobacco, rice, and other crops. Advances in wealth followed increases in slave ownership shortly thereafter. The connection was direct and linear. Owning slaves served as a critical benchmark of one's social and economic standing, and it indeed represented the embodiment of one's individual freedom. Possession of slaves freed one from having to work the fields or toil for someone else. A slave owner was the master of his world. Even if one owned no slaves, he still aspired to do so since it represented one of the principal manifestations of wealth and respectability in the region. Cultural norms set the standard that others sought to emulate.

As Americans continued their westward migration, many brought their slaves into the new territories while others hoped to purchase their own chattel with a few good harvests in the unspoiled land. They would attempt to replicate the great wealth and the social norms that slavery had brought along the Atlantic coast further inland. In doing so, they ensured a variety of things, including the spread of slavery and a market for slaves idled by soil exhaustion in the East. The migrants became inadvertent foot soldiers in the struggle not only to maintain the delicate balance of slave and free states in the U.S. Senate, but also to feed the voracious needs of the international textile market. Global capitalist demands for southern cotton proved seemingly inexhaustible, tying the old world to the new world in an economic system fueled by race-based labor exploitation.

America and slavery expanded together as the Market Revolution gave rise to consumerism and the concomitant demand for raw materials. Although the pace of this growth varied from place to place and time period to time period, the nation's imperialist desires continued without abatement. The trouble for this growth posed by slavery, which first emerged during the Missouri crisis, would remain a dilemma as America actualized its manifest, capitalist, and imperialist destinies.[18] When tracing America's growth from a tiny sliver of settlements along the coast to a global power astride two oceans, it becomes clear how central the frontier has been to the nation's development. Historian Frederick Jackson Turner built his career on the famous "Frontier Thesis" which linked the formation of America's institutions and basic character with the conquest of the "wilderness." Turner recognized that the slavery battle was tied to this process, yet he did not fully grasp the capitalist market forces which served as the true catalyst for continental conquest. Open spaces represented more than just the site of potential homesteads; they served as contested economic territory over which would be fought one of the epic battles in the nation's early history. America's growth became a dual-edged sword; it represented expansion and prosperity, just as it initiated controversy over slavery. Acquiring western land might have been perceived as America's manifest destiny in the 1840s, but it also hastened the nation's dissolution as it brought two conflicting economic systems with divergent foreign policy needs into constant conflict. Territorial aggrandizement came at a heavy price.[19]

War with Mexico in 1846 rekindled the slavery debate, temporarily hushed but not fully silenced by the Missouri Compromise. For those who earlier missed Jefferson's fire bell, it was ringing again, only this time more loudly. Representative David Wilmot of Pennsylvania thrust the slavery question into the debate concerning Congressional appropriations for the war by offering a rider that any territory acquired from Mexico would be closed to slavery. Although never enacted, the so-called Wilmot Proviso revealed that passions over slavery had not abated. Out of the conflict in Mexico emerged the Compromise of 1850, composed of a series of laws that satisfied few on either side of the slavery divide while enraging the extremists on both sides. Abolitionists looked at the proposals and lamented such things as the aggressive Fugitive Slave Act and the protections provided for the interstate slave trade they contained; whereas proslavery advocates bristled at what they considered the assault on constitutional property rights inherent in popular sovereignty provisions and the banning of the slave trade in the District of Columbia evident in the compromise. Although doing little to solve long-standing regional discord, the Compromise succeeded in dispatching the immediate contentious issues surrounding the newly acquired western territories and the growth of slavery. Despite the compromise, southern lust for additional slaveholding lands both at home and increasingly abroad remained undiminished. Regional tension, although briefly stilled, remained high. A look to the future indicated no end to the animosity.[20]

In the middle of the debate concerning the compromise, Mississippi congressman William McWillie stressed that "the Union is in danger" while casting blame for the situation into the hands of northern politicians. "It is for you [northerners]," McWillie stressed, "to determine what are to be our future relations. The agitation comes from you; you are the actors and upon you rests the responsibility. The South asks nothing but equality and justice—she can never take less."[21] The Mississippian's comments capture the hypocrisy of the age as he leveled sweeping broadsides at those in the North while depicting people from the South in benevolent terms. Despite his protestations, it is clear that southern politicians, by viewing every national debate through the prism of slavery, sowed as much discord as their much-lamented abolitionist foes. Indeed, so vital was slavery to the future of the region and to its conception of itself that nothing short of the acceptance of slavery everywhere would seemingly silence southern protestations. Things kept deteriorating and with it increasingly went any hope of persuading outsiders that slavery should be protected. Passage of the Kansas-Nebraska Act in 1854 raised the already high sectional tensions to a theretofore unseen level, just as it marked the demise of the Whig Party. Only the Democratic Party remained as a truly national political organization.[22]

The lengthy debate over the territory of Kansas fanned the flames of discord, just as it revealed the long-term southern objective of expansion. Abolitionists and slaveholders flooded into the territory, violence erupted, and no one found satisfaction with what resulted. Kansas statehood was eventually shelved, leaving in its wake bitter sectional animosity. Common ground between the North and South became difficult to find. Summarizing southern opinion on the growing abolitionist challenge in 1854, South Carolina senator A. P. Butler observed, "If, however, they mean to go on with this agitation, I give notice, as far as I can speak for the south, that, if they keep it up, they must do so at the peril of the Union."[23] The cords which bound the country together continued fraying. Proslavery theorists found the prospect of winning over others an elusive objective. Most critical, southerners such as Butler began crafting their narrative solely within the framework of "us versus them" and thus failed to account for the critical reality that genuine abolitionism, in the form of the desire to end slavery everywhere in America without exception, represented a minority voice in the North. The tone of southern polemics by the late 1850s became more celebratory, more self-serving, and more designed for regional consumption with the goal of swaying Yankees conceded. Some southern theorists even advanced the notion that slaveholding societies were superior to those without the peculiar institution. Likewise, hints of disunion were increasingly becoming threats of secession. Southern rhetoric had changed from placing slavery within the context of the existing federal union to making it the bulwark of a "superior" southern social order that remained faithful to the Constitution from which the rest of the nation strayed. A line in the sand was being drawn.[24]

Two events signaled that a rapprochement with the North could not occur. First, John Brown's 1859 raid on the federal arsenal at Harpers Ferry under the auspices of a grand yet ill-conceived scheme to arm slaves throughout the South crystallized the sectional tension that had intensely divided America for a generation. Some abolitionists celebrated Brown as an avenging angel who vowed to wipe the sin of slavery from American soil through the only means left untried: bloodshed. Although many abolitionists themselves blanched at the thought of violence, they found the zeal with which Brown undertook his crusade worthy of praise. This lionizing of the troubled Brown played poorly in the South, a region hypersensitive to slave insurrections and outside criticism. To be sure, most northerners were not Garrisonian abolitionists. Opinion in the North ranged from the minority segment of abolitionists that sought to eradicate slavery to antislavery proponents who desired to limit the expansion of slavery to create a lily-white West and the remainder of the population which did not consider the topic worthy of consideration. The Free Soil and Republican parties, both northern entities, tended to oppose the expansion of slavery while arguing that slavery where it existed remained constitutionally protected. The drive to limit slavery's spread stemmed far less from moral compulsions against placing the slave system there than from a desire to keep the land free from the enslaved whose presence, they believed, degraded the value of labor. More often than not, antislavery advocates envisioned a free-soil West as a bastion of white supremacy devoid of Black inhabitants. Indeed, many white northerners opposed the outright emancipation of slaves without repatriation out of fear that a freed Black population would eventually find its way to the North, a prospect welcomed by few.[25]

Despite the absence of anything approaching a consensus on slavery above the Mason-Dixon Line, southerners perceived a different reality. For most, the mayhem threatened by the Brown episode ended additional consideration of the nuances in northern opinion. From that point forward, it became a simple matter of either supporting slavery where it existed as well as its expansion or opposing the institution everywhere. Abolitionists and antislavery advocates were thus reduced in southern opinion to a single devious whole. Anything but wholehearted support for slavery represented an attack against the entire white South. Brown's raid marked a symbolic turning point in the history of the region. It was rooted in what white southerners perceived to be the inevitable consequence of teaching northerners to belittle the South so that they no longer "respect our rights or refrain from acts of violence and of injury."[26] Other episodes naturally contributed to southern fatalism, but few had as clear a causal connection with the decision to secede as the failed Harpers Ferry raid. From that point forward, support for secession grew as the region's leaders imagined the emergence of a ceaseless campaign to stymie their expansionist tendencies while simultaneously trampling their property rights. The federal union once considered by white southerners as a protector of slaveholding interests had adopted an adversarial tone with the region. Many southerners believed the South should secede because the destruction of the slave system was the oft-unstated goal of the region's adversaries. Disunion increasingly loomed as a plausible outcome of the growing regional rancor.[27]

Abraham Lincoln's election in November 1860 as a Republican and therefore a sectional candidate representing a political party that championed free over slave labor served as the second, more immediate catalyst for secession. Harpers Ferry prompted some southerners to discuss disunion. Lincoln's election set in motion the process whereby secession became the majority opinion in the region. During the 1860 campaign, Lincoln gave no indication that he had any intention of interfering with slavery where it existed. Despite this seeming moderation, the Democratic Party fractured during the election with the northern wing supporting Stephen Douglas, who tepidly championed popular sovereignty, and the southern wing embracing John Breckinridge, who promised to protect one's right to bring slaves anywhere in the common territory. Division filled the country, undermined the last remaining national political party, and opened the door for Lincoln's election. As late as his inauguration in 1861, an event that took place with several southern states already having departed the Union, Lincoln reaffirmed his campaign resolution that he did not believe the Constitution sanctioned legislation to abolish slavery. Until the end, Lincoln sought to avoid conflict, just as he tried to coax white southerners back from the brink. Wishful thinking rather than cold logic informed presidential actions at this point.[28]

Despite Lincoln's outward moderation on the slavery issue, the drive for disunion took root across the region and spread as a result of an aggressive campaign on the part of immediate secessionists to sell the region on the need for prompt and decisive action. For the conspiratorially minded fire-eaters, the success of Lincoln's strictly regional campaign indicated a future in which the abolitionist crusade would culminate with an all-out push to destroy slavery. Although Lincoln himself stated publicly his lack of power to interfere with slavery where it already existed, members of his party, who took a more aggressive approach, would no doubt be emboldened by the election results and demand sweeping change. Adopting a wait-and-see approach would only spur abolitionist initiatives. The time for action had arrived. Writing to his constituents following the 1860 election, Mississippi senator and future president of the Confederate States of America, Jefferson Davis, remarked, "The argument is exhausted. All hope of relief in the Union through the agency of committees, congressional legislation or constitutional amendments, is extinguished, and we trust the South will not be deceived by appearances or the pretense of new guarantees."[29] In short, Davis recommended "speedy and absolute secession" from the Union without consideration of last-minute appeals for peace.[30] The victory of a purely sectional party revealed that the South's days as a slaveholding power were numbered. At the time, the industrial North with its paid labor ethos dominated the national government. Any hope that the South could construct a vast slaveholding empire on the American continent and overseas within the existing union evaporated. If northerners did not consider directly assailing slavery at that point, they would surely do so in the near future; all the while, they would push through Congress legislation that would slowly and systematically strip the South of its rights until slavery became illegal. Far better to fight the battle now against the antislavery forces before they grew too powerful and, perhaps more tellingly, while white southerners still had the lust for battle. Immediate action seemed the most logical choice for a growing number of the region's white citizens.

Although the exact percentage of the white southern population that supported disunion will never be known, historians are certain that the majority of them eventually came to favor the move. When the cry for secession rose, even those outside of the plantation belts supported disunion not because they had slaves threatened by emancipation, but because they believed in the social and cultural conventions created by the institution. Many southern whites undoubtedly recognized that their own social standing, always tenuous, would suffer if those slaves were freed. Nothing united white southerners more than skin color; it forged a people with diametrically opposite economic agendas into a collective. What benefitted the planter did not always benefit the yeoman or poor white person. Yet planters regularly dictated the scope of political discourse in their home states, and in the process, ushered legislation through their state governments that often served only the elites. Economic divisions mattered little because whites had a common interest in maintaining the status quo. Much of the growing political voice won by the yeoman during the early nineteenth century that resulted in universal white manhood suffrage went toward protecting the region's peculiar interests. Planter elites needed to placate the plain folk around them who had become politically active, welcoming their counsel and often taking their suggestions. Even if they disdained the practice of interacting with their social inferiors, they did so out of necessity for they were all free white men and therefore preservers of the republican ideology that precipitated the Revolution and produced the Constitution. At the same time, plain folk and poor whites needed to operate within the context of the prevailing social system; they had to work with the planters since the region's aristocracy headed the political order that gave all whites respectability. Take away slavery, and poor whites would lose their precarious social standing, locked forever in competition over marginal lands and shrinking markets with thousands of newly freed slaves—this time without the assistance of local patriarchs. Inertia thus became a powerful force, joining both rich and poor based solely on skin color as little else united them. In the final analysis, if the yeoman turned against the planter, the foundation of the slaveocracy would crumble. The fraternity of whiteness proved a lasting arrangement that continued long after the institution that gave it birth—slavery—disappeared and would shape the region's history long after the guns that destroyed it quieted. It took a war of unprecedented devastation to derail the secession movement and the system of human bondage that gave it life. Yet that same war failed to eradicate the basic assumptions that undergirded the antebellum southern social configuration even as it dismantled the apparatus favoring regional imperialism. A new and more volatile stage of southern history followed.[31]

After the war, that which gave whites perceived equality was torn asunder as all social classes scrambled to survive in a post-slavery world. Decades would pass before the region regained some semblance of its pre-war prosperity. In the interim, uncertainty reigned for many whites as they sought to rebuild. Poor whites who often struggled before the war, found themselves adrift in a world where they confronted thousands of new economic competitors. Although the freedmen would certainly retain a diminished status temporarily, some of them would no doubt prosper, eclipsing some whites as they rose. Status anxiety figured prominently for many whites as they foresaw a day that the one thing that exalted them—their skin color—no longer shielded them. Industrious Black farmers would compete for scarce quality land, and their harvests would flood already glutted markets. In a world turned upside down, nothing seemed certain and no one was safe.[32]

Faced with the dissolution of the world they knew, white and Black southerners confronted a challenging new reality. For the former slaves, emancipation, although certainly a time of joyous celebration, brought with it the realization that freedom meant the end of certainty. No home, no food, and no money or resources served as the counterweight to the exaltation of freedom. Many Blacks took the opportunity to leave the plantations on which they were held in bondage to find their fortune elsewhere, literally and figuratively escaping the memory of their old life. Others remained close by, entering into labor contracts and procuring, for the first time, wages in exchange for work. They were still "persons with a price," but this time, they at least had some say in the value of their labor and their place of employment. Liberation for many slaves thus represented the freedom to move. Their movement, in turn, compounded the difficulties confronting white southerners who were obsessed with keeping them corralled for their own economic gain.[33] Emancipation threatened the wealthiest southerners with utter devastation. Slave labor and staple crop plantation agriculture formed the foundation of the massive wealth accumulated by the region's elites. For them, losing slavery meant a catastrophic loss of capital. Each slave held a value determined by market forces that tended steadily upward during the nineteenth century. A man's slaves represented a substantial portion of his wealth and, for some, the only means of cultivating and harvesting crops. Their loss turned rich men into poor men overnight. This proved especially true for those of marginal wealth or those heavily leveraged.

With sentiments regarding the importance of race so ingrained, it is not surprising that immediate steps were taken to hold on to a semblance of the pre–Civil War status quo. Liberation merely altered the nature of the region's race-based social order; it did not destroy it. When new southern state legislatures were chosen after the war, the extent of the unrepentant spirit became manifest. Many of the very men who led the region into secession again sat in southern statehouses. A principal concern for this group of politicians was defining the status of the newly freed slaves. Equality proved an alien concept on their agendas as keeping the freedmen in a position close to bondage served as the objective. Repressive Black Codes emerged as each state's basic statement on the freedoms they were willing to grant their former bondsmen. Exhibiting the sentiment common among white southern politicians as they tackled the dilemma of defining the rights of former slaves, Mississippi governor Benjamin G. Humphreys observed before the state legislature in November 1865 that "the negro is free, whether we like it or not; we must realize that fact now and forever. To be free, however, does not make him a citizen, or entitle him to social or political equality with the white man."[34] Humphreys' comments underscore the attitude that governed the actions of white southerners for generations to come. The likelihood of anything approaching equality was not on the table. Although each state fashioned its own laws, several items proved universal. For the first time, Blacks now possessed the right to own property, enter into legally recognized marriages and contracts, and other basic rights. At the same time, state codes typically precluded Blacks from serving on juries and prohibited interracial marriage. Controlling the mobility of former slaves also represented a major concern. Planters still needed agricultural workers and thus demanded some mechanism to check post-emancipation Black ambulation. Not surprisingly, the states of South Carolina and Mississippi led the way in implementing vagrancy laws which gave local magistrates the freedom to arrest Blacks who could not demonstrate employment. Deliberately vague in construction, such laws provided local elites what they wanted: workers. "Vagrants" faced arrest, fines, and hiring out until their societal debt was paid. Other states passed similar laws such as those mandating apprenticeships or even prohibiting employers from enticing away workers with higher wages. Regardless of the mechanism involved, southern states sought to retain as much as possible the master and slave relationship that once existed. For the freedmen, who faced emancipation with nothing save for the fruits of their labor, the post-emancipation South offered few promises. The imposition of discriminatory Black Codes that stripped them of even this possession muted the joyous celebrations upon emancipation. Federal intervention appeared to many northerners as the best way to get a handle on the fast-deteriorating situation in the South.[35]

White intransigence despite defeat raised the ire of many northern Republicans who considered the absence of southern remorse particularly agitating, episodes of violence against those newly freed further elevated concerns that the region proved incapable of handling the post-slavery transition without firm oversight. One observer of the South in the immediate aftermath of emancipation ominously remarked, "From this time forward, the entire white race of the South devoted itself to killing Negroes."[36] Violence was an everyday occurrence as the region sought a new status quo following the war. The chaos prompted many to seek a mechanism to stamp out the swirling unrest. Radical Republicans wanted the South punished for its decision to break up the Union so that it might learn a lesson in humility that even a war that devastated the region could not accomplish. These Republicans placed much of the blame for the southern response on President Andrew Johnson and his lenient policy of reconstructing the region. They wanted to wrest control of the South's return to the union from the president, and place it in congressional, and therefore less conciliatory, hands. According to radical theorists, southern states, through the act of secession, forfeited their rights as states and, as such, existed as conquered territories subject to military occupation. Before the defeated territories gained readmission, they needed to pass through a period of semicolonial tutelage during which they would be forced to embrace all manner of change, including the acceptance of legal and political equality for their former slaves. Congressional elections in 1866 swung the radical faction of the Republican Party into a dominant position in Congress and with that Reconstruction slipped from President Johnson's hands. Wasting little time, Radicals passed sweeping Reconstruction laws in 1867 designed to punish the South. Through their actions, the radicals procured for the freedmen many of the rights and privileges not immediately bestowed upon them when emancipated.

The aggressive federal action, in turn, elicited fierce white resistance to Washington's authority. The Reconstruction South was a volatile place in which "illegitimate" Republican governments and the freedmen who were their most significant constituency faced a steady stream of violence and intimidation at the hands of the region's white population now stripped of much of its political power. The animosity engendered during the period did much to shape the region's future and influenced the course of race relations for decades to come. The American Civil War forever destroyed the Old South by undermining the slave-based version of the "southern way of life" celebrated by the region's white inhabitants. How the South adjusted to the social alterations necessitated by war laid the foundation for its second race-based social order. Turning the other cheek and moving on was certainly not in the offing, at least for white southerners, who harbored a grudge regarding post–Civil War policies that lasted for decades. Confederate general Richard Taylor summarized southern hostility against Reconstruction policies thusly: "The leaders of the radical masses of the North have inflicted such countless and cruel wrongs on the Southern people as to forbid any hope of disposition or ability to forgive their victims and the land will have no rest until the last of these persecutors has passed into oblivion."[37] Considering the tone of Taylor's remarks, it is not difficult to envision the resulting injustices committed by the white South both during and after Reconstruction. Future generations of white southerners exploited regional animus toward Radical Republican policies as they attempted to strip Black citizens of their recently secured rights. Indeed, segregation emerged, in part, from the carnage of the Civil War and the perceived depredations of Reconstruction. Federally mandated Reconstruction officially ended in 1877; however, for white and Black citizens of the South, the forces unleashed in this period would remain contested into the twentieth century. Free of outside influence, white southerners turned to building a new more inward-looking racial order, while Black southerners fought to secure and advance their political and economic rights.[38]

Later repealed by federal legislation, the repressive Black Codes passed prior to the onset of Radical Reconstruction revealed the direction the white South would gravitate toward once federal troops went home. Although emancipation precipitated almost immediate segregation in schools and hotels, full-scale state-sponsored segregation manifested in a slower manner. "Separate but equal" eventually emerged as the guiding principle of the New South, serving as a mechanism by which white southerners could draw a color line without running afoul of the Fourteenth Amendment. Over time, custom morphed into law as local officials began mandating segregation in a variety of venues. The federal court provided its stamp of approval to the burgeoning separate but equal system through several key decisions. In 1883, it ruled in the *Civil Rights Cases* that federal laws, such as the Civil Rights Act of 1875, only covered discrimination by states, not by individuals or private corporations. In the 1896 *Plessy v. Ferguson* ruling, the court fully embraced racial segregation by holding that state-mandated separate but equal facilities did not violate the Fourteenth Amendment. From there, segregation had legal sanction. It would soon permeate all areas of public intercourse in the South.[39]

After the Civil War, the South topically recreated itself, yet just beneath the surface evidence of continuity appeared. The terrible conflict produced only a partial alteration of the rule of white supremacy. Despite Radical Republican efforts to change the region, race remained a central feature of southern life. Decades after the cessation of hostilities, the social mores of the region exhibited only a slight change. Even the arguments employed in the defense of slavery saw resurrection in defense of the emerging system of segregation. It was still about preserving the Constitution as the "founding fathers" intended. It was still about states' rights. It was still about Thomas Jefferson, James Madison, and the Kentucky and Virginia Resolutions. It was still about John C. Calhoun and the *Exposition and Protest*. Most of all, it was still about outsiders trying to alter the "southern way of life." Any study of the New South underscores the continued importance of the Old South. At least when it came to the region's intellectual tradition, time often stood still. When the South's first racial system came under attack, white southerners took the ultimate step of leaving the Union rather than submitting to outside intervention. The manner in which the region reacted when its second racial system faced intense opposition reveals how the region had changed and how it remained the same.

As segregation spread, southern state legislators sought to purge remaining African Americans from the voter rolls, thus completing their assault on Black equality. Populist threats of a fusion with Republicans in the 1890s hastened the spread of "electoral reform" throughout the region. Bourbon Democrats trembled at the implications of poor whites uniting with Blacks based on their common economic hardships. Fears of "Black rule" returning provoked a thorough reformation of voter qualification laws. The adoption of poll taxes and literacy tests, in conjunction with ever-present physical intimidation, all served to block Black suffrage while shrinking the white electorate by striking from voting rolls those at the bottom of the economic ladder who did not fall in line with the Democratic Party's pro-white agenda. By the start of the twentieth century, the South was developing a new race-based social and political order to replace the one dismantled by the American Civil War. Jim Crow governed all social intercourse, while mass disfranchisement shrank the electorate and limited political reform. With debate thus stifled, the Democratic Party quickly became the only show in most southern towns. Outside of the Republican presence in isolated locations, such as the mountains of Tennessee and North Carolina, a slate of often unopposed Democratic candidates was the only choice for voters. Political discourse took shape in the context of a unidimensional party system that guaranteed southern politicians elected to the United States House and Senate could expect to stay there for a long time, building lots of seniority in a national legislature where time in office determined one's political power. In election cycles where the Democratic Party gained control of Congress, the white South had its soldiers strategically placed to block legislation antithetical to its thinking. Jim Crow had multiple layers of defense. It had the support of state governments, the sanction of the nation's highest court, and the national legislature, disproportionately governed by southern influence, there to protect it.[40]

In its infancy, segregation required little defense beyond a simple statement that Blacks were inferior and incapable of full integration into the community. This belief was rooted in the fear that Blacks outside of the so-called "civilizing influence" of slavery would retrogress to their "natural" state of barbarism. Perceptions existed that Blacks would not work, would engage in petty crimes to take care of themselves, and inevitably undertake more serious offenses including murder and rape. The latter fear grew more pronounced in the years following emancipation. By the

1890s, the number of stories in southern newspapers that chronicled Black depredations especially involving the rape of white women mounted. One chronicler remarked in 1889, "Rape is the most frightful crime which the negroes commit against the white people, and their disposition to perpetrate it has increased in spite of the quick and summary punishment that always follows; and it will be seen that this disposition will grow in proportion as that vague respect which the Blacks still entertain for white skin declines."[41] Most reports of Black wantonness lacked substantiating evidence, placing the veracity of these accounts in question. Nonetheless, in this milieu, segregation gained strength, spreading throughout the South as a mechanism to return white control over the Black community and thus to halt the Black population's alleged declension. At the same time, it served as a tool for reestablishing white male dominance in the region following the embarrassing defeat of the Civil War and outside occupation during Reconstruction. Reinstating regional racial customs, even if in an altered form, served the purpose of buttressing white supremacy at a time when threats to tradition appeared everywhere. As Jim Crow spread, many northerners tacitly accepted white oppression of the Black minority in the South rather than challenge what many believed to be a naturally occurring social phenomenon: racial separation. Ultimately, most white northerners in this period harbored similar racial sensitivities as their southern counterparts and proved more than comfortable with segregation in their own neighborhoods. Despite their freedom, African Americans in the North faced constant economic repression and social separation before and after the Civil War that derived from widespread acceptance of Black inferiority above the Mason-Dixon Line. Until the population of the North expanded to include many more African Americans, few politicians from that region saw any need to question segregation or the racial mythology that formed its foundation. Change, however, loomed on the horizon.[42]

Over time, anthropologists and sociologists broadened American understanding of race and culture. Their research revealed the flaws behind the racialist ideology which posited that governmental systems, cultural achievements, and all aspects of a society's and an individual's development and potential for future advancement were determined by race. Research by twentieth-century scholars began exploding this mythology one tenet at a time by underscoring the host of factors that shaped any given country and its people. Environmental factors along with societal traditions rose in significance as the vital forces that dictated cultural manifestations. Under this construct, no culture could be defined as superior or inferior to another, just different based on a series of mitigating factors. Race, which had once been considered a central historical force shaping nations, diminished completely in its explanatory significance as a growing number of scholars embraced the idea that it was a culturally created construct that had no meaning beyond that which each society ascribed to it. This modern racial ideology marked a significant departure from the prevailing national consensus that witnessed the advent of segregation with hardly a challenge.[43]

Dissemination and acceptance of the new paradigm would take time, but as the twentieth century progressed, it became increasingly important for white southerners to advance a defense of their racial institutions that transcended a simple superior versus inferior dichotomy even as the racism inherent in their positions remained unchanged. They were following in the footsteps of their antebellum forebears who codified their defense of slavery when the institution came under attack. Despite scholarly efforts to undermine the racial hierarchy present in America, there remained a large contingent of white southerners, some of whom were academics in their own right, who looked at the situation around them and proved reluctant to accept equality, at least until some changes took place. Capturing the prejudices of the time, poet and novelist Robert Penn Warren noted in the early twentieth century that the southern white man "wishes the negro well; he wishes to see crime, genial irresponsibility, ignorance, and oppression replaced by an informed and productive negro community."[44] Until this chasm with exceedingly subjective criteria was crossed, white southerners, as Warren's remarks suggest, would remain uncomfortable with any push for equality. Rather than permit sweeping change in light of new research, the white South dug in its heels to resist. As in the past, southern race theorists and regional champions reemerged when segregation fell under intense scrutiny.

American involvement in World War I, both as a supplier of arms and later as a combatant, sparked a war industries boom. Many factories struggling to meet demand—a demand they would never completely fill—expanded their operations, while opening new plants to capitalize on the conflict. Employers needed to keep the production lines moving. Spurred by potential employment, African Americans found the prospects of decent pay a powerful force to leave the South in search of both economic and political opportunities in northern cities. Although many failed to find the expected promised land, most enjoyed greater freedom than possible in the Jim Crow South and certainly better wages. As for the long-term consequences of the Great Migration, many migrants settled in preexisting Black communities in northern urban centers. This demographic shift, a trend that spanned both World Wars, revolutionized politics in northern cities. As northern Black communities grew, so too did their political voice. In many states, Black constituents held the balance of power come election time. Seemingly overnight, Blacks went from being a largely forgotten minority to a key constituency. Once indifferent to segregation, many northern politicians transformed into champions of racial justice as the communities they represented changed. With Black people being politically active and organizations such as the National Association for the Advancement of Colored People (NAACP) promising election-day retribution to politicians not attuned to the struggles of Black America, segregation and its satellite institutions could not long stand unchallenged.[45]

Casting about for a remedy to the mounting civil rights push, a growing number of the South's national politicians grudgingly came to recognize they needed to soft-pedal their racism in hopes of garnering enough congressional votes to shelve objectionable legislation. Antilynching fights in Washington during the 1920s and 1930s prompted awareness among southern politicians that they could no longer rely solely on race in constructing their defense of Jim Crow. Failure to do so, they feared, might hasten more aggressive efforts to dismantle *de jure* segregation. No doubt, many northerners still embraced the old racialist perspective well into the twentieth century, but few openly espoused it as time progressed. Northern elected officials struggled with appearances, as they sought to avoid seeming too friendly with segregationists, even if they sympathized with southern arguments. In 1938, South Carolina's U.S. senator James Byrnes, warned constituents of what the future held when he commented, "It is difficult for one not a member of Congress to realize the sectional feeling now evident against the South."[46] By the dawn of the 1940s, a perception emerged among southern leaders in Washington that an assault against segregation was inevitable. The South's Washington leaders, in turn, utilized every tool at their disposal to arrest the push for racial justice while it still existed on the periphery of the Jim Crow edifice. A legislative foray against lynching was one thing; an attack on Jim Crow represented a threat of a much greater magnitude. Preventing such a battle became the primary objective of the South's Washington delegation. To garner the support of politicians who now represented states with a strong Black voting presence, southerners needed more race-neutral arguments for segregation that would enable them to sell their vision of reality to others. Gradually, a growing number of the South's national politicians began abandoning the strident racism that served as the foundation of regional explanations for segregation in exchange for a coded dialogue that enabled them to obscure regional hate behind a smokescreen of logic and legality. Although the myth of Black inferiority remained a consistent theme advanced on the local level until the very end of Jim Crow, national politicians and even several state leaders, beginning in the late New Deal era, abandoned, albeit episodically, their overt racism in exchange for more edifying constitutional claims in an effort to stymie advances in African American rights.[47] South Carolina's virulent racist politician Ellison "Cotton Ed" Smith, for example, took the time to clarify during the 1942 legislative battle to repeal the poll tax in the middle of WWII that "so far as the race question is concerned, it is just a smoke screen; it has nothing to do with this horrible onslaught on the Constitution."[48] Georgian Walter George similarly remarked during the same debate that "there is no issue of race, and no question of race, color, or creed involved in this discussion."[49] In this sense, the prosegregation discourse differed from the proslavery one as southern politicians attempted to downgrade the centrality of racial prejudice in their worldview. In a changing world, segregationists began adapting their tactics to stay ahead of larger social and cultural shifts in the nation. Try as they might, however, modern intrusions such as television undermined any effort to keep segregation from becoming an American pariah.

Pressure in Washington for laws designed to tackle the South's racial order coincided with an array of legal challenges to segregation across the region, along with widespread public demonstrations against racial injustice orchestrated by Jim Crow's victims. After having fought a war against racial injustice overseas, the nation stood ready for change. More importantly, the African American community immediately recognized how the fight in World War II spoke directly to their personal struggles for justice, which commenced long before the conflict. The Double V Campaign, promising victory against injustice at home and overseas, captured the spirit of the times. Change was in the offing.[50] Mississippi's Theodore Bilbo, who unabashedly championed white supremacy, commented on the potential impact of the war: "I think we are going to have so much trouble with the negro soldiers when they get back from this war that everybody will be willing to let them go to Africa."[51] In this environment, a growing number of white southerners began recognizing that the pressure pushing against them was only growing and would not cease until the entire system of racial separation collapsed. By the end of World War II, some white southerners viewed the mounting critique of their region from not only outsiders but also from within, as a harbinger of disaster. Cold War pressures on the United States to live up to the ideals expressed in the nation's founding documents only added to concerns that change would visit the region. Internal and external forces pushed white southern leaders to scramble for mechanisms to mitigate the pressure compelling change long before the direct attack on *de jure* segregation was joined. This time faced with an implacable foe, which was arguably more threatening to the region than the abolitionist movement since it permeated every community in the region, white southerners responded in an unexpected fashion.

The moment of truth for segregation's defenders came in the aftermath of the 1954 *Brown v. Board of Education* decision. Today, historians embrace the idea of the long civil rights fight and recognize that a coalescing of forces before the landmark case gave rise to the mature movement witnessed in the 1950s and 1960s. At the time these forces were taking shape, however, few whites, save for southern political leaders, recognized that an unstoppable wave of historical change was already crashing down upon them. Long before most of the region's white population grasped the strength of the national campaign against segregation, the African American community around them was actively resisting the oppression they confronted in ways both big and small by steadily advancing the drive to dismantle Jim Crow. Early evidence of grassroots discontent was dismissed by the region's whites, who viewed signs of Black recalcitrance as isolated and insignificant occurrences. The indifference of white supremacy's champions to the aspirations of regional Blacks, in turn, went a long way to ensuring that segregation stood even less likelihood of survival than the ill-fated slave system. By the time the majority of segregationists recognized that something was amiss, it was already too late. Instead, white southerners were awakened to the forces arrayed against them by *Brown* and organized themselves accordingly in an effort to check the integration of public accommodations which they believed was still possible. The decision thus touched off a wave of hysterics similar to the one produced by John Brown's Raid on Harpers Ferry. For all the talk of states' rights tossed about in the 1950s and 1960s, however, only a handful of the South's leaders took the states' rights argument to its logical extreme. Segregation's defenders would not revisit the secession issue–that was a lesson learned the hard way by their forebears. Shocking paroxysms of violence broke out as white southerners bitterly fought the rising tide against them. On the surface at least, it appeared as if the region was spiraling into lawlessness. But public perception is often formed by the most sensational story, not the more mundane. Many moderate leaders, who often personally detested civil rights, offered a tempered response to the changes hoisted upon them, stopping short of advocating for a climactic last stand. These tepid champions of segregation recognized the futility and danger of such thinking and pulled the region back from the brink. Indeed, few practical politicians veered toward an all-or-nothing challenge to integration, revealing, at least in part, southern acceptance of national political power and the limitations of their own aspirations.

No longer bound by the imperative to export their racial order, twentieth-century southerners adopted a cordon defense in hopes of keeping the civil rights fight from intruding too deeply into the region. Each paid lip service to the idea of challenging court mandates but would fight the battle for segregation within the context of the existing federal order. Unlike southerners a century earlier, twentieth-century southerners did not bow toward disunion; they leaned toward "massive resistance," a vaguely defined phrase that threatened much difficulty, but its caveat of "all lawful means" underscored the New South's adherence to the inviolate Union. A sweeping array of poorly coordinated resistance efforts ensued, with little in the way of a cohesive plan driving them. Once the region embraced the inflammatory and hyperbolic notion of "massive resistance" it gave voice to the region's most reactionary racist element, which pushed aside any and all "moderate" solutions. Violence engulfed the region, making the already strained constitutional claims made by the region's defenders that much weaker. In essence, Jim Crow segregation faced its greatest threat with little seeming chance of success. The *Brown* decision escalated perceptions that external, and increasingly internal, threats would engulf the white South. Sabers were rattled, old arguments reemerged, and violence occurred, but defenders of the institution entered the fray without wielding the ultimate weapon—secession—or seriously considering the resurrection of its lesser cousins interposition and nullification. Although many would resurrect the rhetoric of the Civil War, they stopped short of advocating disunion.

Segregation's defenders would seek legal loopholes, employ delaying tactics, and threaten before admitting defeat against "overwhelming odds." Indeed, unlike nineteenth-century southerners, twentieth-century ones fought the archetypal "good fight" without having to exit the union. It was never seriously considered. The tropes they employed revealed the powerful sway of Old South rhetoric, whereas their tactics starkly contrasted with those utilized by previous generations. White southerners tried all they could to arrest integration yet found themselves checked repeatedly by the courts, by Congress, and by grass-roots protests. Everywhere they looked, their worldview came under attack. Resigned to the outcome, Georgia's Richard Russell, the politician responsible for organizing the failed southern resistance efforts to the sweeping Civil Rights Act of 1964, dejectedly commented after the bill's passage: "All that we can do is swallow hard and hold our heads high, knowing that we did everything humanly possible to further the cause of constitutional government."[52] Russell, like many of his political allies, understood that the fight for Jim Crow was over.[53]

Embracing the myth of the Lost Cause to buoy morale in the defeated South, many segregationists hoped that their own "heroic" last stand would assuage constituents and mark the peaceful end of the fight. The southern effort to salvage the racial isolationism it embraced after the Civil War failed. Once the central myths behind segregation's existence began melting away, there existed nothing to replace it. This failure points to an obvious conclusion: there was never a reason to maintain separate facilities save for hate. On every level, segregation proved a net loss for the South. It drained resources which were desperately needed in the impoverished area, and it prevented future investment in the region owing to concerns large manufacturing interests had about establishing their businesses in a region teeming with racial unrest. Segregation kept the region locked in a bygone era ensuring that as the twentieth century advanced, the South remained firmly grounded in the nineteenth. No amount of southern references to the Constitution in the halls of Congress could obscure this painful reality. The consequences of segregation were disastrous for the region's future growth.

In the aftermath of the climactic legislative showdowns over civil rights in the 1960s, the South experienced substantive change. Its political orientation clearly underwent a sizable shift as growing numbers of the region's loyal white Democratic voters began transferring their allegiance to the once-reviled Republican Party. This political realignment was truly momentous considering the long-simmering hatred of the GOP in the South since the days of Lincoln. Throughout the twentieth century, southern politicians hurled insults at the Republican Party accusing it of being the true party of civil rights and hence the catalyst of all of the changes that transpired in the period. For example, Alabama's John Sparkman noted to Democratic voters prior to the legislative showdown over the Civil Rights Act of 1964 that "nearly all of the Republicans are against us as they have historically been."[54] More skeptical observers however recognized the national Democratic Party bore much of the responsibility for civil rights and the growth of federal authority. Older southern politicians remained loyal to the Democratic Party. If for no other reason, they derived what power they had in Washington from their standing within the party. A younger generation of politicians cast off their ties to the Democratic Party which had seemingly abandoned the interests of the region. Bitterness ran deep as southerners pondered the irony of how the Democratic Party that was responsible for so much mischief in the mid-twentieth century was saved from obsolescence after the Civil War by the very region it now attacked. The Republican Party, which had long embraced commercial and industrial growth, also championed fiscal conservatism and anti-big government stances which naturally resonated with southern voters. Once the national Democratic Party turned its back on the racial mores evident in the region—a trend that commenced during the New Deal—and the legislative showdowns over civil rights in the 1960s ended in failure, it was only a matter of time before white southerners found a new home in the fiscally and socially conservative Republican Party. Ironically, African American voters who had long been denied basic rights in southern states run by the Democratic Party gravitated to that organization with the passage of the Voting Rights Act of 1965.[55]

In the twenty-first century, the political landscape of the South no longer closely reflects the "savage ideal" depicted in Wilbur Cash's *Mind of the South.* Presently, urban centers throughout the region, which were reconfigured in the second half of the twentieth century by white flight, embrace a more liberal orientation which stands in stark contrast to the rural and small-town South which remains wedded to the conservative principles that once dominated the region. Even with all of these changes, the race-centered dialogue of the past is never far from the surface. In many contemporary southern elections, an urban versus rural electoral cleavage often plays out along racial lines, only now with African Americans having a voice in how they are governed. Despite promising signs, the widely heralded post-racial South—and indeed post-racial America—appears to be a way off. Much of the rhetoric emanating from the South throughout the nineteenth and twentieth centuries persists into the twenty-first. Today, conservative ideals centered on property rights, individual choice, and limited government are wielded in a race-neutral manner. However, their centrality to modern conservatism and to national political discourse remains a clear reflection of the continued influence of the southern fights to preserve slavery and segregation in America. Recognition of this connection is not meant to imply that modern conservative politicians embrace a racial ideology today or shoulder any direct responsibility for the injustice of the past. Instead, it merely demonstrates the distinctly southern flavor of contemporary conservative thought. Hundreds of years of southern intellectual history are now distilled in a broad conservative agenda that is popular throughout the nation. Much of American politics has become southernized.

2

The Essential Mythology

Behind every nation stands a pantheon of beliefs that define its essential nature and highest ideals. Regions, states, and even smaller jurisdictions also have traditions and cultural norms that they contend set them apart from the larger whole to which they belong. Such smaller dominions often embrace the ethos of the nation while advancing refinements that unify the local populace and mark them as distinct within the collective. Often, the corpus of ideals that define a group represents an objective to strive for rather than an actual reflection of the state of things on the ground. Principles, in part, are the basis of these beliefs, but so, too, is mythology. They embody that which a group of people desires to be and hopes that they can become. In a land that has harbored both slavery and segregation, America's founding principles of liberty and freedom still reverberated in the South, even if these concepts rang hollow for those outside of the traditional power structure. Many wanted them to be the foundation of the world around them, and for white males at least, they remained a partial reflection of reality. Throughout the nineteenth and twentieth centuries, white southerners advanced their mythology regarding the nature of society created by the region's bifurcated racial inheritance. In it was leavened the expected blend of fact and fancy that typifies group identity. Southern racial mythology became an essential regional bond that served as the foundation of the proslavery and prosegregation arguments.[1]

"A better-looking, happier, more courteous set of people I have never seen," wrote Nehemiah Adams, a Massachusetts clergyman, during his 1854 visit to Savannah, Georgia, upon casting eyes on slaves for the first time.[2] As the sojourn of this New Englander continued, Adams adjusted his view somewhat, but in the end, he rationalized that despite the depiction of slavery in Harriet Beecher Stowe's 1852 work *Uncle Tom's Cabin*, the slaves he witnessed "surpass any three millions of laboring people, in any foreign land, in comforts, in freedom from care, in provision for the future."[3] This northern visitor found his expectations concerning the ills of slavery challenged. He read abolitionist literature and even preached on the evils of slavery from his Boston pulpit. In short, he expected to find overwhelming evidence of harsh oppression and broken spirits in the slaveholding South. Instead, he found a buoyant slave population and only passing evidence of the treachery he believed would abound. To be sure, Adams did not ponder the more profound implications of a life lived at someone else's leisure. No thought was given to what it meant to be without the basic liberties and freedoms that Adams himself so enjoyed or even that the perceived joy he witnessed was illusory, a mask meant to conceal one's true anguish. Nonetheless, his comments mirrored those advanced by slavery's defenders for decades. Many proslavery claims originated in obvious mythology, but Adams's account reminds us that myths are not always rooted in pure fancy. Often misperceptions of sensory information, rather than deep awareness, shape how people view the world around them.

As the abolitionist crusade against slavery heightened in the 1830s, white southerners naturally countered with claims that challenged the dark and sinister depiction of regional race relations advanced by William L. Garrison and others. The region's citizens could not accept such harsh criticism without offering a defense that captured their perception of the social order which they defended and helped to perpetuate. Politician James Henry Hammond, who served South Carolina as governor and U.S. senator, observed in a manner reminiscent of the northerner Adams, "I believe our slaves are the happiest three millions of human beings on whom the sun shines."[4] South Carolina novelist and poet William Gilmore Simms, who wrote extensively on the slavery question, added that satisfaction reigned amongst the slaves and that he could think of few people "so happy of mood, so jocund, and so generally healthy," as the South's Black bondsmen.[5] Both Hammond's and Simms's comments reflect the opinion of most proslavery theorists. To admit that slaves suffered in any way would be to undermine the foundation of the region's identity. Even a cursory exploration of the slaveholding districts in the South, advocates contended, demonstrated that contentedness ruled among the enslaved. Naturally, neither Hammond nor any of his cohorts addressed the psychological implications of bondage, just as they made no effort to understand the internal factors that shaped the external attitudes and actions of the enslaved. To expect them to do so, however, is to commit an anachronistic fallacy. Before the days of modern psychology, few thought that the singing and smiles of the slaves were anything but an outward manifestation of their inner satisfaction. Today, of course, psychologists recognize that people adopt a variety of defense mechanisms to cope with intolerable conditions, mechanisms that often deliberately obscure inner hurt. Hammond, who did not have the benefit of modern psychotherapy (or the work of contemporary historians), could only conclude that signs of conviviality underscored overall slave happiness. Proslavery advocates reported on what they saw and on what they wanted to see, emphasizing that which bolstered their claims while conveniently downplaying that which challenged their sanguine view. This union of myth and reality spans the proslavery crusade and extends to later fights in defense of segregation.

Assertions that the slaves "loved" their masters were linked with contentions that slave owners reciprocated these sentiments. The enslavers under this construct cared for their slaves and came to view them as part of their extended family. In 1829, wealthy Florida planter and slave merchant, Zephaniah Kingsley Jr., describing this phenomenon, observed, "A patriarchal feeling of protection is due to every slave from his owner, who should consider the slave as a member of the family, of which a slave constitutes a part, according to his scale of condition."[6] White southerners boldly proclaimed that "there are few ties more heart-felt, or of more benignant influence, than those which mutually bind the master and the slave,"[7] or at least that was how math professor, clergyman, and attorney Albert T. Bledsoe chose to depict the relationship in his proslavery writing. Mutual respect and admiration between whites and Blacks served as the explanation most often given for the alleged happiness of the slaves. A slave, according to educator Thomas R. Dew, "generally loves the master and his family."[8] Dew clearly toed the standard line championed throughout the South that the enslaved looked upon their oppressors as benevolent keepers rather than malignant abusers. It is noteworthy that Dew added the adverb "generally" to his remarks. No doubt, Dew, like many others, recognized that not all slaveholders earned the unvarnished adoration of their captives. That he mentioned the possibility of caveats at all is telling when one considers the treatise's purpose of celebrating the positive good produced by the institution of slavery. Obviously, something caused Dew to equivocate rather than make his statement on master-slave relations categorical. Such elision on his part did not represent any overt duplicity as no one categorically claimed that all enslavers proved kind and benevolent—only the vast majority of them. For Dew, most "evidence," which took the form of white hearsay, indicated that the slaves looked fondly upon their masters. The backbone of all variations of the proslavery argument revolved around the basic assertion that those held in bondage remained happy and respected their enslavers. Under the guise of this outlook, examples to the contrary proved too few to quantify. If one looked in the right places, paternalism was evident everywhere. Also critical in assessing Dew's comments was their proximal relationship to the Nat Turner slave revolt. The very existence of the violent episode pointed to obvious trouble in the white southern paradise. If things proved as sanguine as most white southerners depicted, there would be no need for equivocation. The Turner episode influenced the absence of categorical certainty in Dew's comments as it clearly highlighted the profound dysfunction evident in some plantation districts. Dew carefully straddled the line in stressing the overall benevolence of the slaveholding system while necessarily leaving open the prospect that reality did not always live up to the mythology.

Antebellum white southerners never denied that transgressions against the paternalist ethos occurred. They always left open the prospect that a few bad apples existed in every bunch and that the excesses of such individuals, in turn, accounted for overt manifestations of slave unrest such as infrequent revolts.[9] For them, the issue remained that abusers represented a small minority of slaveholders, not the majority as abolitionists suggested. Opponents of slavery depicted a world in which brutality reigned and slaves received daily beatings by lecherous masters. White southerners read those claims and found abolitionist charges slanderous. Quick to defend the handling of their own slaves, white southerners grudgingly admitted that some in their midst proved less beneficent, thereby indicating that they recognized the limitations of the paternalist ethos and conceded that a nugget of truth, in turn, informed abolitionist claims. Writing in 1838, former South Carolina senator William Harper urged white southerners to pressure neighbors who mistreated their slaves, since an abuser "casts a shade upon the character of every individual of his fellow-citizens, and does every one of them a personal injury."[10] Harper, who penned his defense of slavery in the early days of the abolitionist crusade, sought to cleanse the institution of the violence that reformers found most odious and that potentially triggered slave unrest. Proslavery champions held out hope that lessening the brutality of what they considered a generally benign institution might prompt acceptance from slavery's detractors that the institution warranted a place in American life. The fact that this belief rested on the shaky foundation that antislavery forces would concede to a less violent form of oppression proves beyond the point as most proslavery theorists remained convinced that the system they defended represented a positive good. To them, the correlation was direct. Abuse spurred northern outrage. Ultimately, southerners believed that if they corrected the most glaring abuses evident under the slaveholding system, the cacophony of opposition to the institution from outside the region would dwindle to a handful of abolitionists. Southern "benevolence" would yield, they hoped, widespread northern indifference to the existence of slavery in America, permitting the South to continue the racial status quo with minimal outside interference. This "logic" proved irresistible yet hopelessly shortsighted and regrettably resilient. Future generations of white southerners espoused the same misguided outlook that tempering the excesses of their race-based social orders would mollify those determined to change the region. The results proved similarly tragic.

Rather than being wholly negative, some even argued that the abolitionist movement only made southern slavery stronger. Slaveholder and proslavery theorist Matthew Estes went as far as to postulate that the abolitionist movement had vastly improved the institution as it existed in the South since its impact "in all cases has been to correct errors, remove abuses, and thus soften the condition of the Slave."[11] The rub for Estes was that northern agitators simply did not recognize the enormous steps taken by the white South to make the slave system as humane as possible. It was for this reason that regional tensions continued to mount. Had he comprised his principal treatise in defense of slavery following the fierce debate regarding slavery's expansion that resulted from the 1846–1848 war with Mexico, Estes would no doubt have been even more critical of the abolitionist movement and more doubtful that any action on the part of the South would sway northern opinion. Early nineteenth-century slave owners simply did not conceptualize their opponents as devoted ideological warriors willing to fight at the ramparts when it came to combatting the inhumanity of slavery. History proved them wrong. When later generations recognized that abolitionist forces would not accept southern topical reforms, they still urged the "few" remaining abusive slaveholders to clean up their acts for the effect such a step would have on the proslavery cause in general. Central to regional mythology remained the necessity of depicting outsiders as the sowers of racial discord and the initiators of the outwardly hostile actions taken by slaveholders. Proslavery forces elevated themselves to the role of victim in the antislavery fight, arguing that they confronted a villainous opponent who advanced a free labor ideology that was riddled with flaws. By contrast, slavery represented a system in which the enslaved and the enslavers allegedly derived benefits.

Those in bondage wanted for nothing in the paternalist worldview as the enslavers offered their charges protection from cradle to grave. In exchange, owners believed the enslaved gave their captors enthusiastic adoration while enjoying a robust standard of living. Capturing the essence of this perspective, Matthew Estes commented, "Our Negroes here are in Paradise, in comparison with the Negro Slaves in Africa."[12] As fears grew that antislavery forces would undermine the existing tranquility that allegedly reigned supreme in the region, southern spokesmen found only external causes for slave discontent. After all, if masters treated their slaves with benevolence and if those very same slaves longed not for a freedom that they never knew, then how else might one account for Black hostility? Nothing save for outside provocation became the immediate response as the memory of substantial slave uprisings real or imagined—such as those involving Gabriel Prosser (1800), Denmark Vesey (1822), and Nat Turner (1831)—diminished over time. As the frequency of large-scale and violent slave unrest dipped, it became easier to peddle the myth that white benevolence accounted for the alleged tranquil race relations in the region. Where peace and paternalism abounded, unrest simply could not prosper. Abolitionists garnered ferocious and sustained condemnation for they were "Satan" in the guise of a reformer seeking to disturb the region's delicate equilibrium.[13] The impact of the antislavery campaign found its way to the South, causing some to claim that because of this pressure, "we have to draw the rein tighter and tighter day by day to be assured that we hold them [our slaves] in check."[14] James Hammond, always a curious chronicler of events, touched on a contradiction in southern logic which in many ways vindicated abolitionist rhetoric, just as it exposed the malleability of the paternalist ethos. The South Carolinian admitted that restrictions on slaves were expanding, despite the oft-touted presence of paternalism, while offering a suitable explanation for this departure from the ideal: abolitionist propaganda duped slaves into believing that life in freedom would be to their benefit. Hammond's comments reveal that southerners, out of necessity, had readjusted the extent of their paternalist goodwill. At the same time, his reflections point to a more sinister motive behind white southern actions. Although not stated publicly, Hammond's remarks shed light on a significant factor behind the decline in large-scale slave revolts. By carefully restricting the actions of those in bondage, slaveholders limited the prospect of cross-plantation interaction between the enslaved, thereby circumventing a key vector in the exchange of rebellious ideas. In further curtailing the freedoms of the slaves, plantation owners did much to bolster the perception that tranquility governed their communities as they did away with the nexus of forces that generated rebellion. Stifling oppression rather than benevolent oversight shaped this development; however, as with any mythology, the truth proved less important than the desired perception. White southerners identified the absence of substantive rebellions as proof of paternalism's existence. Of course, white southerners had more than just Yankee abolitionism and slave volatility in mind when they recommended kind treatment of their bondsmen. Something other than ethics and morality was at play.

Writing at the start of 1845, James Henry Hammond reduced things to their economic core by stripping away the paternalist veneer to expose the capitalist root that made slavery so vital to southern interests. As Hammond saw it, treating slaves with "kindness," was "necessary to our deriving the greatest amount of profit from them."[15] As expected, the myth of tranquil southern race relations remained balanced with the economic realities of the plantation. Slaveholders in most cases did not beat their slaves mercilessly, not solely because they abhorred the practice as they often emphasized, but because, by resorting to such barbarity, they would injure or possibly kill what they considered a valuable commodity. Until the end, slaves were viewed as financial investments. While this vision shocks modern sensibilities, we must remember that the capitalist ethos which guided master-slave relations often mitigated the excesses depicted in abolitionist literature. The profit motive, not necessarily white southern magnanimity, dictated treatment. At the same time, Hammond's remarks point to the larger connection between southern slaveholders and the global marketplace. Located at the heart of the textile industry, which served as the economic life's blood of many industrialized nations, was cotton agriculture and the enslaved people who made it all possible. Despite southern slaveholders denouncing slave mistreatment, their purpose, whether intended or not, was to feed voracious international cotton markets by any means necessary, even via self-serving flashes of benevolence. The paternalist ethos which stressed benevolent slave treatment was grounded in the vision of reality shared by many white southerners regardless of the purity of their motives.[16] The fact that Hammond's 1845 comments were reprinted in a widely circulated compendium of proslavery articles in early 1860, points to the longevity of his influence, the salience of his ideas, and the persistence of southern devotion to the alleged benevolent treatment of the enslaved.

Rather than chronicling reality, proslavery arguments advanced an ideal in depicting the slaveholding South that remained consistent across the antebellum period. In many ways, they helped create the mythology that defined and shaped the region's identity. Proslavery claims proved simple: this is how we live, and this is what we aspire to be; leave us alone and this is what we will become. Finding historical examples in which theory did not live up to practice is easy enough to accomplish. Scholars have scoured the historical record to explode the assumptions which informed southern musings concerning paternalism, all to reveal that slaveholders often deviated from the lofty standard that they established. Despite the self-evident weakness of their assertions, proslavery advocates recognized the need to retain an idealized depiction of slavery in the face of very public criticism of the institution. When outsiders cast aspersions on others, invariably the "insiders" seek to defend that which makes them distinctive. If a key feature of that distinctiveness also provides the community with considerable wealth, the strength of the myth grows more intense and more widely believed. Paternalist writings were not necessarily meant to be a facsimile of southern society as it existed on the ground any more than early capitalist defenses of the free labor system were meant to be an idealization of the truth devoid of an extensive discourse on how the reality of factory life included as much grinding poverty and oppression as it did upward mobility. The notion of benevolent masters overseeing cheerful bondsmen became an elemental truth in southern self-image formation. Idyllic representations of everyday life lent more than a touch of nobility to the slaveholding minority. Treating proslavery treatises as anything but a written manifestation of what the region wanted to be rather than what its white inhabitants knew it was misses the point. Such treatises created the ideal and reinforced what regional champions liked to consider the most commonly found iteration of the South's racial order. The presence of cruel masters and unhappy slaves did not make paternalism unreal to them or diminish its importance in shaping future actions. It remained in place without challenge as a defining regional guidepost.

Many fall short of the ideals of the groups they belong to—professional, faith-based, or social—but such standards are not then summarily abandoned because of their unattainability. People still strive to achieve them as they order society and create the boundaries that establish the norms of the group. Even if few white southerners lived up to the ideal, they were, nonetheless, judged by their peers, in part, on how close they came to attaining the standard, and they, recognizing the importance of appearing as a paternalistic master, strove to become the embodiment of the coveted image. Criticizing the paternalist ethos as a bundle of lies obscures the very reason proslavery arguments developed. For white southerners, most of whom embraced Christianity and believed they were good exemplars of the faith, explanations that "softened' slavery's rough edges while elevating its practitioners were necessary features of regional intellectual life. Responding to accusations regarding the inherent injustice and lack of liberty evident in slaveholding communities, Albert Bledsoe bluntly stated, "The institution of slavery is designed by the South not for the enlightened and the free, but only for the ignorant and debased."[17] Bledsoe left little doubt as to the need for the continuation of the paternalist caretaker state made necessary by the presence of a large number of enslaved persons whom he considered of dubious morality. Paternalism shaped regional development and buttressed societal norms. It was important precisely because it offered a semblance of stability and legitimacy to an otherwise problematic institution.[18]

The value of slavery extended beyond the social order; it became the basis of a worldview from which white southerners established a sense of their own identity and one from which they made judgments about the world outside the region. So convinced were they of the quality of their social fabric that they challenged outsiders to travel to the region and see with their own eyes the benevolence that abounded. U.S. senator A. P. Butler of South Carolina opined in the early stages of the fight over the Kansas-Nebraska Act that those who visit the region, "who have lived amidst slaveholders, who have partaken of their hospitality, and have seen the administration of justice and all the graver forms of civilization there" are "better reconciled to the institution of slavery than that class and school of persons who read and take in their notions from *Uncle Tom's Cabin*."[19] In short, southerners were proud of what they had created and were convinced that if outsiders objectively explored the situation on the ground in the region, they, too, would recognize its positive attributes. Blacks, so the argument went, were elevated by their bondage, but so were the region's whites.

Race and class regularly found expression in proslavery arguments as a means of reassuring those outside of the plantation belt that all regional whites supported the status quo even if they possessed no slaves. Although most proslavery advocates focused on the benevolence of the institution or its economic necessity, others dedicated, at least part of their attention, to the myriad of benefits slavery allegedly afforded whites regardless of their slave ownership. South Carolina statesman John C. Calhoun observed in 1849 that the exalted status that slavery granted whites afforded them "pride of character of which neither poverty nor misfortune can deprive them."[20] In 1857, prominent social theorist George Fitzhugh of Virginia, building on his previous efforts to champion the supremacy of the southern social, cultural, and economic order, heralded the existence of an enslaved Black population as a critical ingredient in making "whites a privileged class," since it exempted "them from all servile, menial, and debasing employments."[21] As regional discord mounted, James Hammond augmented Fitzhugh's work by more forcefully laying out his "mudsill" theory. On the floor of the Senate in 1858, Hammond began, "The greatest strength of the South arises from the harmony of her political and social institutions. This harmony gives her a frame of society, the best in the world, and an extent of political freedom, combined with entire security, such as no other people ever enjoyed on the face of the earth."[22] After sketching the contours of the superior nature of southern society, Hammond turned to providing an explanation for this splendor. He continued, "In all social systems there must be a class to do the menial duties, to perform the drudgery of life. . . .

Such a class you must have, or you would not have that other class which leads progress, civilization, and refinement. It constitutes the very mud-sill of society and political government."[23] Lest there be any doubt concerning the group in southern society that constituted the mudsill, the South Carolinian explicitly added, "fortunately for the South, she found a race adapted to that purpose to her hand. . . . We use them for our purpose, and call them slaves."[24] Little more explanation than this is required to understand why most white southerners wanted to believe, and ultimately accepted, the myths surrounding regional racial norms. Everyone from rich to poor had a vested interest in preserving the status quo as all of them benefitted either directly in the form of financial gain or indirectly via social gain. If no other reason than providing a perpetual mud-sill class for the South existed, then the institution of slavery performed as needed by muting class conflict and buttressing planter interests when circumstances might have warranted something else.

Basic assumptions regarding Black inferiority undergirded southern mythology. The issue proved so central that it permeated all aspects of southern thought. Indeed, a belief in a racial hierarchy informed every proslavery defense regardless of its slant. It proved so elemental as to require little more than passing reference to the alleged absurdity of any social scheme predicated on racial equality. On the floor of the U.S. Senate, A. P. Butler summed up the overarching belief in a racial hierarchy: "Abolitionists cannot make those equal whom God has made unequal."[25] An extended disquisition on the role of race in shaping nineteenth and twentieth-century southern social orders follows in Chapter 3. Individuals of African descent found themselves in bondage, according to proslavery assertions, because of their alleged inferiority. When fashioning arguments that touted the peaceful relations between the races, it was always advanced that Blacks could hold no other position besides the one they inhabited owing to their debased origins. Hammond's famous mudsill remarks clearly depicted the enslaved as occupying the only status befitting them. Nothing but long-term exposure to "superior" European cultures could keep them from reverting to their innate state of barbarism. In part, the racial order of the South worked because it was the only one possible. Blacks were uplifted through exposure to superior culture, whereas whites were similarly elevated by the presence of degraded "others." Summarizing this perspective, Jefferson Davis, commented in 1859 on the relationship between master and slave: "Living peaceably together each is the better for the presence of the other."[26] That so few questioned the prevailing order underscores both the level of control that slave owners had over southern politics and the extent of popular support for all facets of the mythology. True opportunity existed for very few in the antebellum South. Stifling both physically and psychologically, the South's racial order kept most of the region's population in line by the sheer force of its existence. Framed as something inevitable, slavery existed as the best possible social arrangement given the peculiarities of the region's development—or at least that was how the most invested preservers of the order chose to define it. With limited exceptions, the white majority either embraced the status quo or at least passively accepted it by remaining indifferent. Few raised their voices against the prevailing order, which if public figures such as Butler and Davis are to be believed, directly benefited them regardless of their social standing. Later, during the American Civil War, thousands marched to their deaths in defense of regional interests that did not always serve personal ones. Powerful indeed was the pull of identity.

The mythology of the region necessitated the preservation of the order—slavery—that gave it life. Without human bondage, the South would become just like the North and would teem with class and presumably racial unrest. South Carolina's Charles Pinckney, who served in the Continental Congress and participated in the creation of the 1787 Constitution in Philadelphia, remarked during the controversy surrounding the admission of Missouri, that the slaves in the American South were treated far better than the workers of Europe, before adding, that if one took "the situation of the free negroes now resident in New York and Philadelphia, and compare them with the situation of our slaves, he will tell you that, perhaps the most miserable and degraded state of human nature is to be found among the free negroes" there.[27] As Pinckney's comments highlight, white southerners believed they had crafted the perfect social order and they exhibited a willingness to defend that order against all detractors. The perspective shared by Pinckney in the early nineteenth century proved widely popular, persisting right up until the outbreak of the Civil War. According to proslavery advocates, as long as outsiders did not stir the pot, slaves would receive even better treatment than that which they already did and would continue to receive it into the future. As preservers of an allegedly superior order, white southerners had a vested interest in maintaining the system that gave, at least all white men, power. Although most white southerners did not own slaves, they benefitted both in their communities as well as in their families by the master-slave dichotomy that informed regional social interactions. To preserve this order meant protecting the slaveocracy, which as antislavery and abolitionist sentiment mounted and as the pull of fire-eater rhetoric gained strength, drove the region toward disunion. Southern arguments in the 1820s and 1830s focused more on the benevolence of slavery. By the 1850s, this emphasis shifted to include sweeping statements regarding the superiority of the slaveholding system and the nefarious intentions of northern abolitionists. With territorial growth checked and attacks against the institution mounting, white southerners found their place in the nation endlessly assaulted. Their "perfect" order faced such affronts that the region's place within the Union was called into question. James Hammond offers the best coda for any exegesis on southern willingness to safeguard regional institutions against external threats while also indirectly reaffirming the superiority of the southern order. "If the abolitionists are prepared to expend their own treasures and shed their own blood," he observed, "let them come."[28] As Hammond revealed, emancipation could not take place without violence in large part because Yankees sought to recast the South in the image of the North. More than slavery was at stake. As external pressures pushed the South into a corner, the appeal of disunion grew. Hopeful of establishing an independent nation, the South created a short-lived confederacy following secession. The experience of the Civil War magnified the innumerable flaws in the region's mythology.

Nothing signifies the failure of the southern social order better than the ongoing effort on the part of the enslaved throughout the Civil War to abandon their captors at the first hint of a federal military presence in the surrounding countryside. Imploding the mythology of Black contentedness, African Americans fled enslavement at the first opportunity, disrupting the economy and undermining white rule at every turn. Their efforts eroded the Confederate fight and dampened morale as Black challenges to the regional status quo proved omnipresent. The most important myth of the white South suffered a devastating blow as the region's allegedly superior social order frayed and its armies met defeat. Far from content, the enslaved coveted freedom and undertook considerable risk to secure it. In a world turned upside down, the Civil War brought everything the white South believed about itself into question. A critical nexus of forces coalesced and, at least outwardly, slaughtered an array of sacred cows in the region, offering a glimmer of hope that something new might emerge. The hope for change proved illusory.[29]

Slavery's demise prompted a period of readjustment in which the races struggled for equilibrium. To be sure, few white southerners gave thought to any plan that hinted at equality. Left to their own devices, the region's inhabitants would have kept the freedmen in as close to a condition of bondage as possible. Following an attenuated period of Presidential Reconstruction in which the return of southern states to the Union was designed to take place as fast as possible with the production of new state constitutions that outlawed slavery, Radical Republican administrations from 1867 onward promptly replaced existing Democratic ones as outsiders sought to reconstruct the vanquished South by making it pay for disunion. Federal intervention resulted in the passage of the sweeping Fourteenth and Fifteenth Amendments, in addition to the disfranchisement of many whites involved in the Confederate war effort. Having lost the war, the white South commenced a campaign that ultimately found it winning the peace at a terrible cost. Violence swept the region as "illegitimate" Republican governments faced a torrent of psychological and physical abuse. Elected officials as well as rank-and-file GOP members, including hated scalawags and newly enfranchised Blacks, faced constant intimidation. The northern will to reconstruct the South soon ebbed and along with it went the fortunes of the Republican Party in the region.[30] By the late 1870s, white southern Democrats were back in power busily restoring the rule of white supremacy. Segregation emerged slowly after the war before its spread quickened in the 1890s on the way to becoming an all-encompassing system in the early twentieth century, albeit one with extraordinarily shallow roots. When Reconstruction ended, white southerners went to work crafting a new narrative that again allowed them to lord over the African American population around them. Segregation in the South, like slavery before it, demanded a mythology of its own that made it appear as a timeless institution rooted in natural law. Construction of a cohesive defense for segregation commenced right away. When slavery came under sustained attack, the white South rallied behind its social order. Segregation's birth, especially in the wake of the volatile Reconstruction period, necessitated the same response.

Forging a mythology for segregation posed many challenges with the institution's short duration being the foremost impediment. Slavery existed for more than two hundred years in North America before the need to formulate a consistent defense of it emerged. With such a long history, no one alive in the 1830s could remember a time when slavery did not exist. For them, it was something that had always been there. The same could not be said for segregation. Consumed with notions of racial superiority and equally committed to a social order with a preordained mudsill class, the South embraced segregation as a vital institution of stability following years of war and occupation. Likewise, white southerners desired to corral the region's African American citizens, who sought every mechanism possible to advance their status. Denying those once enslaved opportunity was essential for maintaining the rule of white supremacy. Many of its early defenders saw its birth and thus knew its dubious origins, but nonetheless considered restoring white rule in the region "a problem of the gravest importance."[31] In a region turned upside-down, no alternative to the comforting order created by a race-based social system was imagined. Clearly, the region learned a different lesson following the catastrophic Civil War than expected. Instead of traversing a new path, the South doubled down on the need to reformulate society along racial lines.[32]

Although the specific system of segregation adopted in the South had shallow roots, the practice of racial separation was widely evident in the North before the Civil War wherever a substantive free Black population existed. Segregation of schools and neighborhoods both in custom and law proved pervasive above the Mason-Dixon Line, just as economic discrimination delimited the opportunities available to African Americans there. White fears of racial others knew no geographic boundaries. In this sense, the South's approach to the post-slavery world was fully consistent with the prevailing attitude of the nation at large, which at that time was falling under the spell of Herbert Spencer and his Social Darwinist message. Similarly, segregation, although "new" to the South, flowed seamlessly out of the race-based order that preceded it. Contextualizing southern segregation, not as a discreet development, but as part of a long tradition of race-infused cultural norms renders its emergence in the late nineteenth-century South comprehensible. Although the system of segregation was a relative newcomer to the region, a race-based social system in the South had existed for an extraordinarily long period of time. One would have to go back to the very start of America's colonial period to find a South without slaves. Segregation thus fell firmly in the southern, and indeed the American, tradition as it tied directly to the racialist worldview that dominated the nation's early history. When the dust settled following Reconstruction, the New South departed little from the ideas that grounded the racial order in the Old South.[33]

Myth creation requires a believable set of first principles that both set a subject in the best possible light and that edifies believers. Segregation thus needed a plausible series of explanations for its existence that left no doubt of its essential character. Forging the features of that character meant looking back to the days of slavery. Without fashioning a link to the region's past, segregation's defenders could not establish the primordial roots of the institution. Utilize slavery and the task became simpler, yet still challenging. Slavery's demise, so the myth went, granted a race unprepared for freedom extraordinary liberty. Segregation's champions, in turn, placed their cause in the same intellectual stream as advocates of slavery. One theorist noted, "The southern black man at the time of Emancipation was healthy in body and cheerful in mind."[34] As the temporal distance from slavery expanded, so too did the declension of the freedmen. Considering the universality of racist thought in the late nineteenth and early twentieth centuries, any claims utilizing notions of racial inferiority would be accepted with few reservations. Later, this reliance on the "school of civilization" model, in which segregation—like slavery before it—was depicted as uplifting Blacks, required alteration as criticism of segregation and the entire concept of racial hierarchy mounted. Before then at least, the South's heritage is best depicted as a single unbroken thread of continuity in which the system of segregation derived from the institution of slavery both in a sociocultural sense and an intellectual one. Blacks could not flourish without white oversight read the claims of segregationists. Dubious assertions that Black crime skyrocketed after slavery served to underscore the importance of benevolent white oversight. Segregation thereby replaced slavery as the only plausible mechanism of social control given the region's biracial inheritance. Summing up late nineteenth-century views of Black declension, public health "reformer" Frederick Hoffman observed regarding African Americans that "the colored race is shown to be on the downward grade."[35] Out of this perception sprang calls for more rigid racial control.[36]

Efforts to resurrect paternalism in the New South gravitated toward the

Jim Crow promise to restore beneficent white oversight in the region. As much as this notion meant in the Old South its usage and future in the new one encountered many roadblocks as the twentieth century progressed, not internally where the region's whites rarely questioned its relevance, but externally as national perceptions on race shifted. Mythology had its limits as much had changed since the days of slavery. With the Black population out of bondage, many white southerners no longer considered it their obligation to look after them. Paternalism, if it ever existed at all, assumed a different form. Blacks were still considered childlike and in need of constant white oversight; however, unlike the situation that existed under slavery, most whites no longer considered it their responsibility to assist the African American community now spatially separated from them. Families freed from enslavement found themselves removed from the web of "benevolence" that provided for their basic needs. Proslavery author, Albert Bledsoe could not resist speculating upon what would befall the South should emancipation ever become reality. According to Bledsoe, the decoupling of southern whites from southern Blacks would occur so that "in one or two generations, the white people of the South would care as little for freed Blacks among us as the same class of persons are now cared for by the white people of the North." In a prescient moment, Bledsoe continued, "The prejudice of race would be restored with unmitigated violence.... And they will feel the rigid exclusion from society of the whites and all participation in their government."[37] Bledsoe's vision became a reality. Keeping African Americans at arm's length in the New South became more important than the caretaker role southern whites once touted. Historian Philip Bruce observed about race relations in his home state of Virginia in 1889 that "the diminished intimacy of the relation between master and servant is reflected with exaggeration in that growing social spirit which is moving the negro and white man with equal force to withdraw still further from each other."[38] What developed was a hodgepodge of often contradictory ideas concerning the roles of whites and Blacks in the post-emancipation South. Only the reign of white supremacy remained consistent. If theorists such as Bledsoe got anything right, it was certainly their forecasts regarding the future social ostracism of the freedmen. The post–Civil War South was not a friendly place for African Americans.[39]

Born out of fear and distrust, Jim Crow allowed white southerners to claim they admired the Blacks that they knew while maintaining a social and spatial distance from them—not because they did not like them, but because it was natural. Similarly, the need to separate was reinforced by the fear that African Americans with little white oversight would commit all manner of crimes thus making segregation a matter of public safety. The myth of segregation elevated the criminalization of Blackness to rote gospel and made regional whites increasingly wary of the African American population around them. In essence, the central myth of Jim Crow revolved around the ability of southern whites to keep southern Blacks in their place. Antebellum southerners primarily viewed their slaves as happy and content, albeit always a potential threat owing to their "savage" nature that white control corralled. Southerners in the first half of the twentieth century looked upon the Black population as without knowledge of "truth, integrity, virtue, self-restraint, industry, courage, patience and purity of manhood and womanhood."[40] As a result, the imposition of harsh Jim Crow justice ensured the swift and often brutal treatment of any Black person who transgressed the fast-evolving racial etiquette of the region. Death or incarceration represented the only options for African Americans who challenged the South's new mythology. Rampant brutality against the region's Black population, while keeping them outside of the social circle of whites, became the foundation of Jim Crow's stability and served as a catalyst for the horrible violence to come.

Despite the ever-present racial unrest in the region, southerners steadily defended segregation while embracing a paternalistic tone that had all of the earmarks of the antebellum order. White southerners utilized paternalism to justify their continued oppression of minorities, even if with less forcefulness than their predecessors. This time, the emphasis shifted from how they treated their charges like members of the family to how they liked and respected the Blacks that they knew. Long-time U.S. senator Allen Ellender of Louisiana, for one, observed, "I am not opposed to the minority races, particularly the colored people. We are their friends, and I believe the responsible element of the colored people are cognizant of the fact that the South treats them better than their Northern Brethren."[41] Under the New South mythology, white southerners allegedly respected known Blacks, but no longer felt the need to extend to them the protective cloak of economic assistance. White respect for southern Blacks, in turn, revolved around the latter's willingness to play along with societal expectations. Indeed, by the twentieth century, most southern whites emphasized that they did not wake "up every morning looking for ways to oppress," to which could be added the assurance that they also chose not to assist. Louisiana's Russell Long noted, "I will not fight the negro—I have always been his friend and I will continue to be so."[42] Such remarks capture the new paternalism of Jim Crow. We like the Blacks we know, the theory went, and we do not oppress them, at least not directly. That was it. Despite the fondness expressed by whites for some Blacks, segregation's necessity was predicated on a sinister outlook regarding African Americans that had clear intellectual ties to the "school of civilization" model popular before the Civil War.

Old South paternalism necessitated that the worst abuses in the slaveholding system be mitigated, in part, to alleviate abolitionist pressure. Even if such abuses were only topically and ceremoniously remediated, discussion of them proved an important feature of nineteenth-century southern paternalism. Segregationists confronted similar external outcries as they navigated the negative publicity caused by wanton violence in a region which claimed that racial harmony existed. As in the antebellum era when the actions of abusive slaveholders received public condemnation, twentieth-century southern politicians devoted considerable attention to corralling the white South's frequent gravitation toward extralegal forms of justice, such as lynching, that dismayed outsiders. The shockingly high lynching rates from the 1880s onward, along with concomitant public outcry against the abuse, prompted many regional leaders to call for restraint. By the 1920s, the NAACP made the antilynching fight the cornerstone of its national agenda, raising awareness of the crime like never before and forcing the South to defend itself in the public arena. Similar to the outlook of their forebears, southerners harbored no interest in getting rid of the system of segregation which spawned the horrific incidents; they merely sought to end the egregious public spectacle aspect of these violent outbursts to still outside discomfort while retaining the volatile system that gave life to the atrocities. South Carolinian James Byrnes speaking against antilynching legislation in the 1930s observed that "it [lynching] is going to be remedied by the education of our people and the development of a sentiment that will uphold the men in public office who courageously perform their duty."[43] Texas's Tom Connally joined Byrnes in calling on the South to better police itself to keep northerners from imposing laws that would strip them of their autonomy. "We want to demonstrate to the world," Connally noted, "that the Southern people are making a heroic effort to control this situation and that they are succeeding."[44] Despite the criticism of spectacle lynching embraced by some, white southerners made no effort to address the systemic injustices and basic assumptions rooted in the Jim Crow system that gave rise to regional atrocities thereby ensuring that racial violence would continue albeit in a different form. Even after a statistical decline in the number of lynchings in the region, white southerners found themselves under attack, just as their forebears did after their own aggressive campaign to mitigate the dark pall that hung over the slave system due, in part, to its own excesses. As in the Old South where some slaveholders, no matter the pleas to temper their mistreatment of slaves, continued their abuse, there remained segregationists who, despite calls to avoid racial violence, trended toward lawlessness. In the 1940s, liberal Claude Pepper of Florida wrote with disgust regarding what he labeled "the tragic failure of the white extremist to realize the necessity of the law handling such matters [alleged Black crimes]," and he continued, "Eventually the Federal Government will step in in such cases and while there will be bloodshed a few times the courts will eventually gain the mastery of the mob."[45] Pepper clearly understood that unrepentant southern behavior would bring far more outside interference to the region than if southerners admitted limited culpability for the excesses committed in the name of Jim Crow and commenced a campaign to bring it under control.

In the face of regional violence and outside condemnation, segregation's champions never ceased their devotion to their racially divided world and thus patterned their mythology in order to engrain separation in southern minds. Most white southerners could agree upon several things. Blacks and whites would separate naturally, preferring segregation to integration.[46] Evidence to the contrary stemmed directly from outside interference. Under this construct, everyone in the South, regardless of race, wanted separation. Although signs of resistance proved everywhere apparent, segregationists summarily dismissed this evidence. Before long, however, pressures against the region began to precipitously increase, placing the tenuous mythology of the region in peril. After WWII, Black servicemen who were exposed to the more liberal cultures of Europe struggled to reintegrate into southern society. Returning with battlefield decorations and pride in accomplishment, Black veterans confronted a society unwilling, despite their heroic service, to grant them a seat at the lunch counter. Not all adjusted, often paying with their lives for transgressions both real and imagined, as white supremacists deliberately targeted African Americans in uniform to deny them dignity and any hint of equality. Stings of oppression were everywhere. Capitulating in the face of white intolerance was an option many no longer would permit.[47]

By the 1950s, southerners peddled hard the myth of regional racial accord that faced disruption only when outside agents injected themselves into the region. Our social order is perfect, they observed, a product of much deliberation and the consequence of cultural and social wants. We exist peacefully albeit separately together. Violence happened infrequently and without the blessing of regional authorities. Arkansan George McClellan, for one, proudly explained, "We have no race problem in the South," before excoriating northerners for economic discrimination against the region which he opined was the true reason for African American poverty and lack of upward mobility.[48] Tranquility, not simmering social angst, was the norm. Outsiders wanted to destroy this accord, in part out of ignorance, but increasingly to curry the support of newly enfranchised Black voters. According to many southerners, northern politicians—in an effort to cater to Black voters for temporary gains—were willing to lock themselves into perpetual servitude to those voting blocs, thereby establishing a vicious cycle in which every year, new and more sweeping civil rights proposals would come before Congress. Bluntly stating the political expediency that southerners believed informed the northern push for civil rights, Texas senator Tom Connally mocked supporters of such laws. Connally asserted, "They do not believe in it, but election time is coming, and 'we must get these colored votes, because if we do not get them somebody else will get them.'"[49] Southern segregationists had it all figured out, or at least they thought they did. Segregation's spirited defense fell short of its objectives for a variety of reasons not least of which was its protectors' utter naiveté when it came to the aspirations of the region's Black inhabitants or the larger shifts in racial attitudes occurring outside of the South.

Growing national acceptance of theories debunking notions of superiority and inferiority in exchange for cultural and social explanations for perceived racial differences placed segregationists in the difficult role of stubbornly defending an anachronistic, not to mention illogical, social order. The alleged shortcomings found in the African American community that had once convinced southerners to initially embrace segregation and northerners to turn the other way soon failed to hold intellectual water as questions regarding the flawed foundation that prompted Jim Crow mounted. Despite this problem, southern apologists merely noted that those living outside of the South, who did not reside among a large number of African Americans, could not understand why segregation proved necessary. Champions of segregation depicted racial division as necessary "to enable the white people of the South to live in contact with large numbers of Negros without the loss of the identity of their ancient culture and their racial purity."[50] Until the end, they continued touting well-worn assertions concerning the unique ability of the white South to address the region's biracial inheritance. Louisiana senator Allen Ellender, for example, bluntly observed, "It is my honest belief that the South is better acquainted with the problems of the negro and knows best how to deal with them than the North does."[51] Echoing Ellender's remarks, fellow Louisianan Russell Long similarly observed regarding the growing racial turmoil in the region, "I firmly believe that if we in the south are left alone that we can work out this problem just as we have had to work out our problems in the past."[52] Struggling to preserve what their forebears had created, white southerners took every opportunity to herald the absolute necessity of racial separation as the only mechanism capable of corralling the region's African American population while bringing peace and stability to all.

By the mid-twentieth century, segregationists still believed that southern Blacks were happy and content, while also harboring great concerns regarding the potential for Black lawlessness once immediate and direct white oversight no longer prevailed. As expected, they staunchly defended the need to perpetuate the racial system they controlled by asserting that the evidence of iniquity highlighted by civil rights advocates proved more illusory than real. Southern Senate leader Richard Russell of Georgia, who frequently pilloried the African American community, felt comfortable claiming in 1957 that "I yield to no man in his concern for and efforts toward equal and exact justice before the Law for our Negro people."[53] Russell's comments are consistent with those made by others. Indeed, segregationists saw no irony in their defense of segregation and their self-professed admiration for the Black population that was held back because of the prejudice they supported. Time after time, white southerners asserted that they genuinely cared for the region's Black population and that external forces proved the only stimuli that stirred internal regional dissent. The segregationist myth demanded strict adherence to the basic assertion that peace reigned in regional race relations and that whites and Blacks recognized and understood their places in the system. Remove its protective cloak, however, and the region's Black citizenry would invariably spark racial conflict. Despite his assertion that "some of the finest people I have ever known are Negroes," Richard Russell still emphasized at the dawn of the 1960s that "the Negro, as a race, has the highest rate of crime of any sizable ethnic group in our country."[54] Russell's paranoia regarding alleged Black criminality, which in his mind made segregation a necessity, captures the essence of the region's post-slavery mythology. No matter how many times Russell and other national political leaders attempted to dress up their beliefs by following a more edifying line of argumentation in challenging the legality of various civil rights laws, the fulcrum of their position forever remained racial bias. Until the end of the segregation fight, white southerners were wedded to the retrogression model popularized in the post–Civil War South that itself had its roots in the school of civilization model which preceded it. The unbroken intellectual line joining the Old South and the New South stretched deep into the twentieth century.

Local and state violence made the prospect of any successful fight for segregation on the national level impossible, just as it exploded the mythology holding that the region could best handle its racial problems. The South's Washington leaders struggled to keep a lid on the excesses in their respective states, especially following the Supreme Court's 1954 *Brown v. Board* ruling. That those leaders never fully stymied local passions reveals their assertions concerning the tranquility forged by Jim Crow were obviously a myth. In the end, segregation's national defenders embraced any and all defenses of the institution, hoping that one or more would strike a resonant chord with non-southerners. For the region's senators and representatives, no amount of moralizing and/or rationalizing could mitigate the impact of the excesses committed in the name of white supremacy on the local level. Senator J. William Fulbright, for example, regarding public perceptions of Arkansans following the violence associated with the 1957 integration of Little Rock Central High School observed, "We have not been a narrow-minded or bigoted people, and yet the rest of the country now looks upon us as such."[55] In the aftermath of the 1961 assault on the Freedom Riders in Alabama, Fulbright again expressed the moderate's dilemma, opining that "those of us who argue that the States are competent to manage their own affairs and particularly to deal with racial problems have great difficulty in explaining such occurrences."[56] Rhetoric and action fell too far apart for even the most naive observer to miss. The worst enemy of the southern myth of tranquil race relations was the southern people themselves. Similarly, few elected officials publicly castigated their constituents for the excesses they committed in the name of white supremacy or seriously considered the possible existence of injustice in the system they defended because they too accepted southern racial norms.

Relinquishing the grip of segregation on the South would, some rationalized, bring economic improvements by way of corporate infrastructure investments—if only the region softened its hardline attitude. Despite the prospect of tangible benefits if some racial mores changed, the majority of white southerners refused to concede anything and fought integration at every turn. Although many did not directly participate in the violence that engulfed the region, they, despite often occupying positions of legal and political power, likewise failed to challenge the forces of evil that operated freely in their communities. The absence of significant opposition to racial injustice is easy enough to explain. Racial separation was widely evident in the public arena and its precepts were reinforced at every stage of southern life. Until the end, segregationist rhetoric stressed that living among African Americans imparted to whites special insight into the strengths and especially the weaknesses of the Black community. Naturally, white southerners rarely spoke openly with the Black people they claimed they knew to gauge how they really felt about being relegated to a second-class status. The racial divide thus spanned not only the public world but, in many cases, the private one as well. An open racial discourse simply could not happen in America for much of the first half of the twentieth century and this proved especially true in the South. As a result, many white southerners profoundly misjudged the level of contentedness with the status quo found in the Black community.[57] From cradle to grave, white southerners grew up in a world where children were taught the benefits of segregation in the home and school and had the message of their superiority reinforced wherever they traveled in the segregated South. Whites went to the front of the line and Blacks to the back. African Americans regardless of age or wealth were deemed inferior by whites without any consideration given to individual achievements. Similar to the slave system before it, segregation entitled white southerners to an exalted social status that many thought worthy of preserving regardless of the potential outcome or the possible economic improvement that might accrue from the infusion of northern capital if only the region muted its hate. Segregation's loss was perceived by many in the same cataclysmic fashion as the prospect of emancipation in the Old South. Despite the pervasive nature of the race-based system, white southern thought, however, never proved monolithic.[58]

Unlike in the antebellum South, denizens of the Jim Crow South were, relatively speaking, more deeply divided on the racial system they lorded over at least in terms of the extremes they were willing to go to defend it. Clearly, a greater percentage of white southerners found the system of segregation of dubious value than their forebears did slavery even if they remained quiet. Careful examination of the segregationist perspective provided by those less devoted to the racial order, yet who had to defend it owing to their holding elected office, underscores that the South was far from unified regarding its corpus of beliefs concerning segregation, especially those involving race. Indeed, southerners offered a multitude of explanations in defense of Jim Crow that proved more diverse than seen in the defense of slavery. In part, evident shifts in the arguments defending the institution reflected the changing nature of the South itself as well as the altered circumstances around them. A sizable minority of southern politicians came to power and toed the line when it came to racial norms, but their fidelity to the institution did not extend much beyond paying lip service to regional myths. Senator J. William Fulbright, for example, is often deemed a "reluctant racist" by scholars in that he went along with the crusade against integration in order to remain in office, not because of a deep-seated devotion to the cause. Nonetheless, Fulbright clearly recognized an important fact about the region that always tempered any doubts he might have about segregation. "In the South," Fulbright remarked, "it [civil rights] does not lend itself to rational discussion, and is essentially a matter of the emotions and passions."[59] Moderate politicians such as Fulbright seldom made biological inferiority the basis for their defense of segregation. Instead, they stressed that Jim Crow was ingrained in the culture and that any attempt to root it out would result in a race war. As such, the Arkansan, despite decrying violence, framed his outlook around the central myth that the South was best positioned to address its own problems. Fulbright might look askance at the excesses committed in the name of Jim Crow, but he opposed any external efforts to corral it.

Texas Republican John Tower, who won election to the U.S. Senate in

1961, condemned the prejudice that existed in the South, remarking, "I hasten to say that as a native southerner I am deeply ashamed of the way we have treated our Negro citizens."[60] However, Tower, like many reluctant segregationists, also observed, "We cannot overturn the mores of a whole society overnight."[61] Instead Tower, like many before him, propped up the old myth that the South should be left to settle its racial problems internally and peacefully for "the greater good of the American Republic."[62] Tower's rhetoric must also be viewed from the standpoint of political expediency. He broke through the solidly Democratic South and won a state-wide Texas election as a Republican. He did not do so by championing racial change; he did so by connecting aspects of the segregationist perspective to Republican efforts to secure a foothold in the region, revealing the framework that would soon bring a sweeping political realignment to the South. Tower's success demonstrated the possible electoral advantage the Republican Party could accrue if it adopted a southern strategy that pandered to the prevalent white racism in the region while employing coded rhetoric emphasizing the sanctity of individual and property rights. All the arguments used in defense of segregation found expression in Tower's rhetoric, however, he first filtered them through a less overtly racial screen before verbalizing them.

Until the end of the legislative battle over civil rights, Tennessee's Albert Gore Sr., who had a demonstrated record of moderation on racial issues, resisted any discussion involving the potential end of segregation. Gore saw it as "surely unrealistic to hope that all bias, preference, and prejudice can be eliminated from our private lives," and he continued, "It would be contrary to generally accepted principles of individual freedom for government to attempt to compel it."[63] Despite their publicly stated distaste for racial discrimination, neither Tower nor Gore accepted regional change through any means save for local institutions—the very same institutions that perpetuated the Jim Crow order. Offering allegedly peaceful solutions to the South's racial problems that were required to work within the Jim Crow framework represented no solution at all. Nonetheless, their proposals fit perfectly within the mythology of the region that defined southerners as peculiarly suited to handle the problems associated with a biracial social order. Even when admitting the wrongs found in the South, white southerners remained wedded to the larger myth that Jim Crow segregation was the most feasible system for the region—at least in their then present. Change, if it were to come, needed to take place by way of an internal force directed by white southerners. Repeating the sentiments of slaveholders who argued that they alone should determine the end date of the institution, twentieth-century southerners made the same assertion regarding their own racial system. Despite the advance of the calendar, time stood still.

The division found in the ranks of the South's national leaders also found expression on the local level albeit in a different form. In the mid-twentieth century, the white South jettisoned, or at least marginalized, public figures who preached a gospel other than defiance informed by the doctrine of white supremacy. Not surprisingly, politicians, who proved less devoted to segregation, circumvented racial sentiments by saying just enough to avoid accusations of being labeled "soft" on civil rights. They still peddled many of the region's central myths, especially the assertion that southern whites understood southern Blacks better than outsiders, making the South best suited to address any future changes to the racial order. For moderates outside of the political arena, the same rules applied. Despite their limited vocal presence, it is important to note that voices of dissent persisted in the region. How successful they were in advancing an apostate position depended on how far they strayed from regional mythology. For example, George Avery Lee, pastor of Ruston's First Baptist Church in Louisiana made no effort to hide his belief in racial equality. He noted, "The Negro is a creature of God, the same as I am. He has a soul, the same as I do. In the eyes of God there is no difference between us . . . the same salvation Jesus brought to me, he brought to the Negro."[64] In the 1950s–1960s, such comments did not sit well among north Louisiana Protestants. Despite his controversial remarks, Lee retained his pastorship and the support of most of his congregation. Although he challenged the racism at the heart of Jim Crow, Lee left a central piece of regional orthodoxy in place in his many musings on race. At the same time he preached the idea of equality in the eyes of God, he emphasized the need for homegrown solutions to the South's racial problems. Lee's emphasis on Black and white southerners coming together to reach a new accord that would dismantle the worst excesses of the Jim Crow system fit firmly in the existing mythology holding that only those who resided in the region had an accurate understanding of the racial order. Lee carefully walked the line when addressing matters of race in the South. He met what he perceived to be his faith-based mandate by touting the brotherhood of man, at least, before God, just as he acknowledged regional customs by stressing the importance of a southern solution to the problem of Jim Crow.[65]

In contrast to Lee, the Christian Life Commission of the Southern Baptist Convention regularly faced the scorn of segregationists, not necessarily because it touted the divine nature of racial equality, but because it stressed the need to embrace the *Brown* verdict and racial change in general. At the Southern Baptist Convention in 1954, the Christian Life Commission issued its report, "Don't Blame the Supreme Court," in which it called for integration as dictated in the *Brown* ruling before adding that "it is time for Baptists and the other citizens of our country to restore to our 13,000,000 Negro people their rights and privileges as guaranteed to them by our constitution."[66] In succeeding years, the Commission's annual report continued stressing the need for racial change. Missing from Commission recommendations, to the dismay of segregationists, was any hint of deference to the established mythology of the South. The Commission, unlike Avery Lee, who did work for the Commission, brooked no compromise with segregationists. To the Commission, God's work superseded the misguided racial etiquette of the South. Protests against the Christian Life Commission were immediate and sustained with state-level Baptist organs rebuking the group and its message. What the regional Baptist convention overlooked in its well-intentioned efforts to promote racial change was the lesson Avery Lee knew well. The majority of the white South believed in the region's central myths. Lee received greater leeway precisely because he wrapped his message of reform in the cloak of southern cultural norms. Lee certainly received his fair share of criticism, but his congregants shielded him since he ultimately preached that white southerners needed to have a place at the table if any future alteration of Jim Crow was to occur. Externally driven change proved too much for the white southern populace to bear.[67]

When confronted with the abolitionist crusade, the white South effectively stifled debate on the issue where it could: below the Mason-Dixon Line. Internal dissenters were silenced, the Black population was oppressed, and outsiders were kept at bay. William Lloyd Garrison may have hated slavery, but he certainly was not about to travel across the region urging southerners to give up the peculiar institution. There remains little doubt that had he attempted such an undertaking, it would have been an extraordinarily short sojourn. Antebellum slaveholders had wide control over the information received by the enslaved. True, word of abolitionism in the North reached the slave quarters across the South, but no corporeal manifestation of the movement or even of Blacks living as anything but bondsmen visited them. Only the enslaved persons allowed to run plantation errands in nearby cities and towns caught glimpses of African Americans in freedom. In short, white southerners in the nineteenth century had considerable control over the extent and nature of information that their bondsmen received. Twentieth-century southerners confronted an entirely different cultural milieu. Try as they might, whites could not stifle all opposition. The Black population, although relegated to secondary social status, remained free to move about, especially to the North. While there, they received exposure to more liberal social customs governing race relations. Although many stayed above the Mason-Dixon Line, modern technology such as the telephone ensured that they could communicate with folks back home, filling them in about a world in which skin color did not necessarily delimit options. A number of them returned after finding the "promised land" held far fewer rewards than expected. Nonetheless, when they returned, they came back changed and armed with knowledge of a different world. Affronted by white racism, many returning Black southern expatriates overtly challenged the prevailing ethos just as they encouraged others to do the same. Allen Ellender's remarks capture the rhetoric often bandied about in the region. In one exchange, he noted, "A southern negro is polite by instinct, but when he comes up north, he gets as sassy as a flea, and with that condition trouble follows."[68] In the mind of many segregationists, episodes of Black recalcitrance stemmed from the influence of non-southern white liberals, who wanted to change the South through a campaign against segregation that they little understood, not from any homegrown sources. Ellender clearly articulated this vision when he remarked that although "there are few agitators among the negro race who want to throw the races together, 99.9% of the negroes in the South would prefer to live to by themselves, separate, and apart from whites."[69] Viewed in light of the dubious data advanced by the Louisianan, the proverbial "outsider" received all of the anger segregationists had to offer. Ultimately, white southerners could not close off the outside world. Likewise, they could not control violent white outbursts at any sign of Black discontent.

Segregationists had no power to block the migration of people and ideas across the Mason-Dixon Line. Technological advances further undermined the white stranglehold over information. Politicians increasingly grasped the potential that television and other media forms had to influence opinion. In 1956, Allen Ellender trembled at the thought that Americans would get carried away by activists distorting media coverage and "succumb to the blandishments of those who would use highly publicized but rare and isolated incidents like the [Emmett] Till case as a vehicle for extending the jurisdiction of the Federal government into purely local matters."[70] Likewise, Richard Russell, in the midst of a filibuster against the Civil Rights Act of 1960, stopped to opine regarding the sit-in movement that its members "were very anxious to start a race riot of terrible proportions. They would like to be able to say through their spokesmen that a terrible incident had happened in the South—so many people killed, so many injured, so many arrested—and thereby prejudice whatever reason is left in the minds" of the American people.[71] As Russell saw it, activists took isolated episodes of racial unrest and spun them into impassioned accounts of simmering injustice. The Georgian, like the Louisianan before him, understood that sensational stories sold copy and if repeated enough they could prompt demands for far-reaching alterations to the southern way of life. Violent racial episodes beamed across the country would invariably provoke change even if such episodes were as rare as southern statesmen asserted. Television thus not only sent images from the outside world in; it also enabled images from within to be beamed out. The latter concern had sweeping consequences. No matter how much effort politicians such as Ellender and Russell devoted to obscuring the truth, the violence that undergirded Jim Crow kept coming to light. Across the South episodes of violence regularly took place, but almost never in front of the cameras. Capturing the turmoil on film went a long way toward debunking one of segregation's central myths that tranquility governed regional race relations. Violence was quickly being recognized as the glue that held Jim Crow together.[72]

In the end, segregationists remained wedded to the mythological assertion that racial unrest occurred with great infrequency in the region since everyone proved happy with his or her lot. After all, nature not nurture prompted the separation of the races, or so went the logic upon which Jim Crow developed. When the South's racial order came under sustained attack by civil rights activists starting in the twentieth century, southern politicians regularly observed that all was well with their society. According to segregationists, even when violence erupted, it was always short-lived and handled equitably on the local level. Without visual images, such assertions proved at least plausible to those living outside of the region. Things changed quickly when video footage became available. True enough, one could still make the claim that such episodes as the 1963 violence against peaceful civil rights demonstrators in Birmingham, Alabama, were limited and the result of deliberate prodding but what could not be explained away was the content itself. No one in good conscience could deem the force employed as commensurate with the alleged crime. Peaceful protests do not warrant police dogs and cattle prods. What the footage revealed was the very real terror upon which Jim Crow was built. Even if violence proved rare, the threat of violence or even death for African Americans, who ran afoul of segregationists for any reason, was an everyday reality. Also, the footage cast serious doubts upon the South's ability to handle its own problems without outside assistance. Few who watched could responsibly claim that the Eugene "Bull" Connors of the region were anywhere close to solving the problems in their locales. Civic leaders in some southern communities no doubt could handle the racial turmoil in their midst by instituting token change while retaining aspects of the existing system, but many others could not. Only substantive reform mandated by the federal government would ensure that African Americans living in communities that lacked more progressive leadership would receive their fair share of constitutional protection. Even if only a few bad apples both Black and white spoiled the bunch, as many Jim Crow supporters maintained, there was nothing the federal government could do but intervene uniformly across the region. The days of haphazard attention to the plight of Black Americans were over. Television helped make social change a reality at the same time that it exploded the myths behind segregation.

Control buttressed white dominance in the Old South. Black mobility remained incumbent upon the caprices of slave owners and only a trickle of information from the outside world entered the plantation. Internal dissent found few venues for expression in the South and outside criticism found fewer still. Furthermore, this bifurcated world ensured an "us vs. them" mentality in which affronts to regional norms were viewed exclusively as the work of outsiders. Limited mechanisms existed for anything approaching a reasonable dialogue on the slave question, a fact that accounts, in part, for the march toward secession. Segregationists confronted a changed world that did not afford them control over a closed system similar to the one their forebears lorded over. Dixie's borders in the twentieth century became increasingly porous, allowing for a much freer exchange of ideas that once unleashed, revealed the mythological character of the region's principal beliefs. Plausible deniability regarding the nature of slavery enabled antebellum southerners to uphold the tenets of their central myths since little beyond an anecdotal examination of their validity occurred. Segregationists, on the other hand, faced prying eyes, internal dissenters, and a growing wave of media interference. Many of the myths they had propagated early in the twentieth century simply could not stand up to the scrutiny they later received. When the myths came under fire, the Jim Crow order lacked the depth of roots to sustain itself. As federal pressure closed in, the internal stability of the region weakened. Demonstrations spread, outside agitators arrived, and massive resisters made good on their threats. Unable to sustain the status quo, the Jim Crow mythology and the racial order it protected imploded.

3

The Link and the Albatross

Defenders of the antebellum order predicated their arguments on the basic premise that a naturally occurring racial hierarchy predetermined those of African origins to positions of inferiority. As Matthew Estes remarked, "the African is naturally inferior to the Caucasian and that he is endowed by nature with certain qualities which fit him for the condition of slavery."[1] One must accept the racialist logic at the heart of proslavery rhetoric for without it, the entire mythos of the region collapses. Ethnocentric prejudices naturally ascribed all that was good in the world and in history to those of European heritage. A dearth of learning, intellectual achievement, and other signs of "civilization," as defined, of course, by those from a western European extraction, typified life in Africa. In an 1837 speech before the South Carolina Society for the Advancement of Learning, William Harper, regarding slavery, asked, "Can there be a doubt of the immense benefit which has been conferred on the race, by transplanting them from their native, dark and barbarous regions to the American Continent and Islands?" Despite the rhetorical manner of his aforementioned words, Harper bludgeons readers with reams of exaggerated data in the remainder of his text, all with an eye toward illustrating that in Africa, "three-fourths of the race are in a state of the most deplorable personal Slavery. And those who are not, are in a scarcely less deplorable condition of political Slavery."[2] Harper's commentary on a benighted African continent serves as just one of many examples of how proslavery authors tied their belief in racial hierarchy with Eurocentric impulses. Putting the matter even more bluntly, James

Hammond wrote, "The African . . . is an inferior race, and never will effect, as it never has effected, as much in any other condition as in that of slavery."[3]

Black people found themselves in bondage, the logic went, owing to natural deficiencies that for most could never be overcome. Repeatedly, slavery's defenders referenced the lifestyles of African peoples worldwide and found their condition uniformly deplorable. Rather than search for the causes behind the seeming lack of advancement among African nations when compared with the European world, they chalked up the disparities to inferiority. Slaveholders justified holding fellow humans in bondage by celebrating the transportation of Africans from the primitive conditions that allegedly existed on the so-called "Dark Continent" to the civilizing influence found on the American plantation. Under their conceptualization of reality, removing people from Africa represented a positive good as it saved them from the heathen, barbaric conditions that existed there. Had they stayed in Africa, their lives would mimic Thomas Hobbes's state of nature, being "nasty, brutish, and short."[4] Nothing but warfare, famine, and deprivation characterized the lot of a typical African, the proslavery literature contended. By comparison, W. Gilmore Simms observed, "The Virginia and Carolina negro is not only superior to the African savages from whom they sprung, but when they have had the advantage of training among the whites, they prove themselves very far superior to the free redmen of the country."[5] Simms was thus willing to concede that at least in bondage persons of African origin could improve their lot if only to a point. Taking nothing else into consideration save for what they believed they saw, proslavery authors made several simple deductions. Foremost, they advanced clear value judgments, holding themselves up as the exemplars of civilization, defined naturally through the prism afforded them by their European ancestry. It stands to reason then, that if they viewed the European tradition as the basis of their own value as a people, they would look negatively at those who deviated from that tradition—hence Simms's willingness to denigrate both African and Native in the same breath even as he slightly elevated the former based on their forced exposure to white society. Seminomadic hunter-gatherers with no knowledge of Christianity certainly did not rank high in the pantheon established by white southerners or others of European descent for that matter. The native peoples of America were thus lumped into the category of barbaric heathens. The farther removed a culture was from the European model, the more "uncivilized" it became. Summarizing the worldview that informed the proslavery cause, Matthew Estes commented, "The white man in all ages has enjoyed a considerable degree of freedom . . . the Negro race, on the contrary, has never advanced much beyond the state of barbarism."[6]

A presumption of inferiority flowed naturally in the days before cultural relativism gained favor whenever a departure from the European norm occurred. When proslavery author E. N. Elliott wrote with certainty that "the negro is an inferior variety of the human race," he spoke not only for generations of slaveholders but for much of the nation. As Elliott saw it, physical and mental limitations hampered Blacks, making it impossible for those of African descent to rise "by his own will and power, from barbarism, and achieving civilization and refinement."[7] Neglecting the incredible cultural diversity that existed in Africa, southern racists condemned that which departed from the expectations of civilization found in the western world. Instead, they lambasted the social and cultural norms of the people they encountered without thought given to the "why" behind the differences they noted. Fire-eater Edmund Ruffin observed it was "both false and foolish" to talk of men being born free and equal.[8] According to Ruffin, an examination of the conditions found in Africa and among those of African descent throughout the globe reinforced the idea of innate Black inferiority.

Starting with this root assumption, slavery's defenders easily fabricated arguments that made plantations a positive good. Indeed, to read the narrative constructed by these southern thinkers is to see how closely intertwined their essential mythology was with regional identity. White southerners were uplifting their slaves by exposing them to all of the riches of "civilization." Far from debasing fellow humans by holding them in bondage, proslavery theorists invested the peculiar institution with almost biblical importance. "Upliftment" served as the preferred term for what slavery did to those in bondage, making the implementation of the system both an economic and, in many ways, a moral imperative. Likewise, it established a connecting thread that spanned all of the major periods in the South's history, tying the antebellum era to the age of Jim Crow and everything in between. The theme of Black inferiority thus found constant expression across the South no matter the period.[9] Similarly, white authors also stressed that Black docility stemmed from recognition among the enslaved that they filled their rightful position in the human order. According to one proslavery advocate, African Americans "feel and acknowledge their inferiority; and in consequence, Slavery is not in the least regarded as a degradation, but as their proper and natural position."[10] Plantation slavery was thus depicted as best for all parties involved. As long as the ever-sturdy hand of white dominance remained in charge, the prevailing order faced few internal challengers. Many theorists believed that slaves left to their own devices proved "too well content with their condition" to consider altering their status through revolution.[11] They would remain enslaved as long as they lived.

If one takes the frequency of commentary on it in proslavery treatises as an indication of how pervasive the notion was, upliftment was a foremost concern for southern slaveholders. Regardless of the author, proslavery writers touted the theme, stressing that slavery only brought positive benefits to the enslaved. Thomas Dew opined, "Slavery . . . seems to be the only means that we know of, under heaven, by which the ferocity of the savage can be conquered, his wandering habits eradicated, his slothfulness and improvidence . . . can be changed."[12] Others proved just as quick to embrace the savage ideal advanced by Dew and others. Author William J. Grayson typifies the perspective of white southerners regarding their charges. Grayson observed that the central feature of Blacks remains their "lazy and improvident" nature.[13] Indeed, Grayson, echoing the sentiments of all such theorists, opined that slavery transformed the "savage" into "an orderly and efficient laborer," since the system "restrains his vices, and improves his mind."[14] Although set twenty years apart, Dew's writing in the 1830s and Grayson's in the 1850s, both authors and indeed generations of white southerners, gravitated toward the same basic premise tied inextricably to the belief in the inequality of man. Albert Bledsoe, summing up the slaveholder ethos in 1856, remarked, "No fact is plainer than that the blacks have been elevated and improved by their servitude in this country."[15] Antebellum whites thus joined their cause to a concept that is horribly racist and inaccurate in today's world but was a rarely challenged fact in their time. The ideas they promulgated became enmeshed in the social and cultural milieu of the region and were passed from generation to generation as established doctrine.

Throughout the antebellum period, proslavery writers noted the beneficial effects that bondage had on those of African origins. A variety of reasons no doubt shaped this emphasis, most of them revolving around the necessity of defending against abolitionist charges that enslaving others was immoral. By adding an ethical component to the institution, slaveholders could pat themselves on the back and celebrate their moral—and racial—superiority. Equally crucial was the absolute certitude with which the upliftment theme was embraced. No explanations followed the platitudes since white southerners generally accepted them without justification or proof. It became a concept so deeply enmeshed in white southern culture that it found expression in practically all southern defenses of slavery. Belief in the inherent inequality of man served as a foundational principle from which all other defenses of slavery sprang. African slavery as practiced in the American South, the theory went, brought inferior peoples, "into continual intercourse with masters of superior minds, information, and morality."[16] This interaction with more advanced people yielded positive fruits, most theorized. According to James Hammond, North American slaves because of their exposure to white influence were granted access to civilization and by extension were uplifted. The extent of this upliftment fell beyond the purview of most proslavery advocates, who typically only stressed that some elevation indeed occurred. Thinkers such as Hammond expected little from those of African descent, making whatever they could achieve the sole product of their exposure to "superior" people.[17] No "nature versus nurture" dichotomy informed Hammond's beliefs; his conception of things was rooted in the notion that nature limited people of African origins. According to Hammond, Africans proved "eminently qualified in temper, in vigor, in docility, in capacity to stand the climate" for slavery, rendering them perfect to assume mudsill status in southern society.[18] What becomes evident in Hammond's remarks is the foundational nature of the belief that those of African origins could only be "uplifted" to a limited extent. Even the best nurturing could not undo the crippling effects of one's origins. In a world in which skin color set the limits of advancement, white southerners found themselves atop the social order that they created. At the same time, few made an effort to provide specific examples regarding how the process of upliftment actually occurred. Whether one looks at proslavery arguments in the 1830s or the 1860s, this central race-based theme of upliftment remained unchanged. With the great power that southern whites held also came the responsibility of overseeing the elevation, however negligible it may be, of those they lorded over. It was a task not to be taken lightly, especially considering its allegedly divine origins.

The opinions of proslavery theorists departed over the exact cosmology of slavery, but not to such an extent that it undermined the key belief in racial hierarchy. This remained a constant. When southerners did try to discern the source of the upliftment paradigm, the Christian God became a central component of the equation. The Old Testament story in the book of Genesis of a curse placed on the descendants of Noah's son Ham, after the latter witnessed his father lying drunk and naked, came to be interpreted as dooming all people of African origins to enslavement. Despite the fact that the biblical account made no reference to color, the mark of scorn levelled on the Canaanites was considered by some to represent black skin. It is no coincidence that this rendering of the Bible became popular in the sixteenth century at a time when the European world began extensive exploration and exploitation of the African continent. Ham's curse, in turn, became a foundational trope for slavery's defenders as it created a divine mandate for the South's racial institution. Thomas Dew most clearly echoed these sentiments by succinctly noting that "God has suited the African to slavery."[19] Considering such a worldview, purveyors of slavery had a built-in explanation for their system that prevented any effort to besmirch them, as abolitionists attempted, with charges of immorality. William Harper, in his 1837 *Memoir on Slavery*, noted, "It is the order of nature and of God, that the being of superior faculties and knowledge, and therefore of superior power, should control and dispose of those who are inferior."[20] For Harper and others like him, slavery had divine sanction. Although touting Christian doctrine, proslavery authors turned the concept of the meek inheriting the earth on its head. Under this construct, the strong not only dominated the world around them, but they had divine authority to do so. When considering the concept of "Manifest Destiny," it is not hard to see how a society that produced a doctrine rooted in cultural imperialism could also provide fertile ground for the various defenses of slavery that had at their root the belief in the strong rightfully vanquishing the weak. As much as some would like to depict slavery's existence as an aberration on the American landscape or as a perverse regional ideal tied to a backward people united in defense of an outdated economic order, it is not hard to place the institution of slavery, and later segregation, in the mainstream of American thought and economic life. After all, the same forces which compelled Americans to conquer a continent also gave them sanction to enslave people of color and later brutalize new immigrants at the start of the twentieth century. God only entered the equation to set the ball rolling. He then departed, leaving the chore of enslavement to his chosen people. As strained as such logic appears today, at the time such notions were contrived, there existed a degree of certitude on the matter that matches our own.

Providence did not blindly pick the American South for the task of uplifting Blacks. The Lord, southerners believed, had a purpose, albeit an opaque one, in bringing the two races together. Often the same theorists who claimed that the powerful had a divine mandate to subjugate the weaker included another thread that ran parallel with the "might makes right" schema. Perhaps to soften overt support for the exploitative use of power among a Christian people, there emerged another thread which more forcefully stressed the divine mandate for slavery. God did not just make one race superior to another and leave them to their own devices; he expected the stronger to uplift the weaker. In an otherwise staid statistical analysis of slavery penned in the 1850s, Thornton Stringfellow wrote, "The South did not seek or desire the responsibility, and the onerous burden of civilizing and christianizing these degraded savages; God, in his mysterious providence, brought it about."[21] Stringfellow, like so many before him, made it clear that the white South bore no culpability for the existence of slavery. Forces beyond white control necessitated the institution. What better way to parry charges regarding the immorality of slaveholding than to ascribe one's alleged transgressions to providence? Antebellum southerners, many of whom were fervent in their faith, found expressions of divine sanction for their undertaking reassuring. If God was for them, to quote a popular Christian verse, then who could be against them? Indeed, for some theorists, religion represented the central feature that lifted African slaves out of their barbarism. In 1859, Edward Pollard, who later helped forge the mythology surrounding the "Lost Cause," stressed not only the elevation narrative so common in the proslavery corpus but also the importance of introducing the enslaved to the western monotheistic tradition, thereby making the institution a clear benefit to those in bondage by offering them the prospect of salvation. Pollard wrote that slavery "elevates him from the condition of a nomad, a heathen, a brute, to that of a comfortable creature, and gives him the priceless treasure of a saving religion."[22] No amount of labor, toil, discipline, and indeed no other contrivance but exposure to Christianity, according to Pollard, brought about the elevation of the slaves. "Savages" needed introduction to Christianity early and repeatedly throughout their lives. Whether or not the Christian message whites permitted their slaves to receive was a controlled one proved beside the point in white southern minds. Since God saw fit for white southerners to forge a race-based social order, slaveholders were obligated to introduce their charges to Christianity. In one of the more shocking reflections on the relationship between the Christian God and slavery, Mississippi minister J. B. Thrasher commented on the benevolence of the institution and on the enslavers who treated the enslaved well by "clothing, feeding, and working them—protecting their lives, and instructing them in the principles of the Christian religion."[23] Slavery, according to Thrasher, was "a purely moral and religious act, and pleasing in the sight of God."[24] His comments underscore the powerful self-delusion which guided the vision of many proslavery advocates. Not only did Thrasher embrace the upliftment myth, but he also asserted that by enslaving people, white southerners were actually performing a divinely inspired task. Although many theorists did not expressly make this case, it is certainly implied in their writing. Some such as Stringfellow, went as far as to claim that slavery in America would only end when "God opens a door to make its termination a blessing and not a curse."[25] In other words, just as God hoisted upon white southerners the responsibility of civilizing their bondsmen, he alone would be (or should be) responsible for the removal of the institution.

Deviations from the standard proslavery line regarding the need for perpetual bondage proved exceptionally rare, but they did occur. In a biblical argument in defense of slavery published in 1860, Charles Hodge, the head of the Princeton Theological Seminary, indicated that emancipation at some future point was possible. As Hodge saw it, emancipation might take place due to "the gradual elevation of the slaves in knowledge, virtue, and property to the point at which it is no longer desirable or possible to keep them in bondage."[26] Although hedged with qualifications, Hodge's depiction of the end of slavery stands in stark contrast to the concepts advanced by practically all other major proslavery thinkers. Hodge in many ways followed the theme of upliftment to its logical conclusion; few others ventured down that path. Of course, Hodge was born and raised in the North, spending most of his adult life in New Jersey, a fact that likely accounted for his willingness to see the enslaved in a different light than southerners. Likewise, although he supported slavery as a theoretical construct, he proved reluctant to embrace the iteration of it that existed in the

South without critique. Hodge's staunch Presbyterian faith gave him pause when he pondered the dissolution of Black families via the slave trade and other southern practices that tended to deny the essential humanity of the enslaved. Like Hodge, many proslavery champions vaguely contended that slavery could alter the very "nature" of the slave, but stopped well short of suggesting that a critical mass could be reached that might render further enslavement problematic.[27] Beyond the simple assurance that a slave's nature might be altered in bondage they would not go, and they certainly did not posit that these changes were permanent. What was never clarified was how and why an altered nature would revert to "barbarism" so quickly, as most proslavery advocates speculated would occur rapidly upon emancipation. If exposure to white southerners brought the level of civilization touted by practically all proslavery authors, then how could the enslaved not one day become so elevated that they should be freed? Most proslavery thinkers opted out of embracing the logically consistent argument that Hodge forwarded by putting an arbitrary glass ceiling above the slaves they described. Rather than conceding the ability of their charges to fully embrace civilization so that they might one day be the equal or at least near equal of whites, they opted instead to make white oversight the linchpin of advancement and race the determining factor in how far one could aspire to go. None conceded that Blacks would one day reach the same level of attainment as whites. Indeed, some such as Matthew Estes postulated that racial inferiority existed not only in white minds but in Black ones as well. Regarding African Americans, he noted "that color, and his natural inferiority, have erected an impassable barrier between him and the white man; he, therefore, never thinks of aspiring to an equality with him."[28] Since the basic notion of Black inferiority was generally accepted, fears that recently freed persons would not behave in a "civilized" manner naturally followed.

Building an ideology around slavery, white southerners created a neatly contained system that validated their use of an insidious institution. They saw the world they inhabited as a peaceful one, in which white oversight uplifted a barbaric people by granting them exposure to "civilization." In the long term, they foresaw the maintenance of that tranquility only in the context of slavery. Push the abolition issue, they speculated, and chaos would quickly override the existing calm, forcing the South "back to its primitive state, in which it is only fit for the residence of beasts of prey."[29] Safeguarding the peace into the future meant preserving the social order that created it—defending it, if need be, at the end of a barrel, rather than relinquishing the stability it established. One of the more outspoken champions of slavery, J. B. Thrasher, asserted, "We, in the South, therefore, believe it to be our duty to God, to ourselves, and to posterity, to perpetuate African slavery, and to extend it as a missionary duty."[30] There can be little doubt that the proslavery ideology resonated with the large majority of the white southern population who viewed themselves in the same crusading light as Thrasher. Their imperialist impulse was, at least to them, driven by divine dictates. They had little choice. Destroying slavery meant anarchy and the end of everything they had struggled to create. The implications of such a seismic change would engulf all of the region's denizens regardless of their slave ownership. No one wanted such an abrupt disruption of the status quo which, in part, accounts for the paucity of substantive discussions on the possibility of a post-slavery future that did not dwell on the likelihood of unmitigated chaos. With the stakes so high, few envisioned a scenario free of lawlessness.

Concerns regarding racial conflict upon emancipation seem peculiarly out of place considering the widespread assurance that docility marked the temperament of the enslaved. How could a people described as peaceful, joyous, and even docile become violent overnight?[31] Some took the position that the docility existing among southern Blacks stemmed from their exposure to southern whites and that through a long-term process, they became tranquil albeit with the threat of the inner savage never far from the surface, especially when beyond the pale of white influence. Outward appearances, however, belied the inner demon that required only a modicum of freedom to emerge. As E. N. Elliot opined, the enslaved were elevated by their bondage; however, "this development is not permanent, but is liable to retrogression as soon as the influence of the superior race is removed."[32] In the end, proslavery champions gravitated toward a simple trope: freedom from slavery brought liberation from white oversight, resulting in a precipitous loss of all of the benefits of civilization accrued while in bondage. Most agreed with this summation and made the concept of emancipation a harbinger of social chaos and dislocation. Without slavery, the South would degenerate into bedlam as the guiding hand of white rule slipped away and those once enslaved retrogressed.

When discussing a post-slavery world, a cataclysmic race war emerged as the most common outcome of emancipation concocted in proslavery treatises. Time after time, in place after place, and theorist after theorist, the argument remained the same. Those of African descent proved so barbaric and so tenuously in possession of rudimentary levels of civilization that even if exposed to those of European ancestry for extended periods, they would quickly regress to their innate state of barbarism following the removal of white oversight. Mississippian Jefferson Davis, for example, commented that regarding the prospects for free African Americans, "the negro could not exist in anything like a civilized condition without the presence of the white man."[33] There was no alternative according to those of Davis's ilk. Freedmen would either have to be shipped to Africa, or they would remain in America where conflict with whites would be inevitable. Whether in the form of correspondence, treatises, or speeches, the theme of upheaval proved so pronounced that it served as a formulaic feature of proslavery arguments which delved into the question of emancipation. Catastrophic financial loss upon emancipation was joined by fears of a bloody race war in sending shivers down the spines of slaveholders. The formula fell along the following lines: "The history of the world has too conclusively shown that two races, differing in manners, customs, language, and civilization, can never harmonize upon a footing of equality. One must rule the other, or exterminating wars must be waged."[34] The bloodlust on both sides of the question necessitated strict adherence to the natural order, which proslavery theorists argued remained rooted in their theory of racial hierarchy.

The consequences of slavery's eradication in America was a subject that southern theorists spent considerable time addressing. Indeed, it became an unavoidable talking point as the nineteenth century progressed and sectional tensions exploded over the westward expansion of slavery. By the 1850s, proslavery advocates devoted great attention to the issue as the prospect of aggressive federal action against the region mounted. Growing abolitionist and antislavery political power exploded following the emergence of the Republican Party and further enhanced southern angst. Any scheme that saw an end to the institution save for those stemming directly from providence filled most white southerners with fear. Minor transgressions committed by the enslaved, such as petty theft, had long been the bane of plantation holders even if most turned a blind eye to it. No matter the level of exposure to the more "exalted" white race, there always remained a residual hint of barbarism among the enslaved, so theorized the proslavery forces in order to rationalize episodes of larceny and other minor offences which scholars today understand as acts of resistance. Serious concerns surrounded the possible removal of uplifting white oversight. Strike it from the equation, and the Black population would "be led from petty to greater crimes, until all life and property would be rendered insecure."[35] Others held, "All accounts agree that the emancipated Negroes are actually declining in civilization: that they are now in a lower state of improvement than they were when in Slavery."[36] Regardless of the thinker, some semblance of discord was expected should emancipation ever occur.

Authors varied in terms of how depraved they believed Black actions in freedom would be. For some, a mere glimpse north of the Mason-Dixon Line underscored that Blacks free from white oversight rarely thrived. It is only "as slaves in the midst of white men, they can and do improve," argued one proslavery advocate.[37] A major reason, such theorists postulated, for Black poverty in northern locations was connected with the absence of the threat of the whip that was utilized on practically all southern plantations. Without it, Blacks, many asserted, "will not labor at all if they can escape it."[38] Repeated assertions that the enslaved tended toward idleness when left unguarded filled proslavery literature. Again, the point remained simple. Slavery benefitted those of African descent in innumerable ways, from shielding them from the interminable wars that plagued their native lands to providing them food, clothing, and shelter. Their emancipated brethren in the North lacked paternalistic white oversight and, as a result, much of a work ethic since they embraced their innate tendency toward sloth. This fast-eroding work ethic, in turn, helps account for the expected uptick in violence. Without a steady income, it was assumed that liberated Blacks would "fall on helpless women and children, the weak and the infirm" to survive.[39] Not addressed in white southern screeds was the larger question of how racial discrimination impacted Black Americans in every setting they found themselves in. Apparent shiftlessness among the free could just as easily have been depicted as the product of discriminatory hiring practices instead of an innate tendency to loaf. As frustrating as it remains for modern readers to see these words and to bemoan the absence of higher-level thinking demonstrated in these outlandish claims, it must be remembered that these utterances remained not the musings of marginal men, but the embodiment of how many white Americans, regardless of region, perceived matters of race at the time. Convinced of Black inferiority, nineteenth-century Americans had no need to question the status quo. They knew with certainty that they had it right. With the assurance of Black depravity, proslavery theorists noted with confidence that those of African descent prefer, "sinking down into the listless, inglorious repose of the brute creation," to hard work.[40] "Retrogression" seemed to them the only possible outcome if abolitionists ever succeeded in carrying the day.[41] The phrase and the concept would not go away, and it would later serve as a justification for why white oversight needed to be returned in the decades following abolition.[42]

Although the history of the American South is the principal subject of this work, it is imperative to reiterate that the racism evident below the Mason-Dixon Line did not exist in isolation or solely among southern theorists. The nineteenth-century belief in a strict racial hierarchy knew no regional bounds. The nearly universal prejudice in America in the nineteenth century manifested itself in different ways from holding people in bondage in the South to the social and economic ostracism of minorities evident in the North. In an unrestrained assessment of race that stressed the near universality of American prejudice in his time, William Harper uttered, "That the African negro is an inferior variety of the human race, is, I think, now generally admitted."[43] Harper intentionally cast his comments in categorical terms highlighting the fact that all Americans, even those outside of the plantation South, accepted Black inferiority. Most northerners harbored little interest in the plight of the enslaved. Abolitionists, who represented a small northern minority, wanted to fully eradicate slavery everywhere in the nation; they did not, however, agree on the thornier issue of human equality. In abolitionist circles, debate swirled around the prospect of free Black membership and leadership in their organizations. By comparison, northern antislavery sentiment, such as that touted by the Free Soil and Republican parties, supported thwarting slavery's extension to the West primarily to create a white man's paradise free of Blacks, not an interracial utopia. At the same time, antislavery advocates doubted the constitutionality of an attack on slavery where it already existed. Relatively clear lines existed regarding white northern perceptions of the institution of slavery. Some hated the institution, some sought to contain its growth, and some gave it no thought. Shifting the discussion toward a world beyond slavery in most northern locations resulted in a blurring of even this certainty. Most northerners did not see equality as a viable solution. They certainly did not treat the African Americans in their midst as equals. Instead, they relegated them to second-class status and denied them access to economic mobility. Outside of the South, it boiled down to a debate over whether keeping other humans in bondage was acceptable, not whether a brotherhood of man should be sought. Racial equality was simply not a part of the equation.[44] Few outside of a small circle of abolitionists desired a society in which whites and Blacks coexisted as equals, especially not in a region with a vast Black population as found in the South. Of those who tried to picture an integrated world free of racial restraints, whether inside or outside of the South, nothing but chaos filled their visions. The risks so far outweighed the potential rewards that only a foolish man would advocate the end of slavery. There was no room for nuance. Capturing the spirit of this sentiment, Samuel A. Cartwright observed, "American civilization, founded upon revealed truth and nature's laws, puts the negro in his natural position, that of subordination to the white man."[45] For Cartwright, the natural order not just for the South but also the entire nation was one in which racial stratification served as the bedrock of the republic. Abolitionists, according to this argument, thus did not just seek to undermine the social order of the South, they were bent on destroying the country.

White southern fears of Black listlessness and petty theft represented but the tip of the iceberg. Equal to the powerful fears of a massive bloodletting brought on by Black retrogression outside of slavery stood paranoia concerning miscegenation. Proslavery advocates embraced a simple formula they claimed was responsible for the collapse of all great civilizations and empires, which, if left unchecked, threatened to destroy not just the South but the United States. In its base form, the theory consisted of three components that flowed logically, one piece following the other. Amalgamation begets mongrelization before resulting in societal collapse. Any people who permitted this process to occur, the theory went, would, in effect, be committing cultural suicide. Offspring of interracial coupling, rather than exhibit the best characteristics of their parents, would instead display the worst features, a trend which over time would diminish the creative vitality of the society which condoned such degradation to take place. In his 1851 biblical defense of slavery, Josiah Priest, commenting on the ill effects of whites commingling with Blacks, observed that "amalgamation with them, therefore, proposes not only the blackening of the skin, but of the blood and flesh, even to the bone, as well as the deterioration of the mental faculties of the progeny of the whites."[46] What made the white southern position so strange was the fact that historically they were the principal force behind amalgamation, but in their eyes, it was Blacks who coveted relations with their racial opposites. Although scores of documented cases depicting white transgressions against slave women often resulting in bastard babies are known, it remained a subject rarely broached in the antebellum era. Of those who admitted its existence, there was a tendency to downplay its scope. James Hammond, for example, remarked concerning interracial coupling that "its character and extent . . . are grossly and atrociously exaggerated."[47] Most sought to explain away its existence claiming that it represented more abolitionist fancy than a concrete occurrence. Still, others accepted its presence, but only so much as it protected the honor of southern white women. Interracial babies undeniably existed on plantations across the South, and, as Mary Chesnut noted, southern women proved adept at locating the mulatto babies on every plantation but their own.[48]

Despite the incredibly significant white role in promoting miscegenation within the confines of the slave system, fears of Black retrogression only heightened concerns of Black licentiousness. With emancipation at hand, many worried that interracial children would proliferate, leading eventually to the demise of the country. The future of the South could thus go one of two ways. It could become a wasteland as racial wars rocked the region, destroying the conviviality that had once existed as whites struggled to keep wayward Blacks in order. Or it could become the literal and figurative breeding ground for the nation's collapse. Adding to the amalgamation-collapse formula sprang another myth that social equality would beget bedroom equality. This binary formula contradicts many of the tenets of the proslavery cause which held that the races would inevitably go to war following emancipation. The confluence of race and gender in this aspect of the proslavery argument is crystal clear. Defending the idealized notion of white womanly purity required the formation of a foil—the Black man, whose lust for white skin knew few bounds and required constant correction. According to one observer, "there is something strangely alluring and seductive," to Black men, "in the appearance of a white woman; they are aroused and stimulated by its foreignness to their experience of sexual pleasures, and it moves them to gratify their lust at any cost and in spite of any obstacle."[49] Considering how tightly the doctrines of white supremacy, Black inferiority, and gender roles were linked in the Old South, any externally forced shift in the status quo would not likely produce permanent change but only the reconfiguration of a new order predicated on the same balance of forces that previously existed. A post-emancipation scenario in which white southerners did not seek the restoration of their authority is difficult to envision.[50]

Consistency often serves as a central feature in establishing identity, even if the very concept that is the subject of the repetition is in error. Commentary depicting those of African descent as inferior appeared everywhere in the region. From newspaper articles to popular literature and treatises in defense of the system itself, white southerners faced constant exposure to the alleged imperatives that made slavery a vital institution. Once ensconced, there existed few reasons to explore the veracity of the claims. When outsiders cast an inquisitive gaze on the region, southerners responded by heralding their institutions more loudly. They saw few genuine alternatives to what they considered the perfectly conceived society around them. Abandoning the institution, even looking at it with suspicion, might yield a result that no one wanted to confront. Dire forecasts of racial violence and widespread miscegenation served to further ensconce the system of slavery in southern life and anchor the necessity of the institution in white minds. Far better to preserve the status quo than risk sweeping changes that might bring a violent future. As most saw it, only external forces, such as those unleashed by the incessant criticism emanating from antislavery forces, had the potential to break the tranquil state, ushering in an era of racial strife. Many southerners proved willing to destroy the union and risk everything in defense of white supremacy that they thought threatened by outside forces.

All efforts to arrest the abolitionist crusade ultimately failed, just as endeavors to preserve the union sputtered with the 1860 election of Abraham Lincoln. At that point, the prospect of a peaceful resolution to regional differences dimmed. Echoing sentiments from throughout the South, the *Richmond Examiner* observed regarding Lincoln's election that "the Government of the Union is in the hands of the avowed enemies of one entire region. It is to be directed in hostility to the property of that section."[51] Slavery was now threatened like never before. Naturally for those atop the southern social order, slavery was more than an abstract concept; it was the very basis of their wealth and identity. For them, losing slavery meant losing everything since much of their wealth stemmed from their chattel. Others too felt that slavery's continuance remained essential to their interests. All they needed for assurance were scores of proslavery treatises peddling dire warnings of the disaster awaiting the South should emancipation occur at a time other than when the region's white citizens directly mandated it. Freed from the plantation, Blacks would roam the countryside robbing and raping as they went. A region that once touted its peace would be subsumed in a torrent of bloodshed. The march to war, however, brought about a conflict that the agricultural South failed to win.

As the war entered its final years, desperation on the southern home front mounted. Elite white women, in particular, found themselves thrust into positions of authority on the plantation and discovered how fragile the mythologized image of regional race relations truly was. To them, fell the task of extracting labor from the enslaved, a job made more difficult by the ever-expanding draft which steadily consumed the South's white male population. Compounding the struggles at home, the enslaved, who always sought advantages within the context of the paternalist order, increased their resistance efforts owing to the clear absence of overt physical threats and assaults issued by white men. At the same time, the enslaved, despite all of the rhetoric touting their fidelity to their "masters," often abandoned the plantation as soon as the opportunity presented itself. As Yankee soldiers neared, the pace of slave labor slowed and the runaway rate exploded. African Americans took advantage of the chaos of war to secure for themselves freedom and opportunity. Making matters even more frightening to white southerners was the decision of many newly freed Black men to embrace the clarion call in Abraham Lincoln's Emancipation Proclamation by enlisting in the Union Army and waging war against the social order that once enslaved them. Far from being hopelessly beholden to their white "masters" as the proslavery argument went, the enslaved seized the opportunities provided by war to strike out on their own. The myths of the white plantation South with its allegedly superior social order and peaceful race relations experienced a seismic setback via the war and resulting emancipation. White women on the home front were the first to discover that the mythological race-infused belief of Black contentedness and docility was false. As the war ground to an end, all of the white South came face-to-face with the deeply flawed nature of their racial assumptions.[52]

With the conflict over, the question of dictating the peace reigned supreme. Landless and moneyless when emancipated, many African Americans faced an uncertain future. Whites, of course, experienced their own dilemma as they sought to rebuild all that was destroyed. Rather than await the actualization of the race war prophecy foretold by proslavery theorists, white southerners did what they could to keep Blacks under their thumb. When Black Codes, which were instituted almost immediately following emancipation, came under attack, something new replaced them. Federal occupation of the region during the so-called "radical" phase of Reconstruction brought threats of Black legal and political equality that were much touted but never fully implemented. White southern violence exploded as efforts to put the "bottom rail on top" faced immediate retaliation. Nocturnal terrorist groups such as the Ku Klux Klan initially intimidated the freedmen before the federal government broke the group's backs through legislation and aggressive enforcement. The dismantling of the first permutation of the Klan did not spell the end of white resistance to Black equality; it just marked a transition to different forms of terrorism. Before long, Reconstruction governments were in full retreat, making the 1877 compromise that officially ended it a moot point. Reconstruction had failed and white southerners, although losing the war, clearly won the peace. With the national government abdicating responsibility for the South, it did not take long for the region to embrace another racial order that was rooted in the profound fears that prompted many to support secession. With the end of Reconstruction and the removal of the federal presence it brought, sweeping racial violence remained the norm as the South's Bourbon Democratic oligarchs reinstated the rule of white supremacy. It is no coincidence that the 1880s and 1890s saw the largest number of lynchings in the history of the region. Newspaper reports from the period chronicled story after story of southern Blacks committing all manner of crime—a clear indicator to many that they were indeed "retrogressing" as proslavery advocates had warned. Although a small percentage of those lynched were alleged perpetrators of rape, the fear of Black licentiousness remained an all-pervasive concern in the region. Blacks found themselves harassed by the southern legal system in innumerable ways for a wide array of crimes, some serious, but many clearly were not. Death often resulted. Regional justice norms dictated that Blacks needed to be kept in their place otherwise they would only deepen the level of their atrocities. Key to restoring white supremacy in the region was safeguarding white women by ensuring African American compliance with the new order. Far better to mete out prompt corporal punishment for Black transgressions, white southerners contended, than to let that same individual off easy, thereby emboldening him to undertake more heinous crimes.[53]

Many have chronicled the rise of Jim Crow in the post-Reconstruction South. Its patterns and development are now widely known. From the onset of separation that began immediately following the Civil War in schools to state-sponsored segregation that achieved national protection in the *Plessy* case, Jim Crow's foundation was built on a complex web of statute and custom that proscribed the locus of interaction between the races. Its stranglehold on the region did not appear overnight, but gradually over the course of many years prompting some to speculate that the post-war South could have become something other than it did if only an alternative path was chosen. The idealist wishes to see a time when things could have been different; whereas the realist recognizes that a social order predicated on racial inequality could not be replaced by one rooted in racial equality overnight, especially not in a scenario which saw one of the races with a distinct numerical and economic advantage over the other. To expect white southerners to treat Black southerners as equals is to overlook time and place. Things did not necessarily have to be as severe as they turned out, but there can be little doubt that the social landscape of the South following emancipation would have had as its basic design a mechanism to ensure white rule. Slavery might have been destroyed but the belief system which had sustained it remained. To onlookers, Blacks had not advanced at all without white oversight, and indeed the alleged increase in petty crimes in the region convinced many that the feared retrogression of southern Blacks that so often filled proslavery writings was taking place. That many of these crimes were exaggerated or the product of circumscribed economic opportunity proved beyond the point. It represented to many white southerners a reversion of theretofore elevated Blacks to barbarism as soon as they operated outside of direct white oversight. Although slavery disappeared, the racism that informed the arguments on its behalf was repackaged in the defense of segregation. Despite emancipation, few white Americans demonstrated a willingness to accept Blacks on equal terms. Segregation thus began as a concept rooted in the very same notion of racial hierarchy that permeated the South, and America, in the antebellum period. Racial attitudes changed slowly, making the South's new social order a matter of limited concern north of the Mason-Dixon Line. Before the Civil War, many northerners rallied to the overtly racist free soil ideology, making it not too surprising that after the war their perceptions of race remained the same. True, most northerners eventually recognized the necessity of ending slavery and even ensuring that Blacks received basic legal and political rights, but beyond that, there was far less of a consensus. Very few were ready for widespread social interaction with African Americans in the public arena, and very few thought that such an arrangement should be pushed on the South. *Plessy* surprised no one as it reflected the overarching national racial perspective. At a time when Social Darwinists preached the "survival of the fittest" gospel, white Americans in the late nineteenth century believed that separating the races seemed to be the natural and inevitable consequence of placing an inferior people in a position of freedom for which they were unprepared. By the start of the twentieth century, few Americans would consider challenging this assertion, and few of them did.[54]

The race-based explanation of the southern social order continued well into the twentieth century. Despite the increased opprobrium with which racial invective was viewed as the century progressed, southern arguments in defense of segregation often included some variation of the retrogression model made popular in the defense of slavery. Notorious race-baiter and former Mississippi governor Theodore Bilbo in his ghostwritten publication *Take Your Choice: Separation or Mongrelization* depicted coerced segregation as the only guaranteed safeguard against "mongrelization." In private, Bilbo went as far as to say that it was through "fear of the White Man that the negro has refrained from committing so many atrocious crimes."[55] Obsessed with maintaining racial purity, even with violence if necessary, Bilbo clung to the notion that "one drop of negro blood in the veins of a white caucasian makes him a negro."[56] Later, Bilbo added, "To preserve her blood, the white South must absolutely deny social equality to the Negro regardless of what his individual accomplishments might be."[57] Bilbo's comments underscore the stark reality of southern race relations as well as the inchoate fear which necessitated racial segregation without exceptions. It all came down to race. Ultimately, the Mississippian returned to two basic facts: racism would remain in America regardless of the desires of some, and "the negro will be discriminated against for the next 100 years as he has the last 300 years."[58] Nothing would change the minds of hardliners regarding the treatment of the region's Blacks. Like Bilbo, most southern politicians were reluctant to shed their belief that clear differences separated whites from Blacks, a fact that made segregation essential to them. How they chose to make their cases varied across time and place, but the notion of Black inequality resonated through the decades. It remained an idea so pervasive in the region, so widely accepted for so many years that it just had to be true—or at least that was how many white southerners saw it. Accepting an alternative narrative meant also conceding that cultural constructions such as segregation were not necessary. In the end, white southerners, despite the information available to them, believed that separating the races in some fashion was the best scenario for all involved. Their essential mythology demanded a stark division of people without concern for individual circumstances. The rationale for that division differed. Some said it was naturally recurring whereas others asserted it was best for all parties involved in order to ensure the purity of racial bloodlines. Regardless of the reasoning for it, segregationists understood that some manner of racial division needed to be.[59]

As the push for racial change advanced in the twentieth century, many white southerners began redirecting fears of Black depravity that prompted segregation to a less overt form of racism that stressed natural tendencies rather than a power dynamic of white lording over Black. Segregationists staunchly clung to the necessity of maintaining the racial hierarchy; however, they tended to pull from a diverse constellation of ideas in its support, leading to an array of idiosyncratic defenses of the institution. At times, it appeared that white southerners threw every conceivable argument they could find at the integration battle in hopes that something bore fruit. References to nature abounded as segregation's defenders looked to the animal kingdom, and hence divine providence, to validate Jim Crow's presence. Bluebirds and red birds (or any other color used interchangeably), did not nest together, segregationists claimed in one of their favorite ornithological references, because it was unnatural for them to do so. Southerners were often bold in their use of this reference. On the Senate floor, for example, Louisianan Russell Long opined, "If the good Lord had intended us to be all alike he would have made us that way."[60] Going further in this line of reasoning, he postulated that different bird species not nesting together was evidence that God did not desire the commingling of the white and the Black races. "We believe," he observed, "without wanting to hurt anybody's feelings, that it is everyone's right to feel proud of his race and to preserve the purity of his race."[61] If left to their own devices, "like" invariably would associate with "like." North Carolina's Sam Ervin succinctly observed that "men segregate themselves in society on the basis of race in obedience to a natural law which decrees that like seeks to associate with like."[62] Applying this limited observation to humanity proved irresistible and frequent. Whites and Blacks, according to this logic, would divide along racial lines without legal mandate, as naturally, some theorized, as oil separated from water.

As during the days of slavery, segregationists noted that a divine force compelled segregation and that same providential hand accounted for any inequalities appearing between the races. Into the 1960s, white southerners remained wedded to the institution. As segregationist logic put it, "men segregate themselves in society on the basis of race in obedience to a natural law which decrees that like associates with like."[63] Natural, God-given, characteristics were alleged to create the myriad of ills that hampered the region's Black population in its efforts to advance. White southerners stared down the grinding poverty that permeated many southern Black communities and declared this condition a byproduct of sloth rather than oppression. Speaking to this alleged inherent inequality, North Carolina's Sam Ervin explained that forced integration represented an effort "to thwart a law of nature and to bring about something artificial."[64] Since God allegedly ordained separation of the races, some such as West Virginian Robert Byrd remarked, "Equality is not a characteristic in nature, nor is it a characteristic among human beings . . . Life is a gift of God, but equality is not."[65] God, in his infinite wisdom, created all of humanity and imbued each race with special gifts, asserted segregationists. These gifts were quite different and not meant to be evenly distributed to all people. Some went as far as to scour the Bible to find evidence that the good Lord expected his people to remain separated. The lengths such individuals would go to cast their white supremacist narrative in a favorable light knew no bounds.

Segregationist pamphlets inundated the South in the mid-twentieth century spreading the gospel of Jim Crow to a vast audience. One such pamphlet, "God Gave the Law of Segregation (as well as the 10 Commandments) To Moses on Mount Sinai," resurrected the insidious biblical curse of Ham by defining God's chosen people as the Israelites, whom the pamphlet's author understood to be the white race. The Israelites were specifically instructed by God to avoid the inhabitants of Canaan, who were defined as Black in the inflammatory circular. Separation thus was not something adopted due to the whims of the southern people or even because of their peculiar prejudices; instead, the Jim Crow system affirmed God's "plan for the segregation of the races."[66] Had he wanted all people to be the same, he would have created them as such, segregationists advanced. Just as antebellum southerners embraced the curse of Ham to validate the enslavement of those of African origins, twentieth century segregationists employed the same biblical story in defense of their racial institutions. These ideas filtered down to the white southern populace from the pulpit. Far from oppressors, segregationists raised race to a moral imperative. Like sought like because God made it so. Episcopal minister James P. Dees of North Carolina wrote, "I think every member of the white and Negro races has the solemn obligation under God to preserve his race from amalgamation, or mongrelization . . . I feel that it is morally mandatory."[67] White southerners were thus not defying biblical injunctions to love their neighbors, they were fulfilling the dictates of their creator by forging a social order that upheld divine wishes or so went the defense of Jim Crow. Under this construct, segregation statutes in southern states did little more than provide legal sanction to the status quo freely entered into by the region's inhabitants. According to adherents of this position, segregation would develop regardless of the desires of well-intentioned reformers. Repeatedly, white southerners chose the simplest explanation, the one that allowed them to adhere to their preconceived notions without critical discourse. Wrapping their prejudices with their faith, as they often did, effectively closed off objective scrutiny of their essential beliefs. Rather than prompting the emergence of a new consensus, the mounting external threats to theories rooted in white supremacy evoked an array of explanations that varied based on the audience and ideological disposition of the theorist but always carried with them a core of racism. White southerners thus behaved in a manner consistent with the actions evident in the vast expanse of human history. They preferred the comfort of the status quo to a meaningful evaluation of the world around them.

Adding to the biological and divine imperatives encouraging like to associate with like, many southern theorists stressed the existence of "race consciousness" among white southerners and presumably among their Black counterparts as well. Georgia's race-baiting governor Herman Talmadge proclaimed, "Each race has its own culture, its own heritage, and its own talents. These are all developed best when the races are not mixed."[68]

Talmadge labeled what he believed to be the innate drive to preserve one's race as "one of the strongest human characteristics," and a "law of nature." According to this strained logic, since race consciousness was a natural law, it therefore was "not discriminatory." No matter how many laws were passed, Talmadge asserted that the natural instinct of race would assert itself rendering integration efforts for naught.[69] Floridian Spessard Holland included a gendered thread to the discussion of race consciousness when he opined that white southern women were the backbone of the segregationist fight as they were the primary force behind the belief that "it is wrong to mix together children of both races in all of the intimate ways that occur in the schoolroom."[70] True to form, Holland also stressed his admiration for the African American community. And like those before him, Holland could not help but close his remarks with the comment that segregation remained essential since "we are different from them in many, many ways."[71] Holland's remarks demonstrated the tendency among white southerners to speak kindly of individual African Americans while lambasting the racial collective. By robustly arguing their fondness for individual southern Blacks, they hoped to advance a public persona which indicated they were more than mere bigots even when their public records suggested otherwise.

During much of the twentieth century, the South fought the war for segregation in a bifurcated manner that played a significant role in its failure to safeguard the institution. In small towns across the South, segregation's defenders often advanced a perspective that Black inferiority and innate depravity made separation essential, echoing the same claims their forebears leveled in the later nineteenth and early twentieth centuries. However, on the national level, politicians sought to downplay the centrality of race in their worldview by crafting arguments rooted in logic and legality. Race, of course, always remained just below the surface; it just found more limited expression in Washington during the 1950s and 1960s when compared to the 1920s and 1930s. Below the Mason-Dixon Line, however, little changed in southern arguments. In the wake of its formation following the *Brown* verdict, the Citizens' Council flooded southern communities with literature heralding the age-old concern that miscegenation begat mongrelization. The *Citizens' Council* newspaper did not mince words when it asserted that "social integration and miscegenation will be seriously detrimental to both races and to our civilization."[72] The fact that this literature rekindled interest in fighting for segregation at the moment of its greatest threat following *Brown* underscores the powerful pull of the racialist perspective in the modern South. Times had changed, but plenty remained willing to brook no compromise in defense of a concept that Americans outside of Dixie were abandoning. At the same time, the white South assertively pushed race to the forefront of regional discourse, it also began quieting internal voices urging even rudimentary reform. Politicians who departed from regional expectations faced election-day retribution from constituents the moment voters sensed one of their elected officials had gone "soft" on the civil rights issue. Those outside of the political arena had more freedom to convey their concerns regarding Jim Crow, but they too had to straddle the line to avoid a wave of retribution from those bent on silencing all voices of dissent that threatened racial customs.

The presence of southern leaders such as those in the 1920s and 1930s who called for nominal changes to limit lynching and other forms of racial violence grew increasingly rare as the 1940s and 1950s progressed. Those unwilling to do so found their careers in jeopardy. Politicians who stressed the need for regional moderation, such as Florida's Claude Pepper and North Carolina's Frank Graham, were voted out of office in the face of a reactionary pushback that deemed even small alterations in the Jim Crow system unthinkable. Defending every aspect of the southern myth increasingly became the norm. Moderate voices still existed, but they typically relegated their comments critical of the racial status quo to the private rather than the public sphere. A legalistic defense of Jim Crow was perfectly acceptable provided its purveyor remained publicly resolute in defense of segregation. Southern leaders could freely embrace constitutional claims without riling their constituents as long as they demonstrated their fealty to regional racial customs. Ultimately, the manner of argument proved less imperative than the perceived dedication to white rule. One such moderate, Tennessee senator Albert Gore Sr., in his personal communication, observed, "I feel that if everyone from the South continues to stand adamantly against anything and everything, refusing to recognize any existing injustices and refusing to accept the inevitable march of progress of events, the tide will eventually break the dam."[73] Like Pepper before him, Gore recognized that white southerners needed to come to terms with the injustices that existed under the system they protected. Yet, unlike Pepper, whose regional apostasy in the public arena cost him his Senate seat, Gore kept his musing private. The climate of opinion in the South did not lend itself to a logical discourse on the topic.

Most regional leaders retained their myopic perspective informed by their belief in a racial hierarchy until the end of the integration fight. Such individuals pulled no punches in demonizing the Black race, utilizing all of the racial invective that existed when segregation first emerged. White southern musings on their perceptions of African Americans were typically direct and pointed to the true rationale for the apparent need for separation regardless of the various race-neutral messages crafted for public consumption that periodically found expression on the national level. Discrimination would always haunt southern race relations unless an outside force acted upon it. Overt racial tropes in white southern arguments that smeared the Black collective with little regard for individual nuances proved common. Virginia's Harry Flood Byrd, who allegedly coined the phrase "massive resistance," exhibited an unrepentant perspective, even in the face of mounting pressure for change, while stressing that integration proved a fool's mission that faced certain failure. As Byrd saw things, any external effort to impose racial equality on the South by misinformed "do-gooders" who thought their actions would uplift African Americans would result in unintended consequences. In response to such a challenge, white southerners, according to Byrd, would merely establish alternative means to secure white supremacy if civil rights advances were ever forced upon the region. Only southern Blacks would suffer from coerced integration.[74] Byrd's comments highlight a central feature of segregationist thinking; even if the region was compelled to embrace change, its citizens would figure out new mechanisms for skirting the law just as they had done following the ratification of the Fourteenth and Fifteenth Amendments. It was a sobering thought. Racism forged by generations of slavery all but ensured that discrimination would persist in the region long after emancipation. Rekindling the popular miscegenation trope first introduced in the nineteenth century, the Virginian also observed, "What our people most fear is that by their close intimate social contact future generations will intermarry."[75] Forestalling this eventuality meant more than just defending an outdated prejudice in southern minds; it meant preserving the republic as more and more people outside of the region looked askance at the region's peculiar racial order. The habits of the past clearly infected the future.

Like Harry Byrd, Richard Russell of Georgia, who was arguably the most important voice in the prosegregation army, could not conceive of the fight over civil rights in any terms save for racial ones. According to Russell, "it has been proven time and again that the integration of the races can only lead to amalgamation and miscegenation and I have never found a case in history where people of mixed blood ever developed their civilization." [76] Russell's comments made in 1960 reveal how central race remained to the white South well into the twentieth century. The Georgian waffled between positions, occasionally appearing moderate, but inflammatory proved his default stance. More often than not, Russell harkened back to the time when southern slaveholders framed slavery as a "school of civilization." According to Russell, "the Negro . . . is the only minority in the United States who has not been willing to work and strive to earn recognition and acceptance. The Negro race and the Negro alone have sought to strong-arm and use physical force to secure the right of association from the majority against the wishes of that majority."[77] Turning the tables on the discussion, Russell dropped his role as defender of the white southern position on segregation and attacked the Black community for wanting equality. Conveniently forgetting the racism that undergirded Jim Crow and delimited opportunities for African Americans, Russell proceeded to condemn Blacks for not working to gain white southern respect.

Joining Russell in questioning African American fitness for full equality, Louisiana's Allen Ellender alleged that "the intellectual and cultural standards of the white race perhaps leave a lot to be desired, but until the American Negro approaches this standard in large numbers, he will not be accepted. This he must do principally and primarily by his own efforts."[78] Ellender like Russell before him, placed the onus for ending segregation on African Americans themselves. Unlike proslavery arguments that made it clear that equality was unattainable, twentieth-century race baiters held out the prospect that white southerners, who blindly accepted the idea of Black criminality, would somehow come to accept African Americans if their condition improved. At least according to Ellender, the real impediment to Black advancement was the Black community itself. Pulling from his grab bag of racist rhetoric, the Louisianan noted the best way for African Americans to improve their status was to drop calls for civil rights and embrace "civil responsibility," which according to Ellender, meant abandoning "filth, illegitimacy, indolence, and crime."[79] Joining his fellow Louisianan, Russell Long noted, "The Negro's best bet—and, indeed, his only hope—is to work toward a basic status of acceptability."[80] Otherwise, Long observed, the Black "race as a whole will be shunned and excluded by the white majority."[81] No clear definition of what constituted acceptability was forthcoming from southern pols who stressed the concept that African Americans needed to elevate themselves before they would be treated with equality. By contrast, some such as Strom Thurmond, noted that African Americans could advance "by getting an education or becoming skilled," but he never asserted that in doing so they would achieve equality.[82] One suspects that the only thing that would elicit approval from the white majority was a change in skin color. The prejudices of race ran deep.

Regardless of the various tones exhibited by segregation's defenders in the twentieth century, a racial dialogue found expression in most prosegregation arguments, even if it assumed a partially coded form. Few ventured from the confines of this reassuring notion. Until the end, southern politicians could be heard addressing the need for segregation using the same claims made by their predecessors a hundred years earlier. Richard Russell lamenting Black crime in the 1960s could just as easily have been speaking in the 1880s or 1890s. Indeed, practically all of segregation's champions claimed to observe that African Americans exhibited some form of racial inferiority. They still returned to the notion that Blacks tended to be lazy and that if left unchecked would resort to all manner of crime. These fears grew especially pronounced as civil rights activism proliferated in the region. As the newspaper of the White Citizens' Council depicted things in the mid-twentieth century, southern Blacks had grown "lazy and dangerous as a result of the new doctrines being taught to them."[83] Although separated by a century, the influence of proslavery writers was not hard to discern in the rhetoric of massive resistance.

White southerners had been born into a society that saw the world through a racial prism. Even as outsiders slowly changed their perceptions, southerners, as they always did, condemned the misinformed do-gooders from afar. Wagons were circled, and many clung to a logic that proved increasingly outdated as the twentieth century progressed. At its heart, the very need to separate the races stemmed from a belief that close interaction between whites and Blacks as occurred outside of the controlled setting of slavery, where the balance of power weighed heavily in one direction, could only lead to racial strife and debasement. Segregation could not stand on its own account if the racism that gave it life fell into disrepute. The inability to forge an alternative to the racialist perspective that informed the defense of segregation reveals many things. Most importantly, it underscores the intellectual bankruptcy of the South's racially motivated social order at a time when evidence debunking its central tenets proved everywhere apparent.

Segregation's champions pivoted to theories regarding life without their racial institutions when confronted with the Civil Rights Act of 1964, which represented the most direct and sweeping threat to Jim Crow. Its passage would destroy the southern racial order, a fact that precipitated considerable musing on the subject. This was not a potential future challenge to the regional racial order such as loomed with Lincoln's 1860 election, but an immediate one. Not surprisingly, many segregationists painted a rather bleak picture of a post-Jim Crow South rife with not just integration, but interracial coupling as well. After years of linking segregation's necessity to fears of Black violence or depravity, segregationists could not easily cast aside their fears involving racial violence and miscegenation. South Carolina's Olin Johnston remarked regarding the end of segregation that "people can expect a dangerous and unpredictable era comparable to the dark days of Reconstruction. This bill [the Civil Rights Act of 1964] will never be enforced without turning our nation into a police state and without the cost of bloodshed and violence."[84] Johnston's comments in many ways mirrored those made one hundred years earlier in relation to slavery's demise. Fears of racial discord might have dissipated for some by the mid-twentieth century, but they still remained for many an ever-present reality. For others, the collapse of segregation led to a profound catharsis in which they accepted, albeit grudgingly, what had transpired. Far from pushing further resistance, they urged restraint, encouraging whites to follow the law of the land. Louisiana's Russell Long did not join those who threatened violence in the face of racial change. Instead, he peaceably remarked, "No doubt this nation will continue to be a nice country to live in regardless of the outcome of the integration fight."[85] Despite his remarks, Long was on record as being fiercely opposed to interracial coupling, which he saw as an inevitable byproduct of efforts to pass sweeping civil rights legislation in the 1960s. In one instance, Long opined, "We think it is absolutely desirable that the white people should continue to be white, and that their children and grandchildren should be the same; and we let our children know that we think just that."[86] Exposing the insidious hand of prejudice that always informed the southern defense of segregation, Long illustrated that even the passage of sweeping civil rights laws would not eradicate hatred in the South. Yes, voting rules and social practices would change as a result, but the racial prejudice that informed the southern worldview since the days of slavery would not end. Instead, it would be passed, as Long asserted, from one generation to the next. Dismantling the legal apparatus of Jim Crow was one thing; undermining the prejudices that created it would not be that simple.

Eventual white southern acquiescence to federal power did not necessarily mean that everyone in the region thought that the landmark civil rights laws of the 1960s were the wisest choice for the region. Wedded to the region's mythology until the end, white southerners believed they truly understood African Americans because they had lived among them all of their lives as had their parents and theirs before them. They alleged that the most important factor shaping outsider opinion on civil rights was northerners' limited direct exposure to African Americans. Northerners who knew few if any Blacks could not possibly understand the shortfalls of the African American community, opined segregationists, for up North Blacks were isolated in urban ghettos far removed from whites. In the South, by contrast, white people grew up around African Americans and as a result had a much clearer understanding of the so-called "vices" inherent in the Black minority than those outside the region. During the debate surrounding the Civil Rights Act of 1964, Georgian Richard Russell chided one of the bill's supporters from the American Northwest: "If one left Helena or Billings, Montana, one would have to ride 2 or 3 days in Montana to be able to find a Negro citizen. I doubt not that many Montanans grow to manhood or womanhood without ever seeing a Negro citizen."[87] Like Russell, Sam Ervin prodded northerners, especially activists, regarding the civil rights issue since most of them were "socially or residentially or financially isolated from the contacts out of which the problem" of race arose.[88]

Segregationists long contended that northerners were willing to push for racial justice as long as it took place in the faraway South. However, they would prove less likely to do so, southerners argued, if and when the civil rights fight shifted above the Mason-Dixon Line. Southerners in these instances were playing to the very real presence of racism throughout the country. They recognized that northerners were far from innocent when it came to intolerance and would recoil at integration efforts in their communities. Politicians from northern metropolitan centers were labeled as pandering to Black bloc voters, whereas pols from states with very small Black populations were deemed as making decisions based on emotions rather than sensibility. Harry Byrd and others regularly denounced civil rights supporters in Washington as championing the cause only as a means of "collecting Negro votes."[89] Once the civil rights fight pivoted beyond merely "punishing" the South and focused on "racial imbalance in the schools and open housing occupancy," politicians such as Richard Russell, suspected that northerners would lose much of their crusading zeal as these programs would invariably target northern communities.[90] Thus, white southerners were quick to identify the hypocrisy of their opponents while advancing astonishingly hypocritical positions of their own.

The "mind" of the South has long been of interest to historians. Whether or not it is fair to say that the South was ever of one mind on anything, it is still reasonable to assert that at least on some matters, especially those regarding race, the white South, despite noteworthy outliers, largely stood as one, and it stood together for a long time on this issue—an issue that permeated the region, informing social interaction, economic exchanges, and outside perceptions of it. The sad legacy of racially motivated oppression regrettably serves as the most salient feature of southern distinctiveness. Although the record suggests the majority of white southerners did not participate in local violence, lawless elements did exist, a fact that made the incendiary rhetoric found in the region dangerous. Many individuals routinely resorted to violence, forever shaping the judgment of history regarding how the South handled the end of segregation. The silent white majority, however, certainly does not escape opprobrium. They supported the violent Jim Crow order in countless direct and indirect ways. They instilled racial prejudices in their children, they financially supported segregationist groups that disseminated the previously referenced racist circulars, and they often verbally accosted African Americans who stepped outside prescribed racial roles. Had more of them demonstrated the necessary intestinal fortitude by pushing back against the lawlessness, as well as the more subtle forms of prejudice, the discord of the period would have been markedly reduced. Their silence thus is more accurately depicted as complicity rather than cautious enlightenment. The absence of action suggests a level of tacit support.[91]

The legacy of slavery profoundly shaped the twentieth-century South, influencing not only its biracial order but also the defense of it. Many of the racial beliefs which found expression in the proslavery argument reappeared in the prosegregation corpus. Race-centered arguments, for Jim Crow, in turn, unraveled as national perspectives on race changed. Slavery's demise only freed the enslaved; it did not alter how white Americans perceived Blacks. Most whites remained just as racist after the Civil War as they were before it. Founding segregation on the premises of the South's first racial order made sense in the late nineteenth century since the logic that informed it remained salient after the war. As time proceeded, however, white southerners faced the need to address the civil rights issue in something other than racial terms. Despite their intentions, the South's leaders failed to step outside the stranglehold that race, and ultimately the Old South, had on the region. When segregation fell in 1964, southern senators could still be heard comparing themselves to Robert E. Lee's Army of Northern Virginia, refitting post-Reconstruction Era southern rhetoric to meet the needs of a new century. Echoing the spirit of the "Lost Cause," Richard Russell, following the bill's passage, stressed his pride in fighting alongside his southern colleagues who gave "the last particle of ability and the last iota of physical strength in the effort to hold back the overwhelming combination of forces" arrayed in favor of the legislation.[92] Even if unintended, the allusion to the Old South could not have been more apt. Segregation's demise represented not only the death of the institution, but it also served as the final nail in the coffin for the Old South, at least in terms of overt racial appeals. Although chattel slavery ended with the Civil War and the Thirteenth Amendment, in many ways the ideas that informed that institution's defense remained in place throughout the reign of Jim Crow and found expression in an array of insidious institutions designed to oppress the region's Black citizenry. Thus, the Old South died not in 1864 and 1865; it died in 1964 and 1965.

4

The Connecting Thread

Without question, a belief in racial inequality informed the southern position regarding both slavery and segregation. Once slavery emerged as an economic necessity in the South, depicting the enslaved as somehow less than equal to those of European descent became the norm. The same principle influenced prosegregation arguments, since, after all, it would be illogical to create a spatial distance from one's equals in public settings. When white southerners conceptualized the best social arrangement in the region, they did so through a racial prism. They started with a predetermined belief in racial inequality and then constructed a defense of their racial institutions that validated their prejudices. It proved an effective mechanism for rallying support at home and, at least for a period, a satisfactory tool for keeping outside pressure for regional change at bay. Were racism the only mechanism they employed in defense of slavery and segregation, then the claims of the region's defenders would be largely forgettable save for the insight such prejudice provided into regional cultural norms. The fact that they were not testifies to the complexity of the defenses that they forged, and more importantly to the troubling reality that the very same Founding Fathers who secured American independence, forged a practical republican Constitution, and shepherded that republic through the "critical period" provided ammunition for the defense of racial injustice. The bitter legacy of hate, along with the apparatus necessary to dismantle it, were all found within the same Constitution. In one of history's great ironies, a document that enunciated American freedoms was utilized by some to deny basic rights to others. At the same time, the document's contents served as the foundation for efforts to dismantle the systems of oppression it once shielded. Just as champions of creating a strong federal government and greater equality found the U.S. Constitution suitable to achieve their ends, the defenders of slavery and segregation—who always represented the minority voice in America on these matters—found the same document malleable enough to satisfy their own provincial goals. When white southerners, whether in the nineteenth or twentieth century, claimed that they were preserving the Constitution as the founders meant it to be, they really believed what they said, at least in this regard. This point cannot be overstated. Time and again, across the pantheon of beliefs that informed both racial orders stood the consistent assertion that the white South was upholding the Constitution. It was outsiders who wanted to destroy the precious inheritance of the Revolutionary Era by forcing their abolitionist and integrationist beliefs on the South that trampled the most sacred national document. It remained a much-heralded concept in the South transcending the limitations of time and proving without doubt that a continuity in political thought existed in the region. Steadfast devotion to the Constitution became a constant echo in southern state houses across the decades. Its very flexibility made the Constitution amenable to a variety of interpretations, many of which found expression during two of the most significant political debates in American history: the first regarding slavery and the second involving Jim Crow and its satellite institutions.

When southerners pondered the Constitution, their thoughts rarely departed from a static view of the document. Opposed to the notion of the Constitution as a living, flexible set of basic guidelines open to "interpretation," southern theorists typically adopted a fundamentalist approach to it. Elevated to near-divine status, the founders' words became as sacred as scripture in the region. The Constitution thus was a finished product; every power the founders intended for the government to possess was enumerated at the outset. Expanding the scope of the "sacred" text with a loose construction was tantamount to defiling the memory of the founders and the document they created. Except under the most extraordinary of circumstances and via the only constitutionally stipulated avenue available—amendment—could the original document be altered. A sense of permanency thus shaped the southern view of history. Each new reinterpretation of the Constitution brought about by legislative action, executive order, or Supreme Court fiat prompted howls of southern protests against the alleged departure from the intent of the framers. Curiously enough, slavery's and segregation's defenders seemed oblivious to the historical context surrounding the Early Republic. Far from uniform in their beliefs, the nation's founders fought intensely over what the document permitted and what it did not. In the southern interpretation that emerged during the height of the struggle over slavery and which continued well into the fight for Jim Crow, the founders were treated as a homogenous group who were in accord on all things political and social. Naturally, a group willing to distort the reality of their present would also prove comfortable crafting a version of the past consistent with their needs even if that interpretation strayed from the existing record. Slavery's and segregation's defenders conveniently "overlooked" this widely known truth in pursuit of a different narrative more amenable to their interests. Rather than depicting themselves as the defenders of an interpretation of the Constitution that was progressively losing favor, they attached their crusade to a mythical understanding of the past in which the founders were of one mind on all things. Although emphasizing this alleged unity at every turn, the assertion illustrated an absence of a rudimentary understanding of America's Early National period. Despite the evident weakness of southern claims that theirs represented the only plausible understanding of the intent of the founders, this assumption remained at the heart of both the proslavery and prosegregation arguments until those institutions were destroyed.[1]

Lost in southern interpretations are the actual voices of the Founding Fathers themselves, many of whom noted the simple elegance of the document which would allow future generations to reinterpret the manner in which it was implemented without destroying its essential character. Also missing are those voices which sought to eradicate slavery in America and only went along with the inclusion of limited safeguards for the institution in the Constitution to keep the union together following the Revolution. Their short-term concessions were not meant to be a permanent resolution. Indeed, many considered slavery an institution on its way out. The constitutional stipulation calling for the ban on the Transatlantic Slave Trade twenty years after the document's creation lends credence to the fact that slavery was on the downslope and at least some founders intended to close the door on the infusion of new life into the system as early as 1808, thereby hastening its demise. No one in 1787 could foresee the invention of the cotton gin which made cultivation of that crop easier and far more lucrative. Overnight the southern economy was revived and the need for slaves, many of whom were idle due to declining agricultural fortunes, exploded.[2] As the region's populace increasingly fell under the spell of King Cotton, it became critically important that southern leaders freeze constitutional interpretations in place, especially as many northern communities began developing a more diversified economy that threatened the agricultural South. Likewise, they fixed their sights on aggressive territorial expansion and viewed the Constitution as the bulwark of their initiatives which invariably would spread slavery westward. In doing so, they embraced a fallacious argument tied to the situation on the ground at a pre-cotton gin constitutional convention in which several delegates went along with some protections for slavery in the short term with the larger hope that slavery would be terminated in the not too distant long term. The legacy passed from the Founding Founders reached the hands of slaveholders undefiled, and it fell to the latter to uphold it. No further discussion was necessary. Such was the rigidly closed sense of history embraced in the region. Indeed, when it came to the South's relationship with the Constitution, time stood still.[3]

When historians ponder the connection between slavery and liberty, they often harken back to Edmund Morgan's seminal work, *American Slavery, American Freedom;* yet the ideas expressed in it merely reflected what white southerners from the antebellum period to Morgan's own time had long accepted as a fact of life.[4] Leaving little doubt that Morgan's contextual framework fit logically within the worldview that slaveholders themselves embraced, Thomas Dew opined in the early 1830s, "Liberty has always been more ardently desired by slaveholding communities."[5] Going even further in this line of reasoning, Dew admitted that "inferior" Blacks performed all of the "menial and low" tasks in society, but in the process, the Black presence enabled "the perfect spirit of equality" to emerge amongst whites.[6] Naturally, Dew was advancing an idealized portrayal of events, but his commentary reflected more than just wishful thinking. It revealed the way white southerners chose to interpret themselves, underscoring their belief that their society proved superior to that found in the North. George Fitzhugh noted, "Our negroes are confessedly better off than any free laboring population in the world."[7] Unlike the teeming class conflict that permeated northern free labor markets, the South experienced no such problems brought on by rigid social stratification because the region had an enslaved "mudsill" class that not only kept social inferiors in place but also created a sense of absolute equality among those outside of bondage. The fraternity of whiteness that was so celebrated in the South, Dew concluded, served as "both the generator and preserver of the genuine spirit of liberty."[8] In short, white southerners believed themselves the ultimate guardians of the Constitution as created by the founders, precisely because they had a special claim on "liberty" that made them acutely aware of what life without freedom was like. According to politician Robert Y. Hayne of South Carolina, where slaves existed in vast numbers, "Those who are free are by far the most proud and jealous defenders of their freedom. Freedom is to them not only an enjoyment, but a kind of rank and privilege."[9] Fellow South Carolinian, John Calhoun, who for decades championed southern regional interests in Washington, also had strong feelings on this matter, arguing that liberty was "a reward reserved for the intelligent, the patriotic, the virtuous and deserving" or, according to the understanding of the time, a reward that only whites proved capable of actualizing.[10] Calhoun's remarks make clear that concepts such as liberty and freedom, in his mind, were consistent with the existence of slavery, owing to the depravity of the enslaved. He ascribed no higher motives regarding how the founders perceived or might have perceived the races, arguing that they addressed concepts such as liberty and freedom exclusively through a white lens. Liberty, according to John Calhoun, was a cherished commodity, "not a boon to be bestowed on a people too ignorant, degraded, and vicious, to be capable either of appreciating or of enjoying it."[11] Those who lacked the capacity to fully enjoy the fruits of liberty were not and should not be considered as equals in the American Republic opined most antebellum southern leaders.

 Proslavery advocates argued that the fount of liberty flowed from the Constitution's explicit protection of the rights of slave owners. The founders conceptualized slavery as such a critical component of American life that they engrained it in the nation's organic law. Regarding the relationship of the document to slavery, Matthew Estes commented, "The whole framework of the Constitution embraces protection to the South in this important particular."[12] The Constitution, which buttressed slavery, in turn, enabled the region to develop a deeper appreciation for liberty and freedom than their Yankee counterparts who lacked the same comforting and edifying presence of a permanent "mudsill" class. Summing up this perspective, William Trescott claimed, "Republican institutions can never be permanent unless slavery exists as the substratum of society."[13] Slavery and the republican political tradition that inspired both America's Revolution as well as its Constitution were inseparable in the eyes of the South's proslavery forces. Southerners, thus, by retaining a "substratum" in their social order ensured that the embers of liberty always smoldered. By extension, northerners, who abandoned the institution in the years following the Revolution created a society that differed profoundly from that of the South, pulling it away from the allegedly solid republican moorings present below the Mason-Dixon Line. All around white southerners worked the enslaved whose daily existence was at least partially tied to the caprices of their owners. The slaves, who knew nothing but bondage, in turn, did not fully grasp, according to proslavery thinkers, what it was they were living without.

As the North divested itself of slavery and grew antagonistic toward the institution, it also embraced the idea of an activist state predicated on the development of a powerful national government. According to southern theorists, the North first, abandoned slavery, which was crucial for liberty, and second, gravitated toward a strong national government in which centralized power overrode state prerogatives. This process drove the North from the solid moorings planted by the founders into a different territory that celebrated "statism" at the expense of individual freedom. Southerners, who asserted they embraced true federalism as the founders intended, and who incidentally also supported slavery, were actually the preservers of the legacy of the American Revolutionary generation—or at least that was how the region's white denizens chose to depict things. U.S. senator Robert Hayne captured the southern perspective on this issue. He argued, "The object of the framers of the constitution . . . was not the consolidation of the Government, but 'the consolidation of the Union.' It was not to draw power from the States, in order to transfer it to a great National Government, but, in the language of the constitution itself, 'to form a more perfect union.'"[14] Indeed, utilizing this logic, white southerners made the case that their region more closely followed the Constitution and the intent of the framers than did the North. In the often-twisted logic of proslavery advocates, the abolitionist push represented not just an assault on slavery but an assault on the Constitution which so clearly contained mechanisms designed to protect the peculiar institution. Despite their stated intentions, beneath the surface, northern actions threatened more than just the racial system; they also challenged the South's economic interests, which were tied to expansion. Summarizing this position in early 1860, a full thirty years after Robert Hayne made nearly identical assertions during the famed Webster-Hayne debate over the protective tariff, Jefferson Davis stated regarding efforts to dismantle the slaveholding system, "All such attacks are in manifest violation of the mutual and solemn pledges to protect and defend each other, given by the States, respectively, on entering into the Constitutional compact which formed the Union, and are a manifest breach of faith and a violation of the most solemn obligations."[15] One either accepted the southern perspective on slavery or one was aligned against the South and the Constitution. As the antebellum era progressed, the perceived unity between the South's position on all issues pertaining to the spirit and intent of the framers grew clearer to observers below the Mason-Dixon Line.

Southerners never operated in a milieu free of criticism of the peculiar institution. Challenges to the institution of slavery came early in America's history. Even during the colonial period, there existed a strong sentiment that the institution was of dubious moral value, and aspects of it, such as the transatlantic trade in humans, were deemed downright barbaric. Debate during the constitutional convention in Philadelphia highlighted the potential problems that the institution posed for the nation's future. Despite efforts to limit discussion of the issue, the Early National Period saw its presence ever simmering below the surface. With a belief that slaves were property, it comes as no surprise that any initiative to limit the institution was perceived as an assault against the Constitution. As long as the racial dogma that enabled the often-grudging acceptance of slavery remained, it was easier to limit debate on the issue to basic constitutional questions rather than moral ones. Slaveholders thus held firmly to the belief that their slave property could not be taken from them "without full and fair compensation" and only then if a case of great exigency existed. Slave property thus ranked in the same category as realty in southern minds. An undefiled Constitution that safeguarded the spirit of liberty would remain the goal for white southerners across the generations, even if secession, which is not directly referenced in the document, served as the only means for achieving that objective. Writing in 1856 as the swirl of controversy surrounding the admission of Kansas into the union simmered, Albert T. Bledsoe observed, "Although we ardently desire harmony and concord for the States of the Union, we shall never seek it by a surrender of the Constitution."[16] For thinkers such as Bledsoe, the wisdom of the framers was not found in the document's ability to enable governmental change and growth over time; it remained tied to a narrow construction which saw the document as immutable law. It served as the basis of one's independence and, in a Jeffersonian sense, as the foundation of one's happiness. Any property, whether personalty or realty, was held in the same regard by white southern thinkers.[17]

Attacks against slavery were met with an array of responses, but few of them proved of greater longevity than claims that the push against the institution represented a much broader effort to erase basic American freedoms. Fiery George Fitzhugh, whose writings were often extreme even amongst extremists, enumerated the difficulties that lay ahead. Abolitionists, he declared had a multi-pronged plan to alter life not only in the South but across the nation. "First," Fitzhugh noted, "Domestic slavery, next religious institutions, then separate property, then political government, and finally family government and family relations are to be swept away."[18] Fitzhugh devoted little time to linking the drive to end slavery with the theoretical fear of the disruption of the family unit. When he did engage the issue, he depicted what he called "Black Republicanism," as the harbinger of American "socialism." In effect, he asserted that the drive for abolitionism was merely a facade for a more insidious force seeking to destroy not just the southern, but the American way of life. From his vantage point in 1857, Fitzhugh posited that "the North, not the South is the true battleground of the mislabeled abolitionist crusade."[19] Although he offered no evidence in support of his rather bold assertions, Fitzhugh did his utmost to discredit the intentions of his enemies by employing an all too often effective *ad hominem* argument. By criticizing the messenger, he hoped to dilute the impact of the message. Self-righteous northerners might trumpet their free labor system as superior to the slave labor one found in the South, but, if Fitzhugh is to be believed, they were unwitting handmaidens of those bent on destroying the American way of life. Fitzhugh's comments captured the outlook of the South as it stared down the increased marginalization of the region in national politics. Similarly, his rhetoric revealed an effective defensive formula that future generations would embrace as they confronted external threats. Twentieth century southerners would expand upon this theme by stressing the national implications of outside provocations against peculiarly southern institutions. Today, they would argue, the effort is made against a right deemed essential only in the South; tomorrow, there will be a push to dismantle basic liberties across the nation. The contemporary notion of the slippery slope, in which granting minor concessions for social change would unleash an avalanche of future requests each seemingly more disruptive than the one before it, clearly emerged in the antebellum South and would influence regional thinking from that point forward. Astute political observers understood the inevitability of ceaseless agitation against the South.

Despite national and regional changes that raised questions regarding the intent of the founders, white southerners refused to account for these shifts. Their worldview remained fixed to 1787, even if their actual understanding of that time and many of the period's principal actors proved limited. Summing up the southern position on this matter, James H. Hammond boldly asserted, "The South venerates the Constitution, and is prepared to stand by it forever, such as it came from the hands of our fathers; to risk everything to maintain it in its integrity."[20] That Hammond chose not to embellish his remarks indicates that at least in his mind he did not have to. Taking things even further, South Carolina fire-eater Edmund Ruffin went as far as to claim the abolitionist movement's central arguments comported with neither the Constitution nor natural law. According to Ruffin, "most ultra abolitionists, finding that the bible and constitution are both opposed to them, or support the institution of slavery, are becoming denouncers of the constitution and also the bible."[21] Time and again, southern leaders stressed the region's fidelity to the Constitution above all other considerations while casting aspersions on their detractors as being un-American and even godless. As outside pressure to limit slavery grew, so did the South's reliance on the Constitution and the shielding protection it provided for both the region's expansionist impulses and for the institution that gave it life. In the process, they helped to establish the American political tradition of demonizing one's opponents by labeling them enemies of the state.

The evolution of John Calhoun's political thought captures the struggle and change confronted by many southerners during the course of the nineteenth century as their understanding of the Constitution went from being mainstream to strictly sectional. Calhoun was an early advocate of the wave of nationalism associated with the American victory in the War of 1812 before he turned into a bitter sectionalist as the fortunes of his native South Carolina plummeted. In protest against the protective tariff designed to safeguard American businesses from overseas competition, Calhoun set in motion the process that resulted in the Nullification Crisis. He contended that the tariff violated the Constitution for nowhere in the document was the government given the authority to impose taxes to protect industry, only to generate revenue. In addition, Calhoun's home state of South Carolina and its agricultural neighbors confronted markets without protection and were forced to buy more expensive American manufactured goods. Although not necessarily the sole cause of the existing economic malaise, the tariff's impact proved devastating to the nation's poorer states, prompting Calhoun to take notice and shift his outlook. As a result, he labeled the economic travails of South Carolina as being a byproduct of a nationwide political deterioration. At the heart of his critique of the changes that had taken place in America since the adoption of the Constitution was the assumption that the nation had transformed from a federal to a more national orientation, thereby undermining the original intent of the Constitution.[22] To arrest this trend, the South Carolinian sought a mechanism whereby individual states could check federal abuses of power as the push toward national political centralization strengthened. Calhoun, who came to lament the coalescing of political strength in Washington brought on by surging nationalism, observed that the national government "has assumed control over the whole—and thus a thorough revolution has been effected, the creature taking the place of the creator."[23] The very essence of the national union as Calhoun believed had existed at the time of ratification had changed profoundly and in direct opposition to the intent of the framers.

When originally proposed in the 1828 *Exposition and Protest,* Calhoun framed his nullification theory as an effort to provide states with a tool to block the implementation of laws of dubious constitutionality, such as the protective tariff which originated the imbroglio. At the time, Calhoun considered the concept of interposition a logical way by which minority interests could express their discontent with "misguided" federal practices by nullifying unjust laws after careful deliberation on the state level. According to Calhoun, the best approach was a mechanism that afforded the states veto power over national legislation of suspect legality. As the nation expanded both in terms of its spatial layout as well as its economic diversity, the real threat existed that the interests of the slaveholding South would be subsumed by the more populous and industrially minded North. The South Carolinian reckoned that the intent of the framers was to create a stable system in which the will of the people and the will of the states were perfectly balanced in the existing framework. As the nation gradually tipped toward centralization, the rights of individual states began to crumble. Nullification represented his first effort to forge a path meant to preserve what he considered the intent of the framers that stopped short of disunion. If the numerical majority insisted on pushing what some considered an anti-South position, the region, composed of millions of people, needed a mechanism whereby it could negate future objectionable legislation. According to the nullification doctrine advanced by Calhoun, the resolution of a constitutional crisis such as the one raised by the tariff could happen in one of two ways: with Congress repealing the objectionable law in response to a state-level nullification effort or agreeing to a constitutional amendment process that, if ratified, would put to rest questions of legality. The adoption of this moderate approach, he reasoned, would be one way to restore a balanced government by allowing political interest to check political interest in a manner consistent with the vision of the framers.[24]

In his final U.S. Senate speech before his death, Calhoun voiced his opposition to what became known as the Compromise of 1850. In it, he decried not only the South's long history of conceding ground on the slavery issue by going down the slippery slope of compromise in hopes of arresting abolitionist pressure but also the fact that the political deck was increasingly stacked against the region. According to the South Carolinian, "the North has acquired a decided ascendancy over every department of this Government and the entire powers of the system. A single section, governed by the will of the numerical majority, has now, in fact, the control of the Government and the entire powers of the system."[25] Harkening back to his earlier writings, Calhoun noted that the federal system upon which the nation was founded was being dismantled as northerners took full advantage of the existing political structure that disproportionately favored them. As Calhoun observed, the North, owing to its more diverse economy, already possessed a larger population and became a beacon for immigrants who often lacked the capital necessary to purchase land for agricultural cultivation. Couple these factors shaping demographic trends with the bulk of federal tax dollars thanks to northern control of the national legislature being funneled into harbor and road projects above the Mason-Dixon Line and the evidence for why the North was more appealing to immigrants grows evident. Likewise, the South Carolinian posited that all trends then favoring the North would likely compound over time as the gap in political power separating the North from the South widened. Calhoun's musings in 1850 were nothing new to his associates. After all, he had been heralding the dire trends he observed for decades.

Finding a middle ground with the North was no longer an option. Too much governmental power had flowed away from the South. In light of one compromise after another on slavery and the western territories in the nineteenth century, an angry John Calhoun in 1850 uttered in desperation, that the South "has no compromise to offer but the constitution, and no concession or surrender to make."[26] Although vowing to hold the line, Calhoun's reflections came just prior to his death. By this point, the South Carolinian proved no longer willing to concede anything to the antislavery forces especially not the constitutionally protected right to take one's property, in this instance slaves, wherever one wanted. Granting small concessions over time, such as accepting the limitation of slavery's expansion with the Missouri Compromise, in order to safeguard the institution of slavery itself against future attacks had proven a total failure. Ultimately, Calhoun and others like him came to realize that nothing would appease those bent on changing the South. No small concession or limited allowance would arrest the central thrust of abolitionist efforts—the destruction of slavery. Once southerners recognized that nothing they could do would halt the drive to eradicate slavery, they embraced a siege mentality in which they hunkered down in the trenches refusing to give an inch to progress while labeling their actions a heroic defense of basic American freedoms.

To Calhoun and others, it always came back to the Constitution. No matter the nature of abolitionist arguments, whether moral or economic, southerners rested their defense, in part, on the self-evident shields slavery was afforded in the document. Reinterpreting the Constitution's clearly stated provisions was tantamount to, according to Calhoun, defiling the document and altering the very nature of the republic embraced during the ratification process. For proslavery defenders by the 1850s, reassessing the foundational understanding of the document was a no-go, and any deviation from the strict state-centric interpretation they espoused was immediately bemoaned as a threat to the essential character of the Constitution that would by extension result in the death of slavery. According to the South Carolinian, something other than a simple majority should effect the outcome of the country's political decisions; otherwise, there would be no protection for—ironically enough—minority interests. According to Calhoun, the Constitution as then construed, "places in the hands of the stronger and hostile section, the power to crush her and her institutions; and leaves her no alternative, but to resist, or sink down into a colonial condition."[27] Looking to the future, Calhoun saw the ever-expanding population in the North with its industrialized economic order antithetical to the South's agrarian heritage becoming increasingly hostile to the region and its racial institutions. Indeed, Calhoun fully embraced the concept of the slippery slope by the end of his career, even if he did not use the term when he noted that seemingly "small" concessions requested by antislavery forces would inevitably give way to requests for bigger demands. This agitation, according to Calhoun, needed to be stopped "before the great final object at which it aims—the abolition of slavery in the states—is consummated."[28] Calhoun's plan to arrest the trend or at least to mitigate its impact ironically included a fundamental change to the Constitution that he and most white southerners held sacrosanct—the formation of a dual presidency.

Having witnessed his nullification gambit successfully countered by President Andrew Jackson, Calhoun came to believe that nothing short of a fundamental alteration of the Constitution would restore the political balance of power in a manner keeping with his idyllic conception of the past. Calhoun's concerns regarding the prospect of the entire national political apparatus dominated by northern interests elicited considerable effort by the South Carolinian to articulate his thoughts on the "concurrent majority" and how the principle offered a resolution to the ongoing controversy that swirled around slavery without transgressing the "intent" of the framers. "The numerical majority," Calhoun argued, "should usually be one of the elements of a constitutional democracy; but to make it the sole element, in order to perfect the constitution and make the government more popular, is one of the greatest and most fatal political errors."[29] Calhoun pointed to some successful historical examples in which the concept of the concurrent majority informed political decision-making, such as the Roman Republic and the Confederacy of the Six Nations, before circling back to the intended use of the concurrent majority by the founders that derived from the fear of tyranny embedded in classical republican ideology. The Founding Fathers were as frightened by the tyranny of the mob as they were by the tyranny of the monarch. Both potential tyrants possessed the ability to impose their will on others. Calhoun pondered the dire consequences for minority interests if only the voice of the majority was given expression in the national political debate. Even more worrisome was the fact that numerically large minorities (such as the slaveholding South) could be steamrolled by the majority, leading to the onset of a type of tyranny that would dwarf the alleged misdeeds of George III. According to Calhoun, the founders created a governmental system that "is a democratic federal Republic—democratic in contradistinction to national, on the one hand—and to a confederacy, on the other; and a Republic—a government of the concurrent majority, in contradistinction to an absolute democracy—or a government of the numerical majority."[30] His solution to the long-term, seemingly inexorable drive toward unchecked democratic rule which favored the northern half of the nation was a constitutional shift that restored the old balance. In particular, he called for a "reorganization of the executive department; so that its powers, instead of being vested, as they are now in a single officer, should be vested in two—to be so elected, as that the two should be constituted the special organs and representatives of the respective sections [North and South], in the executive department of the government; and requiring each to approve all the acts of Congress before they shall become laws."[31] Despite typically heralding the achievements of the framers, his defense of the dual presidency came complete with commentary that perhaps the architects of the Constitution committed a "great mistake, in constituting a single, instead of a plural executive."[32] The office of the president, according to Calhoun, was invested with extraordinary power that proved antithetical to the idea of popular government. Indeed according to the South Carolinian, the risk of absolutist rule by a sole executive as the concurrent majority collapsed was strong enough to warrant a reconfiguration of that branch of government. A dual presidency would ensure neither section could corral the governmental system in its favor. With an immediate check of a second executive in place, the political climate would transform as leaders from both sections, recognizing that efforts to enlarge their powers at the expense of their rivals were futile, would instead work together thereby "restoring harmony and concord to the country and the government."[33]

To emphasize the strategic weakness of the South, Calhoun, as he did on many occasions, reminded his audience that the region by itself could do nothing to effect the change that was needed. Only northerners possessed the numbers needed to carry an amendment through the ratification process, and, in turn, only northerners could restore harmony between the sections. In the final years of his life, Calhoun, like most of his regional cohorts, clearly placed the onus of responsibility on preventing disunion in the hands of the North. In short, the South could do nothing legislatively to protect its interests; northern politicians needed to thwart abolitionist sentiment that sowed regional discord and embrace constitutional change along the lines of the proposed dual presidency. If northerners were unwilling to change, only disunion offered the South a possible avenue whereby it could continue safeguarding the region's racial order and, by extension, its economic interests. Based on his reading of the situation, Calhoun was offering the North a rather simple deal. Either accept slavery and protect the federal union or continue the assault on slavery and ensure the nation's dismemberment. According to the South Carolinian, "the North may save it [the Union] without any sacrifice whatever, unless to do justice, and to perform her duties under the Constitution."[34] Further negotiations, and more importantly additional concessions, were off the table as only the North possessed the power and resources to adapt its position without the need to make substantive sacrifices. The South would not change its way of life, which the region's defenders asserted was directly safeguarded by the Constitution. In the span of forty years, Calhoun thus transformed from a supporter of emerging American nationalism to an ardent sectionalist. What changed was Calhoun's perspective. As his home state and region faced economic uncertainty and mounting pressure against slavery's expansion, the South Carolinian identified the emergence of a ceaseless war against the South that would only end with the abolition of slavery. Indeed, Calhoun's journey captured the voyage made by the region as a whole. Once aggressively expansionist, the slaveholding South staunchly defended the national political apparatus until that apparatus began working against them. At that point, southerners adopted a siege mentality, stressing that only outsiders could satisfy the South by censoring the abolitionist forces and permitting slavery in the common territory. Calhoun, like the South in general, shifted from accommodation to radicalism. Less than a decade after Calhoun's impassioned plea for northerners to avert the threat of disunion posed by their antislavery rhetoric and efforts to limit the westward march of slavery, fire-eater Edmund Ruffin, along with many southerners, threw up his hands in disgust at the North's perceived recalcitrance on the slavery issue. Ruffin recognized, as did a growing number of southerners by late 1859, that secession would "be the only safeguard against the insane hostility of the north to southern institutions and interests."[35] Just as Calhoun forecast, if nothing was done to quiet the unrest, the South would have little recourse but to abandon the union. Ruffin signaled that Calhoun's prophesied point of no return was at hand. There can be little doubt that had he lived, Calhoun would have agreed.

Antebellum southerners experienced federal pressure against their institutions in a different manner than did twentieth-century segregationists. For one, many of the principle defenders of slavery wrote at a time when the fledgling Republic was in its infancy. Nineteenth-century southerners thus lived through a period in which they observed with their own eyes the centralization of power in the hands of the federal government at the expense of state power. Between the 1830s and 1850s, they bore witness to the alleged defilement of their pure and often mythological notion of the Constitution as it came under sustained attack by those bent on altering the intent of the framers. By checking southern expansion and threatening slavery, northerners appeared determined to thwart southern imperialism and, in the process, undermine the region's economic stability. After the region faced devastation in the Civil War, it also confronted the dual blow of seeing its version of the Constitution with an emphasis on states' rights sacrificed on the federal altar. Although not satisfied with the final outcome, the region acquiesced as it stared down the barrel of a muzzle to the new reality of the national government lording over a perpetual union. All of the mechanisms that Calhoun once labeled as critical to the preservation of the concurrent majority fell by the wayside as national power seemingly reigned supreme. The very vision of the constitutional order that he so carefully sketched in his writings no longer existed in the aftermath of the cataclysmic conflict. Some would argue that it never existed at all. The world Calhoun knew was no more.

Without question, racism informed the white southern understanding of the Constitution. Race provided one with privilege, it imbued one with either potential success or likely misfortune. All whites, simply because of their skin color, had a distinct advantage over all Blacks, even if any of the latter superseded any of the former in terms of financial independence. The South's entire concept of liberty and freedom was tied to a race-based social order: first through the institution of slavery and second through segregation. The latter construction exalted whites albeit in a different manner. It advocated separation of the races because it was believed the races were too dissimilar to permit free commingling. It is not surprising that segregation's champions looked with trepidation at how the modern civil rights crusade threatened to undermine individual rights and freedoms in the same manner that abolitionists once threatened slave property and hence white independence. Twentieth-century advocates for racial change were again assailing the southern way of life, this time threatening one's right to associate with whom he or she wished. The slippery slope of racial reform again reared its head. Fears of overarching racial change compelled by the federal government permeated prosegregation claims as its proponents argued their very liberty and freedoms were being slowly taken away. Lest one misses the parallel, it is unavoidable to juxtapose the themes of liberty and slavery with those of liberty and segregation. Twentieth-century white southerners no doubt believed just as their forebears did that their immersion in a social order that granted white skin an exalted status gave them a special appreciation for "liberty" as they saw firsthand what the absence of liberty meant. Naturally, no segregationist would make this claim loudly in public because the very basis of the Jim Crow order hinged upon its constitutionality—a constitutionality rooted in its statutes guaranteeing Supreme Court-mandated equal, albeit segregated, facilities. To insinuate that Blacks held a degraded place in southern society meant that the legal underpinnings of segregation were in effect voided. Once admission emerged that inequality existed, then the pleas of outsiders would not just be the rantings of those bent on destroying the South, but they would be transformed into noble cries against injustice derived ironically, considering the rhetoric of the white South, from unconstitutional practices. Following the Civil War, efforts to expand the power of the federal government proceeded at a slow albeit inexorable pace that quickened during the Progressive period in the early twentieth century. World War I helped usher in a new era of prosperity and with it a new age of conservatism that came crashing down at the end of the 1920s with the onset of the Great Depression. By design, Franklin Roosevelt's New Deal aimed primarily at fighting the problem of economic depression. Nonetheless, its massive investment of power in federal hands once again awakened white southerners to the need to protect the Constitution from the march toward centralization of government authority. Their forebears had fought the initial campaign in the battle between states' rights and "federal regimentation." They lost that battle and therefore were forced to concede the supremacy of the national government over that of the states as well as accept the perpetual nature of the Union. Several decades later, the battle between federal and state supremacy was rejoined, this time on the periphery as the biggest issue, whether federal power or state prerogatives held primacy, had already been solved in 1865. It did not take long before the government's growth once again brought about challenges to the South's racial order. Segregation and its satellite institutions invariably came under direct attack, prompting calls from southern whites for a strict construction of the Constitution, even though the intellectual foundation of many of their claims had been thoroughly undermined by the American Civil War. Nonetheless, the next round of fighting in defense of southern racial mores unrolled gradually with losses coming in slow yet steady streams for the white South as the region grappled with the implications of heading down the slippery slope of considering minor concessions in the face of cries for sweeping change.[36]

Whereas their slaveholding forebears could point to both direct and indirect ways in which the Constitution protected their chattel, twentieth-century southerners could not as easily look to the document to defend segregation. Segregationists instead turned to a broader read of the Constitution which focused on individual rights and freedoms as well as a clear delineation between the powers of state and national political organs. Interestingly, this twentieth-century fear was not dissimilar to the projections of nineteenth-century southerners who lamented what they considered the seemingly inexorable move toward centralization of governmental power in their time. Such concerns initially appeared in the antebellum period but were peripheral arguments designed to augment the main features of the southern fight in defense of slavery. Central to this outlook was the perception that any and all legislation related to slavery was aimed at taking away the individual liberties of white southerners and centralizing political power in the hands of a tyrannical national government. Southerners in the modern era experienced an even swifter shift toward centralized political power that resulted, in part, from the changed nature of the American nation. The U.S. was no longer a country of small farmers; it was an urban and industrial colossus. The governing strategy that worked in previous centuries would not necessarily work in the twentieth. Starting with the Great Depression, the calls for a stronger national government escalated. Even as the Depression ended, demands raised by the military-industrial complex and later by the sweeping mandates of Lyndon Johnson's Great Society ensured the continued erosion of state power. Against this backdrop of change stood the segregationist forces that witnessed the system they defended being steamrolled by the march of modernity. Rather than concede defeat, they rallied in an all-out effort to preserve segregation under the guise of saving the national republic as intended by the founders. New South circumstances might have differed from those evident in the Antebellum Era, but preserving the Constitution remained at the top of the priority list. The main thrust of the South's defense of a static Constitution changed little across the decades.

Conspiracy theories tend to abound in places where the status quo is under sustained attack or where a way of life is allegedly imperiled. Criticism in such situations takes on sinister connotations, precipitating a response far in excess of the actual threat posed. It is no surprise that when the South's racial systems came under scrutiny, its proponents cast this external opposition in the most devious of lights. To both the proslavery and prosegregation advocates, even mild questioning of the southern status quo represented the opening wedge of a sinister plot to not only undermine the prevailing racial order but also, in turn, the very bedrock of the American political system. Time and time again, this paradigm emerged, linking the region's racial systems with the conservative, inviolate interpretation of the Constitution that informed so much of the region's political heritage. George Fitzhugh's lamentations concerning the sweeping and nefarious intentions of abolitionists in the nineteenth century proved practically identical to those uttered almost a century later by Richard Russell as he sought to thwart civil rights change, not just for what they represented on paper, but for what ill-omens their passage would bring as calls for even more expansive laws followed.

Southern leaders recognized the nefarious forces at work against the region and the nation long before the climactic legislative showdowns over civil rights in the 1960s. Even when limited civil rights-related proposals such as antilynching legislation in the 1920s and 1930s appeared in Congress, regional politicians raised the alarm that it was just the opening wedge for a larger push to end segregation. John Calhoun's charge that the abolitionist movement would ceaselessly demand concessions in spite of compromise efforts was revisited by segregationist leaders who viewed the civil rights crusade as embracing a long-term adversarial approach toward the South that would end only when segregation was dismantled. In 1938, as part of a filibuster against the Wagner-Van Nuys Anti-Lynching Bill, Georgian Richard Russell noted, "If the Senate of the United States should permit itself to become committed to a measure of this nature at the behest of a Negro organization in the United States other bills will follow, and Senators who will be unwittingly caught in the snares of this unnecessary bill will commit themselves to other measures that will strike vital blows at the civilization of those I seek to represent."[37] Joining Russell, Mississippian Theodore Bilbo opined, "Give him this law and then he will demand something else."[38] Further harping on the alleged ill omens portended by the antilynching threat, North Carolina's Josiah Bailey added, "There is nothing to be gained by this kind of legislation. It is merely the opening of Pandora's Box. Senators should understand that. They are taking a step from which there is no retreat. . . . I could get down on my knees and beg the Senate not to pass this legislation, not because of any immediate consequences of it, but of what it leads to, and the precedent it sets."[39] Finally, South Carolina's James Byrnes directing his anger at NAACP head Walter White, whom southern politicians largely blamed for the pressure to enact antilynching legislation in the 1930s, predicted, "He [White] will make other demands, and that those who are willing to vote for this bill because he demands it will acquiesce in his subsequent demands."[40] Southern politicians believed that the clamor for civil rights reform was tied directly to organizational and bloc voter pressure, not to any real fidelity to equality on the part of northern politicians. The 1930s thus represented a major turning point in the way southern politicians conceptualized the forces working against them. Even then, they recognized the dire future the Jim Crow system faced.

In the 1930s, federal antilynching laws were considered the potential catalyst for more advanced proposals. Despite southern successes in blocking antilynching measures, pressure against the region continued with an assault against the poll tax in the middle of World War II as the next threat. As dreaded forecasts that antilynching battles represented the tip of the civil rights iceberg seemingly came to pass, southern politicians recognized that the assault against segregation was already joined. True to form, southerners again stressed the need to hold the strict constructionist line. Mississippi's Theodore Bilbo in 1942 noted regarding the poll tax battle, "This is the first step, the entering wedge, to a centralized government and the wiping out of state lines in this Republic."[41] Governmental change via centralization of power, southerners claimed, not only represented more than the onset of simple reform, but it also served as part of a larger, albeit slow, process which would bring the gradual erosion of state and individual freedoms. So slow was its progress that it often escaped notice, but advance it did, taking this freedom right here and stripping that freedom there. Mississippi senator Wall Doxey, like his state-mate Bilbo, viewed the antipoll tax measure in 1942 with fear as he saw "an effort to pass a law clearly unconstitutional, for no other purpose than political expediency. Those who desire to wipe out the theory of states' rights are happy in the knowledge that at least one milestone has been passed."[42] In keeping with his conspiratorial worldview concerning segregation, Richard Russell concocted a specific trope for voting rights, alleging that if an antipoll tax bill passed, "the sponsors propose to follow it by other legislation which would wipe out all our registration and qualification laws and allow some little Federal official from some other State to preside at every polling precinct in the South."[43] Most southerners, however, stated the obvious fact that abolishing the poll tax required passage of a constitutional amendment since both whites and Blacks needed to pay it in order to cast a ballot.[44] True, it might discriminate on an economic basis but its racial implications were less clear. What mattered to them was precedent. Permitting the passage of a bill on something as seemingly innocuous as an antipoll tax measure, which sought to eradicate a suffrage hurdle that many southerners themselves opposed, meant admission "that Congress can enter that field," and once this happens, "the Federal Government becomes sovereign in that field and can exercise any power to do anything it wishes to do."[45] Echoing the sentiments of his regional colleagues during WWII, South Carolina's "Cotton Ed" Smith opposed what he considered the "gradual but very persistent encroachment upon our dual frame of government," and he continued, "We will wake up one day and find that the power of the States has gone, and that their affairs are being conducted by bureaucrats in Washington."[46] The white South's spokesmen through the years saw themselves as the ones preventing a quicker erosion of state and local authority, all the while recognizing that unless the rest of America woke up, the bedrock principles of the nation's political system would be gone. Just as the ocean's waves inexorably erode and reshape the coast, so too do well-intentioned but misguided activists chip away at the American principles as the founders fashioned them—or at least this was how generations of white southerners believed things to be. The slippery slope concept espoused by southerners like the static vision of the Constitution from which it sprang, linked the Old South to the New in an incredibly tangible manner.

Throughout the discussion of poll tax legislation in the 1940s, southern politicians routinely stressed that race had nothing to do with their fight, as it was allegedly all about preserving the Constitution. Over time, many white southern politicians advanced a line of argumentation that privileged a constitutional over a racial perspective. The question of voting rights in many ways paralleled the discussion of segregation as it was an essential feature of the South's racial order. Without the myriad of impediments placed before Black voters in the region, Jim Crow would have faced an uncertain future from its inception. In a less guarded moment, Mississippi's Theodore Bilbo made clear that "we do not eliminate the Negroes from the ballot box through the poll tax qualifications. It is done by another provision of the constitution of the state."[47] Bilbo was indirectly noting that Mississippi literacy provisions were responsible for keeping African Americans off of the voter rolls, not the poll tax. As such, a state like Mississippi narrowly followed the letter of the law by imposing a literacy requirement on all potential voters yet violated the spirit of the law by utilizing a different standard for "literacy" depending on race. Despite Bilbo's intimation that race indeed informed regional voting practices, southerners throughout the 1940s returned to the oft-repeated assertion that the Constitution clearly left voter qualification decisions to state authorities, who, in turn, followed the letter of the law explicitly without regard to race. Any departure from this states' rights precedent would, to them, represent a step toward "the destruction of this Republic."[48] Even the South's most vocal white supremacists chose to downplay their hate in order to present a unified and what they hoped was a convincing constitutional front against such legislation. Southerners took every opportunity to shift the poll tax debate away from the controversial topic of race and toward a discussion of safeguarding the separation of powers ensconced in the Constitution.[49] Little would change in southern rhetoric over the next two decades even as the intensity of the battle fought against them accelerated.

After World War II, southern politicians began stressing that the civil rights fight would increasingly siphon away individual rights and freedoms. Interestingly enough, whereas southerners in the 1930s talked about an "opening wedge" that would culminate in an attack against segregation, by the end of the 1940s, many of those same southerners linked the drive to dismantle segregation as inherently tied to the future of the country. As pressure for racial change mounted, so did southern efforts to tie their sectional battle to a national struggle for liberty. In following this course, they clearly leaned on the model provided prior to the Civil War in which a different generation of southerners stressed the threat to the nation posed by champions of racial reform. Virginian A. Willis Robertson in 1948, for example, remarked that the region's decision to thwart all civil rights laws, even seemingly innocuous ones such as antipoll tax measures, was essential as such bills represented "another step in the direction of submerging the sovereignty of states in an overpowering central government and it opens the gates for an unlimited invasion of the powers which the Constitution carefully reserved to the States."[50] America's constitutional republic rested on the ability of the South to thwart change, so argued the region's spokesmen. If the government could intervene in the field of voter qualifications, which were clearly left for the states to decide in the Constitution, it could certainly expand its scope in a variety of fields, including segregation and other issues linked to property rights. Alabamian Lister Hill adopted this logic outside of the suffrage issue. Hill remarked during the 1946 debate concerning the formation of a permanent FEPC that its passage "would be the first step toward the nationalization of American business and American enterprise."[51] Southern comments concerning the erosion of basic individual rights, especially freedom of association and property rights, were certainly geared to a broader audience beyond the stalwart champions of white supremacy. In part, they were tapping into the growing suburban voice found in the South and the nation that viewed things like homeownership as the symbol of their lifetime of hard work. To this demographic, the idea that the federal government could tell citizens what to do with their property and force them to interact with those they preferred to avoid ran counter to their conception of American freedom. What these comments also underscore is that long before Richard Nixon's so-called "Southern Strategy," regional politicians had already begun crafting a narrative that deemphasized race by stressing property rights and individual freedoms as the foundation of their opposition to civil rights. Also inescapable is the thread that connects the Old South emphasis on slaves as property rights to the Jim Crow Era pleas that one's personal property was threatened by the government. Later, segregationists would add one's school systems by way of forced bussing. Efforts to shift the narrative to the sacrosanct right of private property demonstrate the calculated nature of southern resistance as well as a broader recognition that simple appeals to race were insufficient to sway potential support their way.

In the 1950s, southern politicians expanded little the vision they shared in the 1930s and 1940s. What became abundantly clear as the battle for segregation entered its climactic stages was the shared perspective proslavery theorists and segregationists harbored concerning federal authority. Virginia's Harry Byrd, for example, responded to one constituent who expressed concerns over the centralization of government power: "I share your apprehension for our future welfare unless there is a return to fundamental principles."[52] Louisiana's Allen Ellender, echoing the words of John Calhoun, lamented the concentration of federal power in all fields when he remarked, "It has been my experience that once government gets its foot in the door, so to speak, the whole leg soon follows it."[53] Federal hegemony needed to be thwarted on the frontier before a foothold was established; otherwise, no effort could roll it back. Extending Ellender's dire warning to its logical conclusion, North Carolina politician Sam Ervin, opined regarding civil rights initiatives, "These proposals are incompatible with the Federal System of Government established by the Constitution, and the basic economic, personal, and legal rights of all of our people."[54] Addressing the growing cacophony favoring civil rights, Georgia's fiery Herman Talmadge boldly asserted that "every fledgling lawyer knows that the real civil rights of every citizen of this country are contained in the first 10 amendments" before adding that "our system of government, as wrought by the founding fathers, is under sustained attack" by those desiring the end of segregation.[55] The roots of southern devotion to an idealized notion of a pure Constitution connected directly to the musings of leaders in previous decades. Southern politicians drew a line in the sand at the first hint of threats against the region's racial order. As the legislative and judicial inroads against segregation mounted, they remained steadfast in their efforts to arrest this drive with inflammatory assertions that the Constitution was being trampled before everyone's eyes in a blind rush to appease minority groups. At a time of sweeping growth of federal power initiated by the New Deal, only the beleaguered South, or so its politicians asserted, held on as true constitutionalists.

At the same time the flames of resistance grew, evidence that a considerable number of the region's white citizens were less than interested in fighting in defense of Jim Crow also emerged. For every southerner prepared to battle the federal government, there were those who did not want to proceed beyond a rhetorical showdown in which they could save face and go about their business. Some, such as the flamboyant J. Strom Thurmond, bemoaned the defeatist attitude he saw among those who should have been the most determined—the region's politicians. In 1961, for example, he wrote a constituent, "The southern will to resist in Congress is not what it used to be and I am trying to refortify that."[56] The following year, Thurmond furthered his pessimistic outlook, remarking that he discovered a general "reluctance up here [Washington] to really fight hard on this subject."[57] It is especially intriguing that at the very moment the South faced the most sustained, persistent push against its racial institutions, some white leaders proved willing to concede defeat without much of a fight. Taking a page from Calhoun's playbook, Thurmond challenged regional inertia. He noted, "The South has already compromised too much and has received nothing in return therefor. I do not see how we can continue to compromise away our principles."[58] By the dawn of the 1960s, Thurmond recognized that accepting any further concessions in the field of civil rights without vigorous opposition would be catastrophic for the region. As Thurmond's correspondence in 1961 and 1962 suggests, finding compatriots to hold the line with him was proving increasingly difficult. One thing for certain, Thurmond, like Calhoun before him, saw no benefit to be achieved by working with the region's enemies. No matter how conciliatory the region was mattered little as the true objective of activists was the complete dismantling of the southern racial order. Those who pursued any path save for outright defiance were subverting the interests of the South claimed Thurmond. Any step toward conciliation would set the region down a slippery slope that would end first in the death of Jim Crow and later in the death of the nation as the country abandoned its constitutional principles.

Civil Rights legislation, even ones with narrow focuses, called for prompt and immediate condemnation throughout the twentieth century. Naturally, when confronted with the sweeping Civil Rights Act of 1964, southerners took things to the extreme, calling out what they considered a direct onslaught against the "bedrocks" of national "freedom, progress, and opportunity: separation of powers, limited executive authority, no special privilege."[59] Texas's John Tower echoed these sentiments, remarking, for example, that the Civil Rights Act of 1964 "would tend to destroy not only checks and balances in the field of State power as opposed to Federal power, but the checks and balances system within the tripartite division of powers."[60] Southern politicians thus staked out an extreme position in which only catastrophic implications flowed from civil rights bills. Resurrecting the rhetoric of the previous century, southerners stressed that more than segregation was at stake; the very survival of the country hung in the balance. The spokesmen for the white South repeatedly trotted out some variation of the central theme that passing the sweeping 1964 civil rights law would set in motion a cascading series of events culminating in the collapse of the nation. Sam Ervin, for example, opined that the civil rights bill's passage meant "the America I have known and loved, the America that believed in liberty rather than Government by regimentation would be supplanted by a police state."[61] Going even further in this direction, South Carolina's Olin Johnston noted, "If we continue to pass on to the Federal Government power and authority, and continue to take power and authority away from the states, we shall wake up some day and have only one government, the U.S. Government of the United States with the States having no rights left whatever."[62] Those who challenged southern assertions that they overplayed the sinister nature of the 1964 law were greeted by the likes of Mississippi's James Eastland who commented, "The Federal bureaucrat is tyrannical. The Federal bureaucrat is arrogant, tyranny would result [if the bill passed]."[63] Foreshadowing twenty-first-century discussions regarding the "deep state," Eastland's conspiratorial outlook concerning federal civil servants was consistent with the paranoid worldview that informed much of the southern fight against racial change. They never looked to the best-case scenario or even a middle-of-the-road outcome, only the worst possible result. Naturally, this type of rhetoric is consistent with ideologues regardless of where they sit on the political spectrum. Opponents of legislation typically focus their angst on the worst-case scenario and urge their supporters that it is best to proceed with caution rather than head down a slippery slope that might lead to unintended consequences. Even a seemingly limited law with the best of intentions could have deleterious consequences. Eastland certainly was not implying that anything good would come of the Civil Rights Act of 1964, but he was reminding his colleagues that nefarious developments could arise even from bills representing seemingly noble ideals. Sticking close to the alleged "intent" of the framers represented the only way to arrest the inexorable march toward "statism."

In 1964, dire forecasts of the collapse of the American political system certainly filled southern rhetoric. Local considerations also loomed large as southerners presented a narrative that saw civil rights as the harbinger of social and political disruption on all levels not just larger national ones. Of course, they vowed to defend segregation to the end, which naturally resonated with their constituents, but they did not stop there. They more overtly than ever expanded the scope of their local critique of civil rights when confronted with the 1964 bill in a manner that might appeal to those outside of the region, all the while clinging to a rigid interpretation of the Constitution. With far greater intensity than exhibited in the past, southern politicians trotted out this bifurcated strategy encapsulated in the reflections of Russell Long who opined that the Civil Rights Act of 1964 represented "a true lynching party on the South, and on our American freedoms of privacy and property and free enterprise."[64] Long's remarks were echoed by his peers in Washington and across the South. Texan John Tower, for one, noted that the civil rights bill was "an out-and-out unconstitutional extension of Federal Government power over the private rights of every American citizen."[65] Alabama's Lister Hill joined Long and Tower in emphasizing the extraordinary power the 1964 law placed in the hand of the national government when he remarked that "if any American has any civil right which should be respected and honored under all conditions, it is his civil right not to associate with another person without his consent or against his will."[66]

The American Revolution and the Founding Fathers were frequently referenced by southern politicians in the civil rights era, especially in the climactic 1964 battle in an effort by segregationists to dress up their largely race-inspired assertions. Hiding behind the cloak of patriotism, many segregationists twisted the thinking of the founders to fit their need for a more elevated line of argumentation. That southerners referenced the founders in no way means that their appeals were linked to a deep appreciation and study of the Revolutionary Age. Instead, they trotted out a vague series of platitudes that the founders, or any American for that matter, would agree with. This trend continued until the end of the legislative battle over civil rights in the 1960s. During the 1964 civil rights debate, Virginia's Harry Byrd, commenting on the dire political trends he witnessed, observed, "Centralization of government power in Washington is the most dangerous trend we face in this country today. It is in violation of the principles of Jefferson, who was a Founding Father of both this Nation and the Democratic Party."[67] Louisiana's Russell Long also boldly asserted that the position southerners found themselves in proved reminiscent of that faced "prior to the American Revolution when the colonists felt they were being imposed upon by the British government and that they were being victimized by it," before he added that modern-day southerners had every right to push back against the injustice they faced as their forebears did in the eighteenth century.[68] Arkansan George McClellan answered critics who accused him of wasting time in a filibuster likewise opted to link his fight with the efforts of the American colonists, remarking that "it was called a Revolution when our forefathers went out, and fought, and died to establish liberty in this land."[69] By carefully framing their narrative, southerners in the twentieth century hoped to legitimize their unsavory institutions. Long, for example, did not dwell on the specifics that drove the colonial push for independence, and he certainly did not contrast those issues with the South's efforts to dress up its defense of segregation. McClellan likewise chose not to flesh out his assertion that his participation in the filibuster against a civil rights bill somehow equated to following in the footsteps of the Revolutionary generation. By planting the seed that some connection existed, these southern patriarchs hoped to elevate their resistance to a heroic level by implying that their screeds against federal regimentation shared a great deal in common with the laundry list of grievances aired in the Declaration of Independence. Although straining credulity, efforts to tie Jim Crow to the Revolution and the Founding Fathers kept coming. Capturing the spirit as well as the vagueness of this approach, Alabama's Lister Hill stressed that civil rights laws "would accumulate overwhelming powers in the hands of the executive branch of Government and grant special privilege to a particular group" and that they, therefore, represented "a political retrogression inimical to the American system as Madison and his contemporary Americans conceived it, and we have cherished it for 174 years."[70] Naturally, Hill offered no further analysis of the situation beyond this blanket assertion. Like his regional colleagues, he framed his discussion in the broadest of possible ways in which a connection to the Revolutionary Era was implied, yet never proven via meaningful analysis. Resorting to the oldest political trick in the book, southern pols painted an idyllic portrait of their defense of an institution that was viewed with increasing disdain by those outside the region.

Although fixing their sights on a narrow interpretation of the Constitution that enabled them to elevate their defense of segregation to the same level as discussions concerning basic property rights and individual choice, southerners were not above appealing to the racism they were convinced existed in the North. Throughout the twentieth century, southern politicians railed against the hypocrisy that they believed drove the civil rights fight. In the 1930s, for example, Theodore Bilbo, reflecting on the disingenuous nature of northern support for antilynching legislation remarked, "If we were to take a secret ballot . . . with every Senator in his seat, and if there were no way on earth for their news to get back to this mongrel population in New Jersey and other States—if no octoroon, quadroon, or mulatto, or anyone with Negro blood in him, could ever find out how Senators voted—this bill would not get 10 votes on the floor of the Senate."[71] So long as the hand of the federal government remained on southern throats, they opined, northerners could smugly decry their benighted countrymen south of the Mason-Dixon Line. However, if the thrust of civil rights activism turned northward, many southern politicians believed the outcry from the very same people who wanted the South punished for alleged racial transgressions would be immediate. Georgian Richard Russell in the middle of the 1964 Civil Rights debate slyly noted, "We shall see how many Senators who say they are so dedicated to the cause of assisting their colored brethren that they are willing to die here in the Chamber to accomplish it, vote when they get down to the two provisions that mean the most to colored people—racial imbalance in the schools and open housing occupancy."[72] Russell was clearly highlighting the dilemma faced by some civil rights activists, who in championing the cause, paved the way for further agitation that would inevitably result in efforts to dismantle the residentially segregated schools and neighborhoods that all knew existed in the North. In doing so he was astutely tying the interests of middle-class Americans, no matter where they resided, to the outcome of the civil rights fight. Unless the push for change was thwarted, the next logical progression in the civil rights battle, some theorized, was to attack residential patterns of discrimination. Naturally, suburban denizens wrapped much of their wealth into a single investment—their homes and by extension, the communities in which they lived. They viewed their property and their local schools as sacrosanct. An assault against them would surely provoke unrest. Richard Russell understood this important fact regarding the *de facto* segregation that permeated northern communities. Throughout, politicians such as Russell stressed the need for outsiders to look beyond the passions of the moment and see the threats civil rights laws posed to individual and property rights protected since the days of the founders. Today, it was the South; tomorrow, Russell warned, it would be the North. Despite throwing everything, including the kitchen sink at the 1964 bill, time had run out on Jim Crow. What southerners confronted was not a temporary gust of political passion as they often claimed; it was the burgeoning of a social movement that would only build momentum as it spread. It was a movement that sprang not just from outsiders as they asserted, but one that developed from within the South's African American community upon emancipation. No amount of moralizing or internal reform would halt this growth. The hypocrisy of a nation touting liberty and freedom while denying the same to its largest minority group was an inconsistency the majority of Americans could no longer sanction.

When the civil rights fight shifted to voting rights in 1965, the stage was set for yet another southern filibuster, only this time to safeguard what was obviously the constitutional right for a state to determine its qualifications for voting—provided, of course, that such qualifications were imposed in an equitable manner. This latter point proved problematic in the South. As in previous instances, southerners had to disingenuously assert that voter laws were fairly administered in their respective states without consideration of race. Segregationists pulled from the same array of ideas in the 1960s as they did in the 1940s. To be sure, some could not resist the temptation to let their prejudices find full expression. Mississippi's James Eastland, for example, opined regarding the Voting Rights Act of 1965 that "not only an illiterate, but one absolutely lacking in all of the attributes of good moral character, or any moron not incarcerated in an institution can be qualified to vote under the proposed legislation."[73] Although Eastland was certainly not alone in utilizing thinly veiled racial invective, the general thrust of the southern case in the voting rights fight was tied directly to the Constitution. Since all of the evidence available then and today points to clear southern efforts to suppress Black voter registration, one must take southern assertions regarding the Constitution in this field with a grain of salt. Yes, the Constitution safeguarded a state's right to determine voter qualifications, but this provision needed to be interpreted in light of the Fifteenth Amendment, which stipulated that race was not to be a factor in determining a person's fitness to vote. Thus, on paper, southern states did not violate the Constitution, but in practice, they trampled all over the document. To dissect their voting rights assertions is to stare hypocrisy in the face.

Southerners such as Sam Ervin admitted that race-based voter discrimination still existed in the South and that those who perpetrated such offenses made it difficult for the region to stave off sweeping efforts to combat these problems. In speaking on the Fifteenth Amendment, Ervin defined it as a "negative mandate" in that it did not grant the right to vote, that it "only prohibits the States from denying suffrage on the ground of race or color."[74] Others such as A. Willis Robertson noted that there would not have been a Constitution or federal union had the national government formulated in 1787 been imbued with the power to establish suffrage requirements.[75] He was not alone in advancing such a theory when tackling voting rights. Even politicians with a reputation for unapologetic rhetoric such as Strom Thurmond pivoted to a more edifying line of discussion when confronted with suffrage measures. He denounced those who would deny someone the right to vote based exclusively on race while decrying the idea of upending the Constitution for the sake of solving the problem. According to Thurmond, the "legislative flouting of the Constitution under the pretense of upholding the Constitution will not advance civil rights."[76] The thrust of southern arguments revolved around the notion that the Constitution did not grant the national government such sweeping powers to interfere with the state voting apparatus. Instead, it was crafted in such a fashion as to ensure that broad concentrations of power were avoided, not just in terms of the different branches of government but also regarding the balance between state and national political prerogatives. Mississippi's John Stennis laid the case out thusly: "It is axiomatic that the Federal Government has only those powers delegated to it by the Constitution. Absent an express or implied grant of authority there is no Federal power. On the contrary, the respective States are the repositories of residual power; that is, authority not given to the Federal Government, nor denied to the States, remains in the States or in the people without enumeration in the Constitution. The Tenth Amendment forever sets this proposition at rest."[77]

In perhaps the bluntest statement regarding southern devotion to an unchanging Constitution, Floridian Spessard Holland asserted, "I believe that the Constitution means the same thing now as it did in 1789. I deplore any philosophy which comes to the conclusion that we have a right to decide now that the framers of the Constitution did not mean what they obviously meant at the time they placed these words in the Constitution."[78] Furthermore, James Eastland contended, "There is nothing in the Constitution . . . which gives anybody the right to vote in the State if he is not eligible to be a voter in that State."[79] Despite frequent appeals to the sanctity of the Constitution, southerners found their assertions falling on deaf ears as Congress approved the sweeping suffrage proposal. Change needed to take place—immediate change in the eyes of many. The time for waiting was over.

History provides the benefit of hindsight. Today, it is known that the dire forecasts regarding the federal government stripping states of the power to set voter qualifications never came to pass. The much-lamented Voting Rights Act of 1965 did as it was expected to do: it opened the franchise to hundreds of thousands of African Americans who had been denied suffrage solely because of the color of their skin. Of course, the fight over voting rights is an ongoing one, yet it is one that plays out in a different milieu than witnessed in the 1960s. Present-day challenges are raised against what is perceived as new impediments in the voter registration process often centered around the presence of an alleged technological divide that inhibits people from completing tasks, such as securing a valid state identification card, rather than overtly denying a particular racial group access to the franchise. Despite some injecting race into all voting rights discussions regardless of the issue, the current debate revolves more around maximizing the number of voters versus ensuring that only those who are duly registered should cast a ballot. Beneath the surface remains the Constitution and the nefarious use of its legacy employed by the defenders of the South's race-based social systems that informs contemporary debate on the issue. No doubt the future will see further discussion over what constitutes a legitimate voter qualification and who gets to decide what those parameters are. Regardless of the battle lines of that future showdown, the ghosts of Jim Crow will never be far from the surface.

5

The Difference This Time

Although white southerners invariably championed a race-based social order in the nineteenth and twentieth centuries, these systems nonetheless differed and had divergent endgames. In turn, regional responses to external threats against the South's respective racial regimes reflected the peculiarities of time and place. As the nineteenth century progressed, abolitionist activism proceeded apace, prompting a mounting chorus of opposition in protest and growing threats of disunion. A lot was at stake considering the devastating economic consequences emancipation posed. Assuming a basic cross-century analysis in which one dollar in 1860 is worth approximately $31.91 today, and utilizing the rough aggregate figure that the price of a slave purchased in 1860 was $800, the average value of a slave in today's money is $25,528. Naturally, this is a rudimentary figure meant to provide context—not a final word. Many of the enslaved were valued higher or lower than the numbers offered here. There are a myriad of other issues to consider when attempting such a computation—including age, gender, and skill sets. Keeping all of this in mind and utilizing only the most basic of statistical evidence in which one slave's value is $800, an entry level planter who enslaved twenty persons had approximately $510,560 in today's currency tied up in chattel. Emancipation without federal compensation would level a devastating financial blow to such an individual. Extend the margin further to include those with considerably larger slaveholdings that cross the million-dollar mark, and it is not hard to imagine why people in this class would view any effort to take away the basis of their economic prosperity with abject fear. Their world and indeed their way of life was at stake. When antebellum southerners drew a line in the sand, it was not a rhetorical one; it was a literal one. Crossing that point meant a full-on assault against a relatively small yet disproportionately powerful minority in the American South. Secession represented to this embattled and privileged class the only logical alternative in a world that seemed increasingly bent on destroying them. Decades of national opposition to slavery and southern expansionism, highlighted to many that no matter what the South did, outsiders would not relent.[1]

The South, following defeat in the Civil War, faced a staggering crisis as slavery came to an end. Billions of dollars were lost when the nearly four million enslaved persons in the region were set free. The often violent Reconstruction period ended with the gradual elimination of Republican rule and the restoration of white Democratic leadership. Despite the return of "home rule," the region would never be the same. The devastation visited upon it by the war and the protracted downturn in agricultural commodity prices in the last decades of the century saw the region limp into the twentieth century. As the economy foundered, the South also took a detour from the promise of economic and political equality for the freedmen advanced in Reconstruction era amendments. Jim Crow and its satellite institutions, such as voter discrimination statutes which made it possible, differed markedly from the antebellum slave system. Businessmen in the region's exploitative industries certainly relied on Black labor and utilized an array of tricks permissible within the Jim Crow economy to keep the region's African American population impoverished and locked in specific locations. However, as the twentieth century progressed, these tools of oppression became less pronounced as more and more of the region's businesses looked overseas for production or reduced their labor force by adopting new technology. In particular, there was less of a financial incentive for segregation especially following the mid-twentieth century mechanization of the region's agricultural production brought about, in part, by African American efforts to find higher paying jobs outside of the region. Without cheap Black labor, southern planters modernized their agricultural operations. The financial loss associated with slavery could be measured in the millions; the same could not be said for segregation, especially not at mid-century. As an institution, segregation increasingly represented a net-drain on the region's fragile economic condition as not only did southern states need to subsidize an array of separate facilities, but their practices also ensured that many businesses would bypass the region in search of territory less teeming with inequity. This latter concern grew more pronounced as the twentieth century progressed. Of course, white southerners still believed in the social and cultural value of Jim Crow, even as they struggled to define its economic necessity. Segregationist leaders heaped scorn on efforts to dismantle the region's racial order. Yet when the moment of truth appeared and a critical mass had been reached in the civil rights fight that threatened the entire Jim Crow edifice, they backed off from an all-or-nothing stance. Violence, of course, would take place, but when it did, it was often the product of local leadership or the failure thereof, not a unified fight as occurred in the Confederate States. So much had changed in the hundred years separating the American Civil War from the South's last-ditch effort to protect its second racial order.[2]

The southern point-of-no return in the nineteenth century became clear in the pivotal period between John Brown's Raid on Harpers Ferry in October 1859 and the election of Abraham Lincoln in November 1860. With mounting dread regarding the impact of the abolitionist movement on the stability of enslaved communities, the seemingly endless stream of what was perceived as "anti-South" legislation, and the dire prospect that a member of the hated Republican Party—which threatened to undermine the expansion of the peculiar institution—securing control of the presidency, the only viable option was disunion. Any other path, some believed, would lead to a gradual erosion of personal freedoms and a consistent effort to dismantle the slave system. John Brown's Raid, which took place on October 16–18, 1859, was promptly condemned by the southern press as being the byproduct of northern fanaticism with regard to the slave question. Most critical, reporters made clear that the attempted insurrection involved outsiders—not native white or Black southerners. Indeed, despite the popular portrayal of the event in the northern press, southern commentators routinely stressed the very white and very northern face of the event. Far from accomplishing its ends, the New Orleans *Times-Picayune* labeled the Brown Raid an abject failure that would "only tighten the bonds of the slave, and to weaken those that bind the white race of the two sections together under one government."[3] Of course, the force of logic also points to another question: if the raid was as limited as the southern press depicted, then why did it prompt such grave concerns in many quarters? Surely something more was at play.

Early in the developing story out of Harpers Ferry, southerners, despite initial attempts to downplay the importance of the raid, understood that a critical point had been reached in relations between North and South. Things could never return to their pre-raid form. At the same time, however, there was ample evidence to suggest that perhaps the abolitionists had gone too far in this "invasion" of the South. A considerable number of voices in November 1859 stressed the great harm that the raid had done to the abolitionist cause in general and that it likely turned many northerners away from the movement out of shock at the wantonness of it all. Members of the New York Democratic Vigilance Association did their part to implicate the Republican Party for the excesses in Virginia before urging its party's voters in the Empire State to reject the "Black Republican" establishment which "either openly justifies or lukewarmly condemns the frauds, atrocities, and murders connected with the Harpers Ferry invasion." Adding an even more sinister thread to the discussion, the leadership of the group opined, "It will appear that Northern abolitionists have long contemplated a war of races; that preparations for it have been slowly and deliberately made; that the recent invasion of the South was not intended to be an isolated one."[4] In the wake of such an occurrence, some argued it was far better to leave the union while there was still something left to fight for. Despite talk of an "irrepressible conflict" in some quarters, there remained a sizable (and arguably a majority) contingent across the nation that decried any talk of disunion or punitive expeditions against the South. Finding a receptive, or interested, audience in support of moderation, however, proved far more difficult than many envisioned.[5]

Less sanguine assessments dwelled on the martyr status that Brown achieved in the North. Despite talk that the raid might mute less strident abolitionist voices, the opposite seemed the case. Many regional newspapers, although soundly condemning Brown's "atrocities," had initially held out hope that the incident would temper northern sentiment against slavery. By mid-November, editorial boards recognized that no ameliorative effect would follow the raid and that "the blood of John Brown will be the cement of the Republican church, and his name the inspiring call to a complete Republican victory at every poll in the North."[6] Before long, the southern press placed Brown's actions solely in political terms and heaped scorn on the hated Republican Party for its allegedly interminable crusade against the South. As the hours counted down before the execution of John Brown in December 1859, white southerners awaited the emergence of what they were told was the conservative majority in the North who would decry the excesses of abolitionists that, they believed, spawned Brown's contemptible actions. Indeed, southerners were heartened by reports coming from some news outlets above the Mason Dixon Line which urged the South to press its case to the northern populace and "rest assured that her appeal to the practical conservatism of the Free States will not be made in vain, if it be made temperately, earnestly, and in good faith."[7] If such conservative voices existed in the North, they did not manifest themselves in the volume suggested by some, prompting a further ratcheting up of fear and paranoia in the South. The intensity of the southern response confounded many period observers. *The New York Times*, for example, posted an editorial regarding the Brown situation which posited, "We have been astonished at the immense outcry raised over that wild and absurd freak of a hard-headed, strong-willed fanatic."[8] Indeed, many northerners found the whole matter dismaying. As they saw it, this was merely the work of a madman. Abolitionists might sing his praise but they represented a minority of northern opinion even at this late date. On the other hand, many of them did not rally to the southern cause simply because they did not see a real cause to rally around. Why coalesce in opposition to a raid that most citizens in both the North and the South strongly opposed? A more sweeping northern response in the South's favor, not indifference, was what southern agitators desired. It was difficult for northerners to get excited over what many considered a nonissue. For most, the whole episode represented the misguided efforts of a mentally unwell man and his small retinue of followers. Far from being the harbinger of a race war or the vanguard of future armed forays into the region, most northerners considered it an isolated incident that warranted little response beyond a shake of the head.[9]

Before 1859 was over, battle lines were drawn as starkly as they had ever been despite clear signs that only staunch abolitionists, such as Wendell Phillips and Henry Ward Beecher, considered Brown anything but a lunatic. The key issue stirring discontent, however, was the decision of the press to highlight the extremists, such as those holding prayer services in northern cities at the time of the revolutionary's death, not the overwhelming majority of people in the region who were not in the least interested in Brown's fate. As much as southerners decried the concept of an "irrepressible conflict" as anti-South propaganda, they were increasingly adopting its perspective as the fallout from the Brown imbroglio intensified. Southern fire-eaters took every opportunity to spin the volatile situation in their favor. They were far less concerned with divining the true nature of northern opinion as they were in buoying southern interest in disunion efforts. Capturing the new spirit taking hold in the region, the *Times-Picayune* observed regarding those who opposed slavery in any form, "These are our deadly enemies, and there can be no fellowship with them, or with those who sustain them, either actively, or by connivance or indifference. It is a proclamation of eternal war, and all who are not for us are for them."[10]

Regional sentiment was clearly drifting toward extremism and a willingness to differentiate between abolitionists who wanted to eradicate slavery everywhere and antislavery advocates who sought to thwart the spread of slavery fast disappearing. According to southern logic, one was either in favor of slavery or completely against it, with the latter camp allegedly being willing to use any means, including violence, to destroy the institution. Going even further, the southern press made clear that a dire future awaited the nation if it sat back and allowed Brown's atrocities to stand without national condemnation. If the nation did nothing, southerners stressed "disunion, civil war, and despotism must be our certain destiny."[11] As battle lines hardened, the South embraced the notion that a conflict was in the offing. Overlooked throughout the process was the wide array of northerners who clearly fell in the grey area. These individuals, likely the majority of the northern populace, were neither friends nor foes of slavery. For them, it was out of sight and out of mind.[12] Despite the indifference of some, a palpable sense that momentum behind disunion was mounting became evident. Unionist U.S. Congressman Roderick Randum Butler of Tennessee, for one, sounded the alarm bells and asked, "Is there no danger apprehended by the Union-loving and conservative people of the grand confederacy from and by the reckless and impudent course of these fanatics [from the] South? I believe, sir, there is great danger. I believe we have much to fear from them. I believe we have men [from the] South who would tomorrow sink the Union into oblivion, if they could advance their own interest."[13] As the initial shock and outrage over the Harpers Ferry Raid abated, it became clear that the very fate of the American nation hung in the balance.

Southern concerns regarding Yankee intentions, nonetheless, were anything but illegitimate. True, northern opinion might not have been as rigid as they asserted, yet the evidence suggests that among vocal northerners, especially abolitionists, Brown was indeed viewed as a savior. In his newspaper, abolitionist Fredrick Douglass routinely glorified the actions of "brave old John Brown."[14] Douglass might not have approved of Brown's propensity for violence, but he clearly supported the larger cause at which it was aimed. Even if the circulation of Douglass's publication was small, it still had an audience, and its membership was infinitely more willing to share its beliefs with the world as compared to those who simply did not care one way or the other. Northerners and southerners were thus stepping into an echo chamber in which the only ideas that found public expression were those dedicated to ideological extremes. Southerners looked to the North for a voice of moderation and found nothing save for vitriol. Hearing only silence emanating from the North, the editorial staff of the New Orleans *Daily Crescent* embraced an alarmist tone, opining that "it [the raid] was intended as the beginning of a crusade against slavery all through the South, to be ended only with the utter extermination of the institution wherever it existed."[15] Georgia senator Alfred Iverson, for one, placed blame for the mounting sectional tension on the Republican Party whose intention it was, he speculated, "to breakdown the institution of slavery by fair means or foul means; if they cannot accomplish it in one way, they intend to accomplish it in another."[16] Rather than attempt to pull the nation back from the brink of dissolution, Republicans, according to Iverson, only strengthened their vitriol in the wake of Brown's raid. Southern extremists viewed their northern counterparts as hopelessly wedded to breaking the region's spirit. With such a recalcitrant outlook, it is little wonder that reconciliation efforts foundered.

Political leaders in both the North and the South heard what they wanted, and each ramped up the intensity of their attacks. Many northern news articles expressed hope that time would heal the wounds of the Brown raid and afford the South the opportunity to defuse its considerable angst in much the same way that southerners hoped northern conservatives would destroy the radical abolitionism in their region.[17] Had it occurred sooner, the impact of the raid might have been limited. Happening as it did, as the nation prepared for the 1860 presidential contest, imbued it with greater significance and allowed it to go a long way to ensuring that the extremist perspective reigned supreme. As the presidential race heated up, direct reference to Brown waned, yet his influence in polarizing the nation was everywhere—apparent even if his name was not. For some, support for the Republican Party was tantamount to a vote in favor of John Brown's actions. The forthcoming election thus assumed even greater importance as many considered it a referendum on the future of the federal union. Senator Clement Clay of Alabama ominously warned his colleagues outside of the South "to labor no longer under the delusion that the southern States do not intend to act" if the sectional Republican Party secured victory in 1860, and he added that "the danger which now environs the country is greater than it ever has been."[18] Should a candidate without southern support secure victory, it would signal to the South that the majority of northerners favored further Brown-like forays and possibly even the end of slavery. The time for compromise was evaporating.

Much attention has been given to the 1860 presidential election. It was after all an epochal moment in American history. Distilling the essence of the South's perspective following the political contest, the Louisville *Daily Courier* grimly remarked, "We see no reason to hope that the war on slavery will ever cease."[19] The ramifications of the contest set in motion a sequence of events that resulted in disunion before culminating in the end of slavery. To Americans at the time, an incredible level of uncertainty abounded. Within weeks of Lincoln's successful election, the call for disunion was everywhere evident in the South. South Carolina might have been the first southern state to secede, but it was not the only one that planned such a step in the wake of the presidential contest. Deep South governors, such as Andrew Moore of Alabama, Thomas Moore of Louisiana, and John Pettus of Mississippi, announced plans for secession conventions before the end of 1860.[20] This was the moment of truth. It would be erroneous, however, to assume that a blind rush toward secession immediately resulted. Many state leaders postured for constituents regarding the need to plan for whatever onslaught Lincoln would bring, yet most adopted a wait and see approach.[21] What this crowd regrettably discovered was that the longer they waited, the more momentum swung in favor of secessionists. It was the latter interest that aggressively sold southerners on the idea that a Republican presidency represented not just a threat to the region's slaveholders but to the very liberty of all the region's inhabitants. Rather than a cooling off period, the time following Lincoln's election until his inauguration saw the region develop into a white-hot fury. Voices of moderation were driven from the field, while extremists gained control over the post-election southern conventions. Talk of a sleeping conservative majority in the North eroded as southerners viewed the election returns as proof that abolitionism had taken hold of northern opinion.[22]

Paranoia, not always facts, figured prominently in the ensuing discussion. Many southern editorials were willing to give Lincoln the benefit of the doubt in so much as it was assumed he would do as he promised: he would obey the fugitive slave provisions of the country and be forthright in his policies. Nonetheless, his antislavery position was unforgivable, and his election came by way of a "conspiracy" of the northern states to dominate the southern states. Proof of the conspiracy, according to southern arguments, resided in the simple fact that Lincoln did not even campaign in the South. As they saw it, the interests of the southern minority were being completely neglected to serve the demands of bitter northern partisans dedicated to controlling the southern half of the country by force. The election returns, noted the New Orleans *Daily Crescent*, "unmistakably indicate the hatred to the South which animates and controls the masses of the numerically strongest section of the Confederacy."[23] This was not democracy, they uttered, but a blanket power grab by one section without a pretense of reaching out to citizens in other regions. As reported by some, "Abraham Lincoln was not elected by the people of the United States as their President. He was elected by the people of seventeen states, combined against the institutions of the other fifteen States. . . . His election was the result of a combination—a conspiracy almost . . . among the non-slaveholding States, to obtain control over the slaveholding states."[24] Because of the alleged cabal-like quality behind the Republican presidential victory in 1860, southerners argued that the election was inherently flawed and that the very foundation of the national government was undermined. North Carolina senator Thomas Clingman observed, regarding the Republican Party victory, "The result is that a sectional party will yield the entire power over all the departments of the Government. . . . We are not only to be governed by a sectional domination which does not respect our rights, but by one, the guiding principle of which is hostility to the southern States."[25] The North Carolinian left little doubt where he stood on the matter. He, like countless other southerners, looked upon the election as the final straw: the last step in the direction of northern hegemony over the political landscape.

Despite the decades-long assertion that slaveholding powers dominated Washington, the 1860 election proved to southerners that they were the true victims of a conspiracy orchestrated by "Black Republicans." Southerners repeatedly asserted that had this truly been a national election, the region would have accepted defeat and, by extension, majority rule. Based on the overt sectional tint to the contest, all bets were off when it came to southern acceptance of the election results. Although optimism for a resolution remained in some quarters, hope clearly dimmed as 1860 came to a close.[26] Naturally, not everyone wanted the region to hastily break away from the Union. Indeed, many white southerners bemoaned Lincoln's election, yet still urged restraint when it came to taking the ultimate step. As this contingent of southerners saw things, the best thing to do was for the region to act in concert while avoiding a hasty decision to withdraw from the union. Patriotic appeals abounded as some stressed the need for the region to drive out the wicked abolitionist minority that appeared to them to be the catalyst behind the anti-South bias in the North.[27] With individual southern states planning or hosting special conventions to address the topic and with South Carolina already out of the Union, the voices for restraint grew more distant. It became clear to all but the most sanguine observer that the South was leaving the Union. There would be no eleventh-hour compromise to forestall disaster. The hour of reckoning was at hand.[28]

Many believed Lincoln's election marked the culmination of a decades-long effort to siphon power away from the South and funnel it in the hands of those determined to dismantle slavery by first blocking its expansion, then by attacking its constitutionality everywhere. Nothing short of northern electors casting their ballots for someone other than Lincoln or, even less likely, the resignation of the president-elect would satisfy white southerners. For those who still wished to operate within the existing federal Union, one other option remained: if Lincoln assumed the presidency, Congress needed to rigorously follow the Constitution and pull as much political power back into its hands as possible as a counterweight to the perceived recklessness of Lincoln and the Republican Party.[29] A change in the status quo was in the offing; only the nature of the shift was not clear. Secession hung in the air as 1860 came to a close. One columnist describing himself simply as "an American Citizen" boldly observed, "If the north will relinquish her unholy war on our institutions, and give us reliable guarantees for all future time, that we shall be treated as equals in this great confederacy, well and good—we shall rejoice at it."[30] On the floor of the Senate, Thomas Clingman echoed similar sentiments. He remarked, "The current of resistance is running rapidly over the South. It is idle for men to shut their eyes to consequences like these. If anything can be done to avert this evil, let those who have the power do it."[31] Despite Clingman's apparent willingness to entertain some form of compromise, he made clear that it would have to be one heavily weighted in favor of the South. In short, the entirety of the North Carolinian's remarks suggested that he held out no genuine hope that an accord could be reached. By this point, the prospect of the North changing the direction of its policies was clearly not going to happen. For decades, southerners railed against northern tyranny and begged those north of the Mason-Dixon Line to alter the nature of public discourse promulgated in the region. Now as the fate of the Union hung in the balance, white southerners again made overtures to conservative northerners who were allegedly numerous. That no response to southern "peace-offerings" was forthcoming underscores how fractured things had become. Mississippi's Jefferson Davis, capturing the essence of the dilemma facing the nation, observed, "Upon you the majority section it depends to restore peace and perpetuate the Union of equal states; upon us of the minority section rests the duty to maintain our equality and community rights."[32] A decade after John Calhoun warned that only the North could save the federal union, his ideas found wide expression across the region. Despite the wishful thinking of those hoping to keep the country together, hope was fast dwindling as the emergent crisis precipitated by the election of a sectional candidate advanced.

Early 1861 brought a wave of southern secessions. Time had run out on those preaching restraint. Ironically, voices of calm did not disappear, and they were certainly not blocked from expressing their beliefs. As secession conventions met, southern newspapers continued to run op-ed pieces composed by those who urged the region to step back from the brink and not follow South Carolina into the abyss.[33] These voices were not censored, but as 1861 ground on and as Abraham Lincoln's inauguration loomed, the powerful southern voices for disunion drowned out naysayers. Despite last ditch-efforts to save the Union, including the Crittenden Compromise which would have safeguarded slavery in perpetuity, efforts at reconciliation failed in large part because neither side wanted to budge on the critical issue of slavery's expansion. Republicans, for example, thumbed their noses at the Crittenden proposal precisely because it would ensure the spread of slavery beyond it southern borders, while southerners, in comparison, refused to accept any further limitations on their right to bring their slave property where they chose. Neither side would relent. Yet neither knew precisely what would happen next. Summarizing the southern position, Alfred Iverson observed, "The southern States now moving for secession will never be satisfied with any concessions made by the north, that does not fully recognize not only the existence of slavery in its present form, but the right of the southern people to emigrate to the common Territories with their slave property, and the right to congressional protection while the territorial existence lasts."[34] Iverson's commentary made clear that the South's expectations were as unrealistic as those found among abolitionists. With neither side willing to budge, the real issue as the new year commenced was how many southern states would leave and what would result.[35]

Even as Americans grappled with the large and small issues surrounding secession, the states that had already left the union wasted little time joining forces. After pushing through secession ordinances, the newly independent southern states met in Montgomery, Alabama, on February 4, 1861, to organize themselves into a loose confederation. Certainly, most of the delegates in attendance did not view their actions as part of a fleeting movement or an innocuous protest effort, but as the first steps toward forging a permanent nation. Even controlling for the very radicalism of the idea that American states could secede and form a new nation, some involved in the movement asserted that the election of Jefferson Davis and Alexander Stephens as president and vice president of the Confederacy respectively suggested that armed conflict with the North was not on the table since both of these leaders were on record as being open to rejoining the Union if basic southern grievances were addressed. This represented wishful thinking as neither Davis nor Stephens saw any path that could pull things back from the brink. Indeed, Davis's final remarks in the U.S. Senate suggested that too much water had flowed under the bridge by that point. Taking a measure of his political opponents, Davis opined that neither they nor the denizens of the South were willing to give up their stated positions. Indeed, Davis observed, "In our judgement the Republicans are resolute in the purpose to grant nothing that will or ought to satisfy the South."[36] The only option remaining was secession. When southern politicians discussed their support for disunion, they invariably returned to the simple perspective that the region was left with no choice. Georgia's senator Iverson, for one, commented, "seeing the storm that is approaching, although it may be seemingly in the distance, we are determined to seek our own safety and security before it shall burst upon us and overwhelm us with fury, when we are not in a situation to defend ourselves."[37] It proved wiser, they argued, to leave the country while occupying a position of strength than to suffer an ignominious gradual loss of power within the union as abolitionists whittled away at the rights of slaveholders until one day all was lost.[38]

Another waiting game commenced. In late 1860, the wait centered on how and when the South would respond to Lincoln's election. The rapid wave of southern secessions in early 1861 prompted the end of the wait. One after another, the southern states left the Union, and their national congressional delegations bid farewell to their northern colleagues. Next, southerners and indeed all Americans waited to see whether or not a shooting war would commence. For some, hope existed that peace would govern relations between the sections turned rival nations. Optimistic that secession could occur without violence, Jefferson Davis, remarked to his colleagues in his last Senate speech, "I hope ... for peaceful relations with you, though we must part."[39] U.S. senator Stephen Mallory of Florida, who later went on to serve as the Confederacy's secretary of the Navy, similarly remarked, "In thus severing our connection with sister States, we desire to go in peace, to maintain towards them an attitude not only of peace, but, if possible, of kindness."[40] As both Davis and Mallory indicated, their ardent desire was for the South to peaceably leave the nation and maintain a spirit of cordiality with the remaining United States. How the game would ultimately play out, they indirectly noted, was almost completely in the hands of the incoming president and his advisers. As far as the South was concerned, it merely wanted to be left alone. Only Lincoln's inauguration and his subsequent actions would determine what happened next. For his part, Lincoln remained silent during the lame duck period before he assumed office save for noting he believed that the Union was perpetual—a concept southerners repeatedly denounced. Furthermore, he openly opposed extending slavery beyond its boundaries at the time.[41] Anyone familiar with Lincoln's rhetoric over the years would not have found anything shocking in the remarks of the president-elect. By this point, southern extremists did not expect much from Lincoln based on his previous record. They were more suspicious of the people who advised him. Even if Lincoln was a moderate, they postulated, he was in allegiance with people dedicated to destroying the South. Far better, they thought, to go down fighting now in defense of liberty than to be slowly defeated by a thousand cuts rendered by anti-South politicians slowly nibbling at the margins of slaveholders' rights.

Lincoln maintained the status quo for one month following his inauguration on March 4, 1861, before setting in motion the chain of events that resulted in military conflict. His inaugural address, although conciliatory and suggesting a willingness to meet southern demands on things such as enforcement of the Constitution's fugitive slave provisions, ultimately pivoted toward the idea of a perpetual union. Lincoln laid out his vision of the nature of the Union and how southern states could not willingly leave the whole without, in effect, the whole agreeing to disband. Should war come, Lincoln observed, it would be due to the actions of the South. Naturally, southerners touted their desire to be independent as well as to avoid conflict; Lincoln reminded them that they could not leave the Union and were therefore, by remaining separate, ensuring that war would come. Confederate president Jefferson Davis in his inaugural address indicated his sanguine desire for the South to live in peace. However, he stated that should the North, or any foe, "desire to inflict injury upon us . . . a terrible responsibility will rest upon it, and the suffering of millions will bear testimony to the folly and wickedness of our aggressors."[42] Whereas the South, as evidenced by the words of Davis, would blame aggressive northern action against the newly formed Confederate States of America for the onset of a shooting war, Lincoln made clear he believed southerners were the provocateurs since their very act of secession represented a rebellion against the United States, not the onset of a new nation. Only the prompt and immediate return of the southern states to the Union could alter the course of history. After unofficially giving the region one month to return, Lincoln took a series of fateful steps that culminated in Civil War. Lincoln's decision in April 1861 to reinforce Fort Pickens in Florida and resupply Fort Sumter in South Carolina were provocative actions that the newly minted Confederate government could not accept and still assert sovereign control over its territories. Lincoln had all but forced the South to defend itself by backing the Davis administration into a corner. The Confederate government responded by breaking the status quo since the Lincoln administration made plain that it would not allow the South to remain out of the union. War had finally arrived.[43]

Much had transpired in the march toward this point. Many state-level histories suggest that a large segment of the South's population was not initially interested in dismantling the Union. It was only the concerted efforts of the planter elites, who controlled many of the mechanisms of power, which brought about secession conventions stacked in favor of disunion. Historians will perhaps never know the true sentiment in the South as the region took the fateful step to leave the country. One thing is certain, however, once secession occurred and the shooting war commenced, the white South for a brief period was overwhelmingly dedicated to the cause. Even those southern states that stood back during the first wave of secession, such as Virginia and North Carolina, left the Union following the attack on Fort Sumter and Lincoln's decision to impose a blockade on southern ports. The bravado with which the region met the conflict soon ran into the cold reality of the terrible nature of war. With but few exceptions, the South played host to almost the entirety of the conflict ensuring that the scarring impact of the war fell disproportionately on its people. The headlong race toward disunion that began with the election of Lincoln culminated in a four-year bloodbath in which everything the South fought for was destroyed. Calmer voices existed in the South, but, in the end, they were drowned out by the demands of the fire-eaters who kept up an incessant drumbeat for secession. Far from achieving independence, the southern war effort culminated in the eradication of slavery and the discrediting of the very idea of disunion. Rather than being deemed sage patriots who fought to preserve an undefiled Constitution, southerners were transformed into traitors bent on subverting the intent of the framers to preserve their race-based social order. Their path back into the union would be similarly bloody and wrenching, but when the dust settled, the region fell back into the patterns of old. Gone was the Reconstruction era Republican presence in the region and its efforts to bring change. In its stead, the Democratic Party, which curtailed the services introduced to the

South via Reconstruction and slowly dismantled the apparatus that provided the region's African American population with access to basic rights and freedoms, returned to power. On the surface, it appeared that the region had learned nothing from the gut-wrenching experience of war and hostile occupation.[44] When the South faced another grave threat to its racial order that was on par with the one confronted in 1859–1860, the response was decidedly different. Perhaps the lessons of the Civil War were not completely lost on the former states of the Confederacy.

Throughout the first half of the twentieth century, threats against various components on the periphery of the Jim Crow edifice appeared on the horizon. Southerners viewed each of these challenges as if they were the harbingers of something far worse. Their responses to relatively minor efforts to make lynching a federal crime and to eradicate the poll tax, for example, were greatly exaggerated when viewed in the context of the actual threat these items posed to the so-called "southern way of life." No matter how many times they stopped the "camel" from getting his "nose under the tent" by blocking such initiatives, the drive to dismantle segregation kept inching closer and closer to the target.[45] Regional political leaders decried the slippery slope that seemingly innocuous civil rights proposals and federal court decisions would set the nation down. Long before most white southerners awakened to these threats, the region's elites recognized that they would lose the civil rights fight if things continued along the same trajectory. Their economic and political antennae were attuned to the dramatic changes coming their way. Over the course of several decades, they tried to arrest this trend while alerting their constituents that ominous forces were moving against the region. Southern paranoia in the early twentieth century turned into abject terror when the Supreme Court took up a series of school desegregation cases in 1952 that collectively became known as *Brown v. Board of Education*. Although the region's leaders adopted a wait-and-see approach after that point, there was a palpable fear of change as they grappled with the possible fallout from an unwanted decision. Prior Supreme Court rulings, such as the 1944 *Smith v. Allwright* case which ended white primaries, were initially met with fear in the region before white southerners realized that other Jim Crow mechanisms ensured the verdict would have a negligible impact on the rule of white supremacy. Previous efforts to change the region invariably appeared to founder on the shoals of vigorous southern resistance efforts. The *Brown* case was different. Virginia senator Harry Byrd, for one, proved pessimistic despite reports in his state's newspapers suggesting that segregation would be upheld. According to Byrd, "there is considerable doubt about this [the court upholding segregation] in Washington, and should it fail to do this, the entire program in Virginia would have to be altered considerably."[46] Byrd's remarks underscore two key features. First, his reservations regarding the court's actions suggest that like-minded southerners were genuinely concerned about a verdict that ran counter to regional conventions. They were not expecting a favorable ruling. Second, Byrd made clear that the region had every intention of challenging a court decision that threatened white southern interests. What form this protest might take was not enumerated at the time, but it was clear that something was in the offing.

When the feared verdict was finally rendered on May 17, 1954, regional statesmen scrambled to get in front of the developing crisis. Some southern politicians believed that concerted action on their part might mitigate the impact of *Brown* as had happened on previous occasions when external forces threatened some aspect of the Jim Crow order. South Carolina's Olin Johnston joined Byrd in stressing the region's leaders were "working together trying to draw up a plan whereby something can be done to help the Southern people."[47] North Carolina's Sam Ervin was also inclined to immediately bemoan the *Brown* ruling rather than wait for a more concrete sense of what the future would bring. Indeed, he maintained a persistent assault against it and all associated with it from the start. To one constituent, Ervin noted, "In my judgement, the decision is the weakest judicial utterance I have ever read. When all is said, the court gives no reason for its opinion other than the fact that some new books have been written on the subject of psychology." After condemning the allegedly flawed nature of the ruling, Ervin proceeded to lambaste the justices who "were placed on the court as a matter of reward for political services. . . . Persons who occupy judicial positions ought not to substitute their private notions for the established law of the land."[48] More measured voices such as that of Tennessee's Albert Gore Sr. understood that change would eventually come to the South. Gore even proved willing to accept at least a modicum of reform. What he objected to was the belief that racial change would occur without fallout. As Gore perceived things, "the customs and mores of the people are not easily set aside, and those who think that public school segregation in the South can be abolished quickly without violence and the intensification of racial tensions, simply do not understand the situation."[49] Unlike Byrd and Johnston, Gore had no plans of participating in organized resistance to the integration edict. Even usually vocal defenders of the South's racial order had qualms about how to proceed in the wake of *Brown*. Some regional leaders usually associated with recalcitrance adopted a different attitude than they previously displayed. Allen Ellender, who rarely minced words when it came to his devotion to segregation, at least in private, urged his constituents to defuse mounting racial tensions. Naturally, Ellender's supporters wanted to know why their senator did not join staunch segregationists in seeking a prosouthern solution by any means necessary. To one friend, Ellender questioned the ratcheting up of intensity: "I frankly can see no good results from following such as course. All that can happen is that many southerners will become aroused and excited and we will have violence. . . . It would worsen rather than improve our position."[50] The 1954 ruling proved bad enough, but it did not come with a timetable for implementation. White southerners had to wait and see how aggressively the court planned to enact its ruling once it delivered its implementation verdict. In many ways, the wait and see period that ensued mirrored that experienced by white southerners on the eve of the presidential election of 1860 or even in the lead-up to President Lincoln's inauguration. One thing was certain after the verdict: the region's citizenry, many of whom did not fully grasp the paranoia demonstrated by their political leaders in earlier civil rights battles, was now keenly aware of what was at stake. All eyes were on the court.[51]

The *Brown II* verdict handed down at the end of May 1955 offered a glimmer of hope for politicians who detested the initial ruling. Although integration would still come, it would occur with "all deliberate speed," a regrettably vague choice of words that provided wiggle room in the South for the emergence of the massive resistance crusade. Despite the notoriety received by those dedicated to fighting in the last-ditch defense of segregation, some southerners pulled back from the brink and urged others to do the same. To be sure, evidence of incendiary language was apparent everywhere in the South in the late 1950s, but there also existed voices urging restraint. A hundred years prior, the Old South marched toward disunion when similarly threatened. Each new outrage against the region brought the fateful day of secession closer. As pressure mounted, the voices of moderation were steamrolled by an inexorable wave of fire-eater agitation. In the 1950s, a similar swell of angst raised by the massive resistance crowd emerged, but it crested far short of the wave fomented by secessionists. Jim Crow entered its death spiral with its defenders orchestrating haphazard attacks against integration efforts wherever they emerged without a single unified and cohesive plan. In this manner, the modern South adopted a reactive posture by marshalling its forces only after courts handed down integration edicts in local communities. By contrast, Old South secessionists embraced a proactive strategy to safeguard their institutions before the direct attack on slavery even commenced. From the 1950s forward, southern states adopted a piecemeal approach that emboldened some local jurisdictions to spearhead limited albeit often violent resistance efforts. Far from unified, the once solid South proved anything but cohesive in the tumultuous 1950s and 1960s. At the very moment when the alleged "boot of federal tyranny" was on the necks of white southerners, the region found itself exclusively on the defensive.[52]

Unmistakable evidence that southern leaders did not know precisely how to respond in the wake of the *Brown* and *Brown II* verdicts can be found in the effort by the region's national politicians to craft what became known as the "Southern Manifesto." After the twin rulings, some politicians wanted the region to make a strong statement that embraced the idea of interposition, thereby directly resurrecting the legacy of the Old South. Despite clear historical lessons that demonstrated the supremacy of the federal government, interposition remained a tool in the massive resistance playbook. In its simplest form, the theory which first found expression prior to the Civil War held that states had the authority to interpose their will between the federal government and the people. As such, it proved the ultimate expression of states' rights, and from it sprang other related concepts such as nullification. Despite the abject failure of interposition/nullification/secession in the past, this constellation of ideas was dusted off in the twentieth century when the region faced its gravest crisis since the election of Abraham Lincoln. Not surprisingly, fiery South Carolinian Strom Thurmond and the more staid yet equally as rabid defender of Jim Crow, Harry Byrd, gravitated to assorted interposition-inspired concepts including dismantling the public school system, and they hoped to convince their regional colleagues of the efficacy of such actions in the aftermath of *Brown II*.[53] Others, however, sought to mitigate the extremism, arguing that interposition was not a viable constitutional remedy for the dilemma the region faced especially considering the less than adequate results secured when previously employed. With clear division regarding the proper direction the protest should take, the decision was made to include the insights of several prominent southern senators whose voices represented a cross-section of regional opinion. Moderates recognized that if modern-day fire-eaters were not corralled, they would propel the region down a path fraught with devastating consequences and, using history as a guidepost, accomplish nothing but regional destruction. What resulted was a committee of southern senators composed of Richard Russell of Georgia, Sam Ervin of North Carolina, and John Stennis of Mississippi—none of whom had a reputation for moderation on the civil rights question, but all of whom were known for their practical political minds. At least publicly, Georgia senator Walter George was credited with spearheading Senate organization on this matter, but his role was limited. Evidence suggests that George was defined as the mastermind of the Manifesto in an effort to sure up his credentials for a pending election showdown against rabid segregationist Herman Talmadge. Earlier, George had said little about the *Brown* verdict, suggesting even further that political expediency placed Walter George at the forefront of this initiative. After weighing his options, the elderly George opted not to seek reelection and face what would certainly have been a punishing campaign against the outspoken Talmadge.[54]

Despite the mounting militancy emerging across the South, the Manifesto drafting committee consisted of men who knew the pitfalls of open defiance. If there was any chance of slowing the end of segregation, it could only come from a public façade of moderation. Extremism on racial matters would not sit well with many following *Brown,* at least on the national level. Southern politicians were entering the endgame, and many of them recognized it. Racial moderates felt compelled to sign the Manifesto even though they doubted the necessity of making a statement on the matter. Such politicians went along for the sake of maintaining their political careers. These moderate voices regularly fielded inquiries from constituents wondering why they were not at the ramparts doing all they could to thwart *Brown.* For them, signing represented a symbolic gesture of their fealty to regional norms, not necessarily a commitment to take action. Because of this difference of opinion, the resulting document represented a hybrid approach that denounced the departure from established jurisprudence in the decision, while promising the use of "all lawful means" to resist its implementation.[55] Capturing the difficult tightrope less radical regional statesmen walked, Arkansan J. William Fulbright labeled the Manifesto "a moderate statement, somewhere between the two extremes advocating nullification on the one hand and the use of troops to enforce the decision on the other."[56] Manifesto draftee, Sam Ervin made clear that the injection of the phrase "lawful means" was intended to undermine the position of those who gravitated toward interposition. In this way, the phrasing had two meanings. First, it was meant to keep white southerners from resorting to violence in defense of Jim Crow, which hindsight reveals did not work. Second, it was a signal to white southerners that unlawful methods, such as interposition which had been tried and found wanting in the past, were not to be embraced.[57] By shelving the interposition issue, the South's national politicians shifted the debate as much as possible away from the most inflammatory options whereas many of their forebears gravitated to them. The difference this time was palpable as many of the region's most high-profile voices either directly or indirectly pushed for restraint. These national southern politicians believed the best path to follow was the one of moderation, in large part because, unlike the Old South which embraced an expansionist ethos, the modern South made no effort to export its institutions. Rather, the region merely desired the maintenance of the status quo. Of course, they had no intentions of completely rolling over, but they saw their only route to at least temporary success as coming via a path that marginalized the most extreme positions in their ranks.[58]

The absence of several prominent southern signatures on the Manifesto certainly raised some eyebrows. U.S. Senator and Majority Leader Lyndon Johnson of Texas held that he was never asked to sign the document owing to his leadership role in the Democratic Party which made it impossible for him to support strictly sectional proposals. Johnson, however, definitely knew of the Manifesto's creation as he was close personal friends with many of the Senate's southern leaders. He could have signed it without much difficulty since his leadership position was in many ways a byproduct of his support from prominent southern patriarchs. Instead, Johnson steered clear of it since he had obvious national political aspirations. Since his chance of becoming president of the United States would be greatly diminished if he embraced such a distasteful sectional statement, he used his national leadership role as a convenient escape hatch. Others such as Tennessee's Albert Gore Sr. did not mince words when it came to the Supreme Court's verdict. As he saw it, "whether one agrees or disagrees with the decision, the decision of the Court is, under our Constitution, the final judicial interpretation of the law."[59] Regarding the Manifesto itself, Gore refused to sign it, noting, "I seriously questioned the advisability of Southerners joining in issuance of this statement. I did not think it would, or could bring any improvement in a delicate and dangerous situation."[60] Furthermore, Gore claimed that his decision was also based on the fact that he received nothing from his constituents one way or the other on the matter. That Gore chose not to sign the Manifesto was far from surprising as he was not someone southern senators relied upon as an active member of their legislative caucus. He would help periodically, but he was far from a stalwart. Although he toed the line when necessary, Gore's central interests were clearly not rooted in the South's racial system.

In the case of Allen Ellender, however, things were different. Although he previously expressed concern over the inflammatory rhetoric bandied about in the immediate aftermath of the *Brown* ruling, he willingly signed the Manifesto. Yet his devotion to the massive resistance fight was limited. Ever since his arrival in the U.S. Senate, he had been a vocal and unabashed race-baiting member of the southern bloc. His response to the emerging massive resistance movement illustrates that at least some lessons from the Civil War experience were learned. Despite growing calls for interposition, Ellender balked at the idea as state governments began challenging federal hegemony. At its heart, he doubted the legality of interposition and recognized that the Supreme Court was the final arbiter on this matter. To a friend, he noted, "I have never believed that I should mislead the people whom I represent by creating and fostering hope of Constitutional relief when I know deep down in my heart there is no hope of obtaining such relief."[61] Going further in this pessimistic fashion, the Louisianan added, "the Federal Constitution is the supreme law of the land; it follows that nothing short of a Constitutional Amendment can change the Court's decision, irrespective of individual or group opinions as to its soundness."[62] Ellender laid it all out. He wanted to find a way to maintain segregated schools; his beliefs on matters of race had not changed at all over the twenty years he served in Washington. Nonetheless, this open champion of white supremacy simply could not envision a scenario in which he could thwart the inexorable decline of Jim Crow. Ellender stood at the precipice of momentous change. He could have publicly told his constituents that the show was over and that they needed to come to terms with a new reality, or he could have taken the path that he ultimately selected. Instead of serving as a friendly voice shepherding the region into a different future, he kept his thoughts regarding the foolhardy nature of southern resistance efforts to himself. Ellender, like countless other politicians of the era, allowed the radical elements to ramp up white resistance efforts thereby ensuring that the inevitable court-ordered change would take place under a cloud of violence. Leaders often fail. In the American South, leaders failed on a herculean level as they held out hope to constituents even when they knew no hope was present.

With the radical element ascendant—or at least proving the most vocal—the South lurched toward massive resistance without a clearly defined plan. States in the rim South, such as Arkansas and Virginia, confronted integration efforts first and lost. These states threw every trick in the book at desegregation edicts, and none of them succeeded in arresting school integration. By the time the fight reached the Deep South, the issue was already decided. Rather than accept fate, however, activists in the region repeated many of the failed tactics tried elsewhere while attempting new schemes—none of which succeeded. In the end, the biggest factor absent in the region was strong leadership. Indeed, many of the South's "moderate" statesmen, although not publicly condemning massive resistance, generally stood on the sidelines and allowed their activist peers to dictate the state-level response. Naturally, it is also clear that even if the most talented leadership in the region was onboard with aggressive resistance tactics, these efforts would have still failed. Without the support of many of the region's political elites, calls for interposition withered as the region pulled back from the brink. Sure there would be violence and even the dismemberment of the public school system in many places, but, in the end, the region never seriously embraced anything remotely similar to that undertaken by their forebears, in part, because they conceptualized their resistance efforts from a static defensive posture. They fought integration with tenacity and often violence. Yet, in the end, they conceded to reality in a manner that starkly contrasted with the all-or-nothing gambit of their forebears. The Old South rushed to secession and war; the New South pondered interposition while embracing massive resistance, a crusade that promised far more than it delivered. The outlook of the region had fundamentally changed from aggressive expansionism to the adoption of a bunker mentality predicated on mounting a cordon defense. Success in such an undertaking could only result from the federal government abandoning its integration efforts—a highly unlikely prospect at the time.[63]

The massive resistance movement caused its fair share of damage and certainly strained race relations in a region where tensions were already high. Efforts to block the integration of schools resulted in a final paroxysm of violence as groups such as the Citizens' Council mockingly linked the concept of southern moderation on the civil rights issue with support for integration. Indeed, the Citizens' Council boldly flirted with the idea of interposition, arguing, "Unless, we in the Southern states do interpose our sovereignty with all of the strength at our command that some day we will have integration or a mixed race here."[64] The unrelenting federal pressure for integration, however, ensured that any such endeavor failed. As defeat followed defeat, Citizens' Council leaders urged members to remain committed to the fight and never surrender even as integration started to take place.[65] Despite promises from politicians that things would remain "segregated forever," integration, albeit usually in a token form, represented the new normal for the region. In the nineteenth century, southerners seemingly spoke with one voice once the secession movement gained momentum. Sure there were opponents of the effort, but over time, those voices were subsumed by the advocates of disunion. One hundred years later, there were plenty of voices calling for action to save Jim Crow. Yet, in the end, their violent and piecemeal efforts to safeguard segregation fell short of their goals.

For some, massive resistance meant utilizing all means at one's disposal to thwart integration. The violent episodes spurred by Arkansas governor Orval Faubus and Mississippi governor Ross Barnett underscore how quickly massive resistance efforts could turn to chaos. Such events were not isolated; they were symptomatic of the fallout brought on by the movement. Indeed, it did not take much for a protest or demonstration to turn when political leaders either directly or indirectly promoted lawlessness. As in the past, white southerners generally considered the resulting deterioration in race relations as a product of outside forces. Provocateurs, who allegedly had non-southern origins, had to be responsible for the mounting turmoil in the region, argued segregationists. Indeed, one of the most common refrains in segregationist lore remained the mythological assertion that if left alone, the South could solve its problems as it always had. Implicit in this assertion was the perspective that outsiders rather than helping southern Blacks did much to undermine the social standing of the region's largest minority group. At no time did they grapple with the obvious discontent of the African American community around them. In the wake of the controversy surrounding the 1957 integration of Little Rock Central High School, Harry Byrd, for example, denigrated President Dwight Eisenhower on the grounds that the commander in chief's actions would "intensify existing bitterness, and will strengthen the resistance of the Southern people to enforced integration."[66] Others went as far as to assert that the episode meant "the tyranny of Russia is upon us when Americans are forced to move at bayonet point by American soldiers seeking to enforce an unjust law on an unwilling and free people."[67] Capitalizing on Cold War fears that communist subversion threatened all facets of American life, segregationists dug in their heels and insisted that outside forces, not internal discontent, spurred racial unrest. As in the Old South, few proved willing to accept that anything save racial harmony existed. Their blindness to the injustice they perpetrated around them, as well as to the countless grassroots resistance efforts which challenged Jim Crow, strains credulity. Rather than see the situation on the ground for what it was, white southerners marched into the future oblivious to the situation that existed in their backyard, but they remained hopeful that their resistance would somehow stymie civil rights advances.[68]

For many southerners, massive resistance meant strictly using "lawful" means to block integration in the manner suggested by the region's national politicians in the so-called Southern Manifesto. Their resistance took the form of picketing, attending rallies, and demanding that their elected officials do something. Much has been made of the so-called silent majority of white southerners—those who fashioned themselves as moderates in so much as they did not support the lawlessness and racial strife that engulfed the region. Among this group, there remained a clear devotion to segregation yet an unwillingness to fight in its defense. They were willing to let Jim Crow die with a whimper. It was this group that understood a new day was coming whether they approved of it or not. Regrettably, much like the moderate leadership in the region, it was also this group which, although numerous, failed to answer the call of history and demand a peaceful transition to a new normal. Indeed, it was the white moderates that Reverend Martin Luther King Jr., in his "Letter from a Birmingham Jail," cast the most scorn upon. These alleged Christian people, King opined, needed to stand up to the injustice around them. Instead, they fell silent and permitted rabid segregationists to take control of the situation in many southern communities. Their silence must also be viewed from the perspective of the vitriol sent their way by the region's more aggressive segregationists. In its newspaper, the Citizens' Council regularly heaped scorn on moderates who they believed "lacked the courage" to stand up for white rule while naively believing that a tempered approach to integration would yield some benefits for the South. Extremists asserted this belief was without foundation for no "moderating force" existed in their opponents' ranks before arguing none should exist in their own. It was all or nothing for integrationists; the same, according to segregationists, should apply to the white South. Public rhetoric in the region tended to belittle those not on the extreme, a fact which no doubt kept the "silent majority" silent.[69] Although they might have disapproved of what they saw, the risk to their person and livelihood proved too great of an obstacle for southern moderates to overcome. They would remain on the sidelines. The presence of a sizable contingent of regional moderates underscores the far from solid nature of the South, not in terms of their belief in a race-based order but in their willingness to fight for its continuation. Perhaps the only thing that unified the white southerners was fear of change.

The changes that befell the South following *Brown* were nothing short of sweeping. Within a decade, the region faced successful legislative efforts to dismantle the entire Jim Crow edifice and shortly thereafter, a drive to eradicate the system of voter discrimination that remained. One ten-year period saw an unparalleled destruction of the South's second racial order. Only the dismemberment of its first proved of more monumental consequence. Unlike in the late 1850s and early 1860s when the primary assault against slavery focused on the institution's expansion, the late 1950s and early 1960s attack on segregation struck at the very heart of the institution. Organized resistance existed everywhere in the region, but its intensity varied, and its prospects for success were never good. More critically, everywhere that massive resistance was employed experienced failure. Every ... single ... one. Massive resistance as it existed in the 1950s and 1960s saw no successes. Defeat after defeat eventually forced white southerners to recognize that nothing they could do would stem the tide of federal intrusion. Demoralization took hold as promises to fight integration with gusto came to swift conclusions and utter defeat. Since the battle was joined at different times and in different locations, those states that faced integration later were disheartened by what preceded them. The fate of resistance efforts in Louisiana is illustrative of what transpired across the South. At one time, New Orleans was home to a well-organized and well-funded Citizens' Council organization. By December 1965, C. E. Vetter, the acting chair of the Citizens' Council of Greater New Orleans, rang the alarm bells to organization leaders that membership had plummeted while resources were growing scarce. As Vetter put it, "white people have about given up and it is a hard job convincing them there is still a lot to fight for."[70] A Council renaissance in the greater New Orleans area, however, was not forthcoming. Whites in the Old South went to battle *en masse* against the prospect of racial change and were overwhelmed by their northern foes. New South denizens suffered loss in a slow, yet steady stream of demoralization. In the face of defeat, Jim Crow's proponents circled back to the rhetoric of the Old South when urging their constituents to move on. They sought to close the intellectual circle that commenced with the cry of "massive resistance" by wrapping their own ill-fated battle to block integration in the myth of the Lost Cause. The battle to defend the South's second racial order resulted in a string of stunning losses, prompting defenders to admit defeat while touting their "valiant" stand against tyranny.

From the start of his Washington career in the 1930s, Georgia senator Richard Russell raised alarms at every bill even remotely linked to civil rights, arguing that despite its mild content, it represented the opening salvo in a war that would be waged against the southern racial order. In 1938, for example, Russell laid out a dire forecast for the segregated South when he opined, "There is no question that if we are finally exhausted and permit the passage of the antilynch bill, it would be followed by legislation to break down segregation of the races in schools, hospitals, churches, restaurants, hotels, bath houses, and all other public places, as well as by bills giving the ballot to every negro, and striking down the State statutes preventing intermarriage of the races."[71] Russell proved wrong about a lot of things, but on this matter, his prescience concerning the slippery slope of civil rights activism was spot on. The Georgian understood that no matter the outcome of individual civil rights related battles, the pressure to enact change would continue until the white South was overwhelmed and the entire Jim Crow edifice dismantled. Based on this perspective, he considered it the goal of the region's national politicians to thwart the onslaught against segregation's heart as long as possible. Despite his considerable success over the years in derailing an array of civil rights laws, Russell only succeeded in delaying the inevitable. The *Brown* decision was the point of no return. The attack on segregation was fully joined. In the coming decade, Russell continued his war against modernity and even orchestrated the longest filibuster in Senate history in a failed effort to stymie the passage of the sweeping Civil Rights Act of 1964. In the face of mounting odds, Russell called for logic and reason to govern the legislative process, but he did not call for violence. Neither did his regional colleagues, all of whom promised to fight encroaching federal regimentation while acquiescing to the end of *de jure* segregation.

A series of letters in late July 1964 following the passage of the Civil Rights Act captures the essence of how Russell wanted to frame the loss. The connection between Russell's musings and the myth of the Lost Cause is unmistakable. No doubt, Russell, who was an avid Civil War buff, deliberately drew upon the verbiage of Confederate general Robert E. Lee's Farewell Message to his troops. Russell noted, "We fought as hard as we could, but our ranks were too thin and our resources too scanty."[72] On another occasion, he observed, "The pressure kept increasing and in the end we were gagged and overwhelmed. Nonetheless, I shall continue to fight for constitutional government with all my strength."[73] Interestingly, Russell stressed that he would continue resistance yet offered no sense of what form such a "fight" would assume. What is equally illuminating is the fact that he went silent on the racial issue, at least in the immediate aftermath of his crushing defeat. To his constituents, Russell stressed restraint. In one letter, he stated, "I have urged the people of Georgia to refrain from violence in dealing with this act and those who really desire to help us in our efforts to mitigate this situation will not incite violence."[74] As far as Russell was concerned, the active phase of resistance was clearly over. He planned to battle future civil rights-linked fights with gusto, but he did not intend to play into the massive resistance crowd any longer. After all, what was left to resist? In an even more pessimistic moment, the Georgian proclaimed regarding the civil rights fight, "The die is cast now, however, and there is nothing that can be done about it."[75] Defeated and dejected, the leader of the southern fight preached acceptance or at least grudging acquiescence rather than defiance. His acolytes followed suit. Had he been as clear regarding the situation the South confronted in 1954 as he was in 1964, at least some of the violence that followed could have been mitigated.

Never the most vocal segregationist, Alabama's John Sparkman, nonetheless, regularly participated with the southern Senate caucus in its fight against civil rights. Like Russell, Sparkman did not mince words when it came to the enormity of the challenge faced by the caucus in 1964. During the record-breaking filibuster against the bill, Sparkman noted regarding the fight, "This is where the battle will be won or lost."[76] Sparkman's comments underscore the terminal nature of the battle over integration. If the southern senators failed, then Jim Crow was finished. It was as simple as that; there would be no further viable resistance should the fight in the Senate collapse. Virginia's Harry Byrd also embraced a less fiery tone than on previous occasions when confronted with the passage of the 1964 legislation. According to Byrd, "We Southern Senators did our best to defeat the bill, but the odds were against us from the beginning."[77] No fire and brimstone promise to enter a new phase of resistance followed. Instead, Byrd like the others asserted that all had been done to stem the tide against the region, but the overwhelming odds arrayed against them finally won out. Emphasizing to constituents the difficult challenges the region's politicians confronted and thereby suggesting that future resistance would be futile, Alabama's Lister Hill noted regarding the outcome of the 1964 fight, "The 71 to 29 vote invoking cloture shows the great odds against which we have been battling," before adding, like Russell before him, "I will, of course, continue to fight in every way I can."[78] Similar to his regional colleagues, Hill offered only vague promises of continuing the fight at hand. The absence of specificity underscores the lack of a Plan B. It was all-or-nothing in 1964. When the battle finished, there remained only platitudes. North Carolina's Sam Ervin left one path opened for the South after the failed filibuster. However, it was a route that would fall beyond the power of the general populace to influence. Drawing allusions to the Reconstruction Era, Ervin observed that many of the punitive laws passed in that period "were ultimately adjudged unconstitutional or repealed because they proved to be unworkable," and thus he held out hope that the Civil Rights Act of 1964 would experience a similar fate.[79] As in the case of the others, Ervin was yet another southern senator involved in the legislative battle over civil rights who offered his constituents not fiery calls for an aggressive response but a lackluster wait-and-see attitude that left the region's ultimate fate in the hands of the court system that was not likely to favor southern legal interpretations. The climactic fight for segregation on the floor of the Senate ended with a simple parliamentary procedure—the invocation of cloture. This group of southern politicians went through the motions, all the while misleading their constituents that something could be done to arrest the civil rights movement. When they failed, they painted for their supporters a scene of a "heroic" final battle to save segregation that ended in the "last ditch." Knowing the uphill battle confronting the region on the civil rights front for decades, the South's national politicians monumentally failed their voters by obscuring what many of them recognized would be the ultimate outcome of the fight—defeat.

And then there was Strom Thurmond of South Carolina. Throughout this period of his Senate career, Thurmond vowed a spirited defense of Jim Crow, including possible resurrection of the concept of interposition while also chastising his southern colleagues for their lack of unity and resolve in the face of the mounting pressure to end segregation being brought to bear on the region. Following the successful 1964 cloture vote, Thurmond offered a restrained vision of his future intentions. He noted, "Although it appears that the battle in the Senate is now over, I am now beginning the fight for repeal because I am convinced that the legislation will create more racial animosity and do more to promote the communist cause in America than any other legislation that has ever been approved by the Congress."[80] Thurmond's reflections warrant special attention considering the inflammatory nature of his racial rhetoric over the years. Rivaled only by Mississippi's James Eastland, Thurmond was a ferocious opponent of racial change who viewed any and all threats to segregation as worthy of opposition.[81] Indeed, Thurmond more fully embraced the concept of massive resistance than most. It is thus not surprising that when he first conceptualized the landscape in the wake of *Brown*, he immediately gravitated toward interposition and sought to steer his regional colleagues towards a direct showdown with federal authority. Instead of taking the fight to the federal government, Thurmond faced roadblock after roadblock, many of which were placed before him by his regional peers. Certainly on the local level, he found many voices who would join his in denouncing integration in the most virulent of fashions. Nonetheless, when he returned to Washington, his southern colleagues often adopted a different approach. They understood things that the aggressive Thurmond refused to, at least publicly, recognize.

A central feature of the southern fight on the national level was an acceptance of just how fragile the region's position truly was. Added to this was the fact that many of the southern delegations in Washington were either lawyers or had served long enough in DC to recognize that nothing could be done to thwart the court's verdict once issued. By 1964, Thurmond had obviously changed. Gone was the one-man filibustering crusader who broke a Senate record with a twenty-four-hour-and-eighteen-minute-long speech against the Civil Rights Act of 1957. Like many white southerners, Thurmond had supported and watched an array of massive resistance efforts crumble in the face of federal pressure. Indeed, everywhere he looked was the wreckage of the order he staunchly defended. In the waning hours before the passage of the 1964 Civil Rights Act in Washington, Thurmond proved less combative than usual. True, he promised he would continue the fight since he argued the bill would raise racial tension in the country rather than solve it. A critical difference, however, is apparent. Thurmond's proposed recourse fell completely in the realm of the legal and strayed considerably from the rhetoric of massive resistance. Even his proposed resistance scheme—seeking the repeal of the civil rights act before it was fully implemented—was a far cry from his former vitriol. In the course of a decade, Thurmond went from pondering all options in his resistance quiver to meekly espousing a repeal effort which even Thurmond as he uttered those words must have known stood no chance of success.[82]

Thurmond's transformation in many ways is illustrative of the awakening taking place among white southerners across the region. Some in the aftermath of the *Brown* verdict were frightened at the changes that were coming and gravitated toward an extremist position early on, vowing to block integration by any means necessary. Many southerners never directly had skin in the game. They watched the failed massive resistance efforts in Arkansas and Virginia and soon realized that no form of opposition would thwart federal power. In those places that directly resisted, even in the Deep South, integration came to pass, efforts to cut state funding for public education failed, and all that remained was a panoply of private academies in which segregation could ostensibly be upheld at least for those with sufficient income. Scorch-and-burn tactics resulted in nothing but racial ill-will and integration. The last remaining option was to concede defeat, relinquish one's former home, and relocate to a new white flight suburb in which segregation rooted in residential patterns rather than mandated by law proved the norm. Tacit admission of failure came in those moments when families packed up their belongings and relocated to new suburbs and from there to exurbs in an effort to keep some semblance of control over their racial destiny. Thurmond's concession that nothing more could be done in 1964 mirrors the reaction of many white southerners when it came to the integration fight. In the mid-twentieth century, the white South chose something of a middle ground. Instead of openly denying the power of the federal courts and government, they dissembled, hoping that an array of tricks and sleights of hand would grant the region time and perhaps a few victories. Instead these efforts met a string of defeats. When Jim Crow fell, it went out with a whimper as the region came to terms with the new normal thrust upon it, often by abandoning territory over which it had vigorously fought in previous decades. The flight to suburban enclaves which offered less crime, good schools, and low taxes accelerated as integration efforts expanded, resulting in a new form of segregation that was defended with socioeconomic rather than racial arguments. Race, no doubt, continued to play a role, but it was no longer the central organizing principle in the region. Rather it was but one of a constellation of issues that informed life in the post-Jim Crow South. The South's overt support for state-sponsored racial orders was at an end. The "fraternity of whiteness" was replaced by the fraternity of wealth.

Conclusion

Comparisons across southern history offer great rewards and considerable risks for historians willing to make them. Ideas are especially hard to contrast along generational lines since they have a meaning unique to the period in which they were promulgated and do not always translate the same across eras. The peculiarities of time and place are critical factors to consider when contrasting periods of regional history separated by many decades. Despite these potential pitfalls, a level of transcendence in southern history is also evident, albeit often obscured by the nature of historical inquiry. In an effort to make complex and seemingly unrelated events more understandable, historians often impose strict chronological frameworks to their studies to break up the panoply of human events into small and digestible bites. For example, many divide the past using external guideposts such as presidential administrations. These temporal parameters impede understanding almost as much as they enhance it for they delimit the purview of a study to an arbitrary, often ahistorical framework. Eschewing conventional periodization, this book links the disparate threads of the Old, New, and Modern Souths together to highlight the key features that have informed southern thought and continue to shape its future yet are often overlooked in traditional narratives that adapt a more narrowly defined approach. Understanding the South requires a full accounting of the ebb and flow of history for much of the region's development can only be grasped as a product of forces that straddle the past and present. In the end, myth more than reality shaped the region's outlook. These myths, however, offer a clear window into the worldview and aspirations of those who promoted them, just as they underscore the continuity of regional thought across generations.

White southerners in the antebellum period exclaimed with confidence that the enslaved population around them was happy. They had few obvious reasons, at least based on their narrow perspective, to suspect otherwise. Compounding white southern ignorance regarding the evils of slavery, the enslaved did not often make vocal their dissatisfaction as the consequences for overt discontent were too great. At the same time, their manifold nonverbal forms of daily resistance went either unnoticed or misinterpreted by those who wielded power. Despite the absence of open rebellion, scores of studies point to an array of resistance tactics embraced by the enslaved as a way to wring concessions from the oppressive system. All of this took place under the noses of slaveholders, who remained oblivious to the defiance around them. Before emancipation, white southerners could say almost without challenge that evidence of rampant slave abuse was exaggerated. Save for the periodic appearance of a published narrative by an escaped former slave, white claims of the benevolent nature of the system were not easily assailed. They lived in what they considered a perfectly formed world in which everyone knew his or her place and challenges to the prevailing system were rare. Ultimately, the Old South proved so insular that comparing its circumstances with those confronted by segregationists operating decades later in a changed environment is not always a direct process. Looking beneath the surface, however, reveals identifiable threads that tie the southern experience together while also illustrating lines of discontinuity.

In the early days of the Jim Crow order, a veil of secrecy obscured from the world the incredible violence upon which segregation was based. With few prying eyes, southerners proudly pointed to how the region had conquered the excesses of lynch law in the early twentieth century by revealing statistics compiled by the Tuskegee Institute which bore out their claims. At the same time, their arguments regarding racial tranquility in the early stages of Jim Crow's existence were readily accepted in that period, as was the mythology of slavery in the antebellum era, owing to an absence of easily circulated evidence to the contrary. Hearsay and conjecture proved the most common forms of evidence against the South's racial systems that were easily dismissed by regional defenders as either fabricated or exaggerated. In the early twentieth century, few Black people marched in the streets challenging segregation laws, owing, in part, to the atmosphere of violence that served as the foundation of the region's racial systems. The apparent lack of open unrest served as sufficient proof for many that goodwill, or at least grudging acceptance, permeated southern race relations.

The second half of Jim Crow's life saw unprecedented turmoil that culminated in the toppling of the entire edifice. As myth after white southern myth was exposed as fraudulent, the onus of guilt when it came to the violent and unjust nature of segregation rested on the defenders of white rule. Pushed against a wall, they reacted as their carefully erected racial hierarchy collapsed around them. White southerners carried on a spirited but futile rearguard effort to block integration and Black enfranchisement. By the 1960s, many realized they were on the losing side of the integration fight. A sizable number of white southerners stood on the sidelines cowered by the radical element about them, all the while remaining dedicated to preserving the racial hierarchy even if they proved unwilling to actively fight for it. Mid-twentieth century defenders of segregation had no choice but to accept, however grudgingly, the presence of outside interference with regional norms. Likewise, circumstances on the ground made it impossible to maintain the façade that all was well in the Jim Crow South. Nothing could keep radio and television from transmitting to the region. Along with this intrusion came a stream of unwanted "propaganda" against Jim Crow. Despite overt signs of dissatisfaction with the status quo emerging all around them from African American grassroots activists, segregationists—until the end of the 1960s legislative battles for racial justice—touted an idealized version of events even when reality pointed to a different conclusion. It is hard to imagine how an educated people could see injustice and discontent everywhere but continue to peddle the myth of tranquility. Yet that is exactly what the region's white majority did.

In the Jim Crow South, segregationists witnessed with their own eyes the Black community resisting the prevailing racial order by participating in demonstrations against the oppression that engulfed them and by lone acts of brave resistance against the indignities that abounded. Not willing to accept the second-class status hoisted on them, African Americans demanded change not just via daily forms of subtle resistance but by way of overt defiance against injustice. Joining them were legions of outsiders, often northerners, committed to the idea of racial change. Within the crowd too were white southerners, who until the more recent past, would never have considered so publicly expressing opinions that differed from the status quo. Taken together, this collective mobilization against segregation did more than any single factor in undermining the South's oppressive racial order. Blow after blow rained down on the "southern way of life," rendering the region's response to the threat disjointed and ineffective, in large part, because the protests so clearly revealed the lies that undergirded regional assertions of racial tranquility. Antebellum southerners never faced such irrefutable evidence of the racial injustice they perpetrated. By contrast, twentieth-century white southerners struggled in the face of affronts to their mythological notion of racial peace and regional accord. Violence represented one response to the external threat, but each physical rejoinder only furthered the resolve of the demonstrators and provided additional grist for an increasingly hostile media which beamed throughout America images that captured the beleaguered defenders of segregation at their racist worst. Integration became a war that the South lost, not only because the South's message proved so antiquated but because the South's actions in the face of the moral crusade for equality proved so contemptible.

Antebellum southerners battled what they considered the hated Republican Party's hegemony in Washington with everything at their disposal, and once the room for political maneuvering had passed, they opted out, choosing secession over what they perceived as subordination. Disunion, thus, served as the only mechanism whereby they could continue their expansionist dreams of creating an intercontinental slaveholding power. White southerners firmly believed their only recourse was secession based on "a widespread and deep-seated conviction that the South, with her institutions, is not safe in the Union."[1] Theirs was ultimately a proactive initiative that failed to secure the desired result and hastened the end of the slave system it was meant to protect. Segregation's defenders already accepted federal hegemony on many things and launched a reactive rearguard effort in an attempt to arrest the further erosion of states' rights. However, once the region acquiesced to centralized authority in certain fields, it became easier to accept the expansion of that hegemony without resorting to the ultimate level of resistance. When the South embraced the concept of "massive resistance" in the aftermath of the *Brown v. Board* case, many of its defenders were not prepared to actually meet the threat posed by integration with the use of such a force. J. William Fulbright, who signed the Southern Manifesto and thus publicly supported the idea of resisting the *Brown* verdict, observed, "Once before when the South disagreed with the policies of the Federal Government, we took matters into our own hands but did not succeed very well. I believe we will have to find some better way to meet this difficulty."[2] History records that despite Fulbright's reference to an alternative course no substitute was created by those considered racial moderates. Compromises regarding segregation, and slavery before it, were not possible. The political atmosphere in the region, whether in the nineteenth or twentieth century, necessitated spirited and ill-fated battles to preserve the region's racial order without regard to the consequences. For the South, it was all or nothing. Slavery and segregation needed to remain as they had always been without requiring substantive reform.

Facing what was perceived as an unprecedented wave of federal expansion into fields once relegated to state authority, especially in the case of civil rights, segregationists fought back with appeals to history that placed them on the same ideological footing as their antebellum predecessors. A critical difference, however, was that proslavery forces always viewed their fight as one tied to external growth; whereas segregationists looked inward and sought little beyond maintaining the status quo, which was under siege from widely recognized outside forces and scarcely mentioned internal ones. Efforts to expand the rights of Black Americans were met with howls of protest centered on the "constitutionality" of a given measure as defined by the region's conservative statesmen. John Calhoun would have been proud as his rhetoric and ideas, even if unknowingly, continued to reverberate in the South long after his death. Whereas the slaveholding interest opted to abandon the union rather than confront federal regimentation, segregationists fought where they could. Then, segregationists accepted, and, in most cases, expected defeat before lamenting the horrible onslaught against the Constitution represented by the newest civil rights legislation regardless of its intent. Capturing the perspective of the Modern South, a dejected Richard Russell in the aftermath of his failed efforts to thwart the Civil Rights Act of 1964 remarked, "While I have grave forebodings as to the effect this step down the road to statism will eventually have, I cannot believe that the masses of our people will for long allow themselves to be led away from the ancient landmark of our greatness."[3] Russell clearly expected his position to be vindicated by the future, making the loss of segregation less painful. At some point, a majority of the American populace, Russell believed, would demand withdrawal of some of the vast power accumulated in federal hands. Today, the nation remains divided over the appropriate size and scope of federal authority. In many ways, this division among the American people has existed from the start of the nation and will likely remain in place so long as the government created by the 1787 Constitution stands. Russell's forecast that the nation would turn against the notion of an activist state has proven accurate up to a point. The rise of the religious right and the strengthening of the conservative Republican Party in the 1970s and 1980s suggested that a substantial percentage of the American people were tired of what they considered the excesses created by big government in the 1960s. It is worthy of noting that the Georgian at the time of defeat did not speculate on the prospect of erecting a third racial order in the South at an unspecified point in the future. Russell, whose entire Senate career was dominated by his opposition to civil rights, perhaps understood in his golden years that the racial order he so vehemently defended would never reemerge.

Tragically, the racial institutions promoted in the South cast a pall over its evolution and patterned political, social, and cultural life there. The perpetual reliance on the prejudice of race was a critical feature of southern resistance efforts throughout the nineteenth and twentieth centuries. It served as the most important and most widely emphasized concept that tied the region together. The centrality of these beliefs on the state and national level since the start of the American nation points to the reality that despite the sweeping legal changes in the 1950s and 1960s, the embers of racism no doubt continued to smolder long after Russell and his fellow obstructionists threw in the towel. Pioneering scholarship by historians such as Kevin Kruse brought about a reimagining of the massive resistance crusade after the passage of the landmark civil rights laws of the 1960s by arguing its adherents carried on the fight in white flight suburbs that blossomed as a result of integration.[4] Tucked away in suburban enclaves, the former champions of massive resistance recreated a segregated world; only this time, it was upheld by custom, not state mandate. Massive resistance did not die with integration, many scholars argue; it was simply renamed and repackaged for a post-segregation world. Its central tenets, including the need for spatial separation, remained unchanged. In this way, the South had been transformed into the North where residential patterns of segregation maintained by local convention were/are apparent. Despite all the talk of the injustice that existed below the Mason-Dixon Line, northern communities were often as prejudiced as southern ones with the only difference being that in the North, discrimination did not take place with state legal protection as the twentieth century progressed. But exist it did. Similarly, southern prejudice did not disappear in the aftermath of the sweeping civil rights reforms of the 1960s; it was simply reconfigured following a distinctly northern model.

Added to Kruse's perspective should be the broader thread of southern intellectual history that began not just with the massive resistance crusade but also appeared initially in the nineteenth century battle to defend slavery. The ferocious white backlash to *Brown* is best understood as part of the larger white southern struggle in defense of an inviolate Constitution and belief in racial hierarchy that found wide expression across the nineteenth- and twentieth-century South. Rather than succumb to the blandishments of outsiders and accept African Americans on some semblance of equal terms after the Civil War, white southerners replicated their old world by forcing Blacks into a subservient social and economic condition via the Jim Crow system. Mid-twentieth century efforts to change the South met with renewed resistance efforts that culminated in yet another collapse of the region's racial system. White flight in many ways represented ongoing southern resistance to the alleged hegemonic rule of the federal government and a logical distillation of southern experiences that began prior to secession. Rather than relinquish their perceived rights, white southerners struck out on yet another iteration of their social order which witnessed the adoption of a more race-neutral narrative predicated on white separation that enabled them to retain some semblance of liberty in the face of what they considered federal tyranny. It is not difficult to discern the antebellum roots of many contemporary suburban hot-button political issues over individual and property rights. At the same time, it must be remembered that a constellation of forces drove "white flight"—not just race. As always, the story is more complex than meets the eye. High taxes, a spike in urban crime, and the construction of new interstate highways in the 1950s convinced many that living outside of America's decaying cities was a sound proposition. By the mid-1900s, people could still commute to their jobs in urban areas before escaping to the safety of tree-lined suburbs at the end of the day. True, integration played a role in the decision to abandon formerly white neighborhoods in southern cities, but like most things, the reality is more complicated than a race-exclusive cause-and-effect narrative permits.[5]

The twenty-first century has seen a renewed interest in the long history of racial injustice in America, not just the variant evident in the South. The peculiar logic of southern race theorists continues to haunt national discourse even if the people using their words or their vision of history are not aware of the provenance of such concepts. Long a minority voice in the country, white southerners conceptualized that those outside of the region were determined to destroy the South's racial inheritance. Although often hinting at the racism that existed outside of the region, white southerners never asserted that their perspective dominated the nation, even as they stressed that their views on government resonated with many outside of the region. Instead, they embraced a siege mentality precisely because their racial ideas were regularly assailed and often fell outside the mainstream. Regardless of whether racism is the singular force shaping America's development as depicted by some or a more localized malady that infected certain locales more than others, the fact remains that the American nation has fallen short of the ideals espoused in the most crucial of all its founding documents, the Declaration of Independence. Throughout America's history, calls for inclusion have existed and continue to shape the nation's political landscape. It was the white South that historically stood as one to block such change, but it was certainly not alone in promulgating injustice on America's minority groups. The entire nation bears the burden of responsibility.

Despite its unsavory history, the South is gradually changing and the future promises further advances, albeit, it seems, at a frustratingly slow pace. Over time, the region has become more modernized and has witnessed its population grow more diverse. In the current age, scholars are finding it more difficult to define what makes the South distinctive. No longer an insular and isolated place, the region is steadily becoming more like the remainder of the country. Likewise, the paranoid worldview and political thought once endemic to the South now finds expression across the nation. Additional time and the further intrusion of social media and other technology into the region will continue to erode unique regional features while simultaneously exporting southern peculiarities to the rest of the nation. Although some lament this loss of identity for with it goes distinct cultural traditions, foodways, and faith-based communities; it must also be remembered that gone too, at least one day, will be the obsession with race that once governed political thought and cultural life in the region. Understanding the South's past and coming to terms with its unsavory mythology and racial customs offers an opportunity to continue promoting the region's efforts to channel its growth and development toward more positive goals while ensuring that it never backslides into the racially paranoid abyss that consumed the South for generations. As the region stands on the precipice of meaningful change, the lessons of history must remain ever present, especially today as many distinctly southern political ideas are now national in scope. In the current rancorous political climate, all Americans should take note of the South's history and the dangers of narrow provincialism and closed-mindedness. Despite its atrocious past, we can learn a great deal from the South, even if these lessons more often stem from its egregious failings rather than its noteworthy accomplishments.

NOTES

INTRODUCTION

1. Samuel C. Hyde, *Pistols and Politics: Feuds Factions and the Struggle for Order in Louisiana's Florida Parishes, 1810-1935* (Baton Rouge: Louisiana State University Press, 2018); Lacy K. Ford, *Origins of Southern Radicalism: The South Carolina Upcountry, 1800-1860* (New York: Oxford University Press, 1988); Kevin Michael Kruse, *White Flight: Atlanta and the Making of Modern Conservatism* (Princeton, NJ: Princeton University Press, 2007); Matthew D. Lassiter, *The Silent Majority: Suburban Politics in the Sunbelt South* (Princeton, NJ: Princeton University Press, 2006).

2. For Reconstruction examples, see: Gregory P. Downs, *Declarations of Dependence: The Long Reconstruction of Popular Politics in the South, 1861-1908* (Chapel Hill: University of North Carolina Press, 2011); Steven Hahn, *A Nation Under Our Feet: Black Political Struggles in the Rural South from Slavery to the Great Migration* (Cambridge: Harvard University Press, 2003); Heather Cox Richardson, *The Death of Reconstruction: Race, Labor, and Politics in the Post-Civil War North, 1865-1901* (Cambridge, MA: Harvard University Press, 2001). For civil rights examples, see: Jacquelyn Dowd Hall, "The Long Civil Rights Movement and the Political Uses of the Past," *Journal of American History* 91 (March 2005): 1233-1263; Jason Morgan Ward, *Defending White Democracy: The Making of the Segregationist Movement and the Remaking of Racial Politics, 1936-1965* (Chapel Hill: University of North Carolina Press, 2011).

3. Michael Perman, *Pursuit of Unity: A Political History of the American South* (Chapel Hill: University of North Carolina Press, 2009). See also: Perman, *The Southern Political Tradition* (Baton Rouge: Louisiana State University Press, 2012). V. O. Key, *Southern Politics in State and Nation* (Knoxville: The University of Tennessee Press, 1984); and: C. Vann Woodward, *The Strange Career of Jim Crow* (New York: Oxford University Press, 2002).

4. Charles D. Chamberlain, *Victory at Home: Manpower and Race in the American South During World War II* (Athens: University of Georgia Press, 2003); Marcus S. Cox, *Segregated Soldiers: Military Training at Historically Black Colleges in the Jim Crow South* (Baton Rouge: Louisiana State University Press 2013); Emilye Crosby, ed., *Civil Rights History from the Ground Up: Local Struggles, a National Movement* (Athens: University of

Georgia Press, 2011); Sharon Ann Holt, *Making Freedom Pay: Race, Violence, and the American South after the Civil War* (Chicago: University of Chicago Press, 2013); Blair M. Kelley, *Right to Rise: Streetcar Boycotts and African American Citizenship in the Era of* Plessy v. Ferguson (Chapel Hill: University of North Carolina Press, 2010); Robin D. G. Kelley, *Hammer and Hoe: Alabama Communism during the Great Depression* (Chapel Hill: University of North Carolina Press, 1990); Mary G. Rolinson, *Grassroots Garveryism: The Universal Negro Improvement Association in the Rural South, 1920–1927* (Chapel Hill: University of North Carolina Press, 2007); James D. Ross Jr., *The Rise and Fall of the Southern Tenant Farmers Union in Arkansas* (Knoxville: University of Tennessee Press, 2018); Sarah L. Silkey, *Black Woman Reformer: Ida B. Wells, Lynching, and Transatlantic Activism* (Athens: University of Georgia Press, 2015); Tyina L. Steptoe, *Houston Bound: Culture and Color in a Jim Crow City* (Berkeley: University of California Press, 2015).

5. C. Vann Woodward, *The Strange Career of Jim Crow* (New York: Oxford University Press, 2002); Edward L. Ayers, *The Promise of the New South: Life After Reconstruction* (New York: Oxford University Press, 1992); Jane Dailey, Elizabeth Glenda Gilmore, and Bryant Simon, *Jumpin' Jim Crow: Southern Politics from Civil War to Civil Rights* (Princeton, NJ: Princeton University Press, 2000).

6. Dan T. Carter, *The Politics of Rage: George Wallace, the Origins of the New Conservatism and the Transformation of American Politics*, 2nd ed. (Baton Rouge: Louisiana State University Press 2000); Darren Dochuk, et al., *Sunbelt Rising: The Politics of Place, Space, and Region* (Philadelphia: University of Pennsylvania Press, 2011); Kruse, *White Flight*; Matthew D. Lassiter and Joseph Crespino. *The Myth of Southern Exceptionalism* (New York: Oxford University Press, 2010); Lassiter, *The Silent Majority*; Lisa McGirr, *Suburban Warriors: The Origins of the New American Right* (Princeton, NJ: Princeton University Press, 2001); Elizabeth Gillespie McRae, *Mothers of Massive Resistance: White Women and the Politics of White Supremacy* (New York: Oxford University Press, 2018).

7. Angie Maxwell, *The Indicted South: Public Criticism, Southern Inferiority, and the Politics of Whiteness* (Chapel Hill: The University of North Carolina Press, 2014).

8. Wilbur Joseph Cash, *The Mind of the South* (New York: Vintage Books, 1991).

1. FORGED IN CONFLICT

1. Warren M. Billings, *Sir William Berkeley and the Forging of Colonial Virginia* (Baton Rouge: Louisiana State University Press, 2004); Kathleen M. Brown, *Good Wives, Nasty Wenches, and Anxious Patriarchs: Gender, Race, and Power in Colonial Virginia* (Chapel Hill, University of North Carolina Press, 1996); John C. Coombs, "The Phases of Conversion: A New Chronology for the Rise of Slavery in Early Virginia," *William and Mary Quarterly* 68 (July 2011): 332–60; David Eltis, *The Rise of African Slavery in the Americas* (New York: Cambridge University Press, 2000); Anthony S. Parent Jr., *Foul Means: The Formation of a Slave Society in Virginia, 1660–1740* (Chapel Hill: University of North Carolina Press, 2003); James D. Rice, *Tales from a Revolution: Bacon's Rebellion and the Transformation of Early America* (New York: Oxford University Press, 2013); John Wareing, *Indentured Migration and the Servant Trade from London to Americas, 1618–1718: "There is a Great Want of Servants"* (New York: Oxford University Press, 2017).

2. Trevor Burnard, *Planters, Merchants, and Slaves: Plantation Societies in British America, 1650–1820* (Chicago: University of Chicago Press, 2015); Michael Guasco, *Slaves*

and Englishmen: Human Bondage in the Early Modern Atlantic World (Philadelphia: University of Pennsylvania Press, 2014); Allan Kulikoff, *Tobacco and Slaves: The Development of Southern Cultures in the Chesapeake, 1680-1800* (Chapel Hill: University of North Carolina Press, 1986); Edmund S. Morgan, *American Slavery. American Freedom: The Ordeal of Colonial Virginia* (New York: Norton, 1975); Kenneth Morgan, *Slavery and Servitude in Colonial North America: A Short History* (New York: New York University Press, 2001); Gary B. Nash, *Red, White, and Black: The Peoples of Early America* (Englewood Cliffs, NJ: Prentice-Hall, 1982); Justin Roberts, *Slavery and the Enlightenment in British North America, 1650-1820* (Chicago: University of Chicago Press, 2015); Peter H. Wood, *Black Majority: Negroes in Colonial South Carolina from 1670 through the Stono Rebellion* (New York: Alfred A. Knopf, 1974); C. Vann Woodward, *American Counterpoint: Slavery and Racism in the North-South Dialogue* (Boston: Little, Brown and Company, 1971).

3. Joseph J. Ellis, *Founding Brothers: The Revolutionary Generation* (New York: Vintage Books, 2002); Sylvia R. Frey, *Water from the Rock: Black Resistance in a Revolutionary Age* (Princeton, NJ: Princeton University Press, 1991); Gerald Horne, *The Counter-Revolution of 1776: Slave Resistance and the Origins of the United States* (New York: New York University Press, 2014); Michael A. McDonnell, *The Politics of War: Race, Class, and Conflict in Revolutionary Virginia* (Chapel Hill: University of North Carolina Press, 2007); Robert G. Parkinson, *The Common Cause: Creating Race and Nation in the American Revolution* (Chapel Hill: University of North Carolina Press, 2016).

4. Max Farrand, ed., *The Records of the Federal Convention of 1787*, vol. 2 (New Haven: Yale University Press, 1911), 364.

5. Farrand, *The Records of the Federal Convention of 1787*, 364.

6. Ira Berlin and Ronald Hoffman, eds., *Slavery and Freedom in the Age of the American Revolution* (Charlottesville: University of Virginia Press, 1983); David Brion Davis, *The Problem of Slavery in the Age of Revolution* (Ithaca: Cornell University Press, 1975); Don E. Fehrenbacher, *The Slaveholding Republic: An Account of the United States Government's Relations to Slavery* (New York: Oxford University Press, 2002); Paul Finkelman, *Slavery and the Founders: Race and Liberty in the Age of Jefferson* (New York: M.E. Sharpe, 2001); John N. Rakove, *Original Meanings: Politics and Ideas in the Making of the Constitution* (New York: Alfred A. Knopf, 1996); George William Van Cleve, *A Slaveholders' Union: Slavery, Politics, and the Constitution in the Early American Republic* (Chicago: University of Chicago Press, 2010); David Waldstreicher, *Slavery's Constitution: From Revolution to Ratification* (New York: Hill and Wang, 2010); Woodward, *American Counterpoint*, 78-106.

7. For Onuf's essay see "Federalism, Republicanism, and the Origins of American Sectionalism" in: Edward L. Ayers, et. al., *All over the Map: Rethinking American Regions* (Baltimore: The Johns Hopkins University Press, 1996). John Ashworth, *Slavery, Capitalism, and Politics in the Antebellum Republic, 1820-1850* (New York: Cambridge University Press, 1995); Andrew R. L. Cayton, *The Dominion of War: Empire and Liberty in North America, 1500-2000* (New York: Penguin, 2005); Kathleen DuVal, *Independence Lost: Lives on the Edge of the American Revolution* (New York: Random House, 2015); Tim Alan Garrison, *The Legal Ideology of Removal: The Southern Judiciary and the Sovereignty of Native American Nations* (Athens: University of Georgia Press, 2002); John Craig Hammond, *Slavery, Freedom, and Expansion in the Early American West* (University of Virginia Press, 2007); David Potter, *The Impending Crisis, 1848-1861* (New York: Harper & Row, 1976); Malcolm J. Rohrbough, *Trans-Appalachian Frontier: Peoples, Societies, and Institutions, 1775-1850*, Third Edition (Bloomington: Indiana University Press, 2008); Adam Rothman,

Slave Country: American Expansion and the Origins of the Deep South (Cambridge, MA: Harvard University Press, 2007).

8. Thomas Jefferson to John Holmes, 22 April 1820, Manuscript letter, Manuscript Division (159), www.loc.gov/exhibits/jefferson/images/vc159.jpg.

9. Charles Pinckney, *History of Congress*, 14 February 1820, 1328.

10. Robert Pierce Forbes, *The Missouri Compromise and Its Aftermath: Slavery and the Meaning of America* (Chapel Hill: University of North Carolina Press, 2009); Matthew Mason, *Slavery and Politics in the Early American Republic* (Chapel Hill: University of North Carolina Press, 2008); John R. Van Atta, *Wolf by the Ears: The Missouri Crisis, 1819-1821* (Baltimore: Johns Hopkins University Press, 2015).

11. David Walker, *Walker's Appeal in Four Articles* (Boston, 1830). David Walker's hostility was equally as inflammatory as that of Garrison. In one passage, Walker noted, "The whites have always been an unjust, jealous, unmerciful, avaricious, and blood-thirsty set of beings, always seeking after power and authority" 20.

12. William L. Garrison to George Sheppard, 13 September 1830, *The Letters of William Lloyd Garrison, vol. 1, I Will Be Heard! 1822-1835*, Walter M. Merrill, ed. (Cambridge: Belknap Press, 1971).

13. Henry Mayer, *All on Fire: William Lloyd Garrison and the Abolition of Slavery* (New York: St. Martin's Press, 1998); James B. Stewart, *Holy Warriors: The Abolitionists and American Slavery* (New York: Hill & Wang, 1976).

14. David Allmendinger Jr., *Nat Turner and the Rising in Southampton County* (Baltimore: Johns Hopkins University Press, 2014); Herbert Aptheker, *Nat Turner's Slave Rebellion Together with the Full Text of the So-Called "Confessions" of Nat Turner Made in Prison in 1831* (New York: Humanities Press, 1966); Patrick H. Breen, *The Land Shall Be Deluged in Blood: A New History of the Nat Turner Revolt* (New York: Oxford University Press, 2016); Kenneth S. Greenberg, *Nat Turner: A Slave Rebellion in History and Memory* (New York: Oxford University Press, 2004); Stephen B. Oates, *The Fires of Jubilee: Nat Turner's Fierce Rebellion* (New York: Harper Perennial, 1990); Governor Floyd quotation from: *Niles' Weekly Register* 41, no. 1059 (January 7, 1832): 350.

15. Matthew Estes, *A Defense of Negro Slavery as it Exists in the United States* (Montgomery: Press of the Alabama Journal, 1846), 227.

16. Lacy K. Ford, *Deliver Us From Evil: The Slavery Question in the Old South* (New York: Oxford University Press, 2009).

17. Anthony E. Kaye, "The Second Slavery: Modernity in the Nineteenth Century South and the Atlantic World," *Journal of Southern History* 75 (August 2009): 627-650; Dale W. Tomich, "The Second Slavery: Bonded Labor and the Transformation of the Nineteenth Century Economy," *Through the Prism of Slavery: Labor, Capital, and World Economy*, 56-71; see also: Daina Ramey Berry, *The Price for Their Pound of Flesh: The Value of the Enslaved, from the Womb to Grave, in Building a Nation* (Boston: Beacon Press, 2017).

18. Edward E. Baptist, *The Half Has Never Been Told: Slavery and the Making of American Capitalism* (New York: Basic Books, 2014); Walter Johnson, *River of Dark Dreams: Slavery and Empire in the Cotton Kingdom* (Cambridge, MA: Harvard University Press, 2013); Seth Rockman, "What Makes the History of Capitalism Newsworthy?" *Journal of the Early Republic* 34 (Fall 2014): 439-66; Michael Tadman, *Speculators and Slaves: Masters, Traders, and Slaves in the Old South* (Madison: University of Wisconsin Press, 1989); Dale Tomich, *Through the Prism of Slavery: Labor, Capital, and World Economy* (Lanham, MD:

Rowman & Littlefield, 2004); Eric Williams, *Capitalism and Slavery* (Chapel Hill: University of North Carolina Press, 1944).

19. Frederick Jackson Turner, *Rereading Frederick Jackson Turner: "The Significance of the Frontier in American History" and other Essays*, John Mack Faragher, ed. (New Haven: Yale University Press, 1999).

20. Charles H. Brown, *Agents of Manifest Destiny: The Lives and Times of the Filibusterers* (Chapel Hill: University of North Carolina Press, 1980); Gerald Horne, *The Deepest South: The United States, Brazil, and the African Slave Trade* (New York: New York University Press, 2007); Matthew Karp, *This Vast Southern Empire: Slaveholders at the Helm of American Foreign Policy* (Cambridge, MA: Harvard University Press, 2016).

21. William McWillie, 4 March 1850, *Congressional Globe*, 444.

22. William J. Cooper, *The South and the Politics of Slavery, 1828-1856* (Baton Rouge: Louisiana State University Press, 1978); Michael A. Morrison, *Slavery and the American West: The Eclipse of Manifest Destiny* (Chapel Hill: University of North Carolina Press, 1999); Steven E. Woodworth, *Manifest Destinies: America's Westward Expansion and the Road to the Civil War* (Alfred A. Knopf, 2010).

23. A. P. Butler, Nebraska and Kansas. Speech of Hon. A. P. Butler, of S. C., in the United States Senate, February 24 and 25, 1854 (Washington, 1854), 16.

24. Nicole Etcheson, *Bleeding Kansas: Contested Liberty in the Civil War Era* (University of Kansas Press, 2006); Michael Holt, *The Fate of Their Country: Politicians, Slavery Extension, and the Coming of the Civil War* (Hill and Wang, 2005); Michael Holt, *The Political Crisis of the 1850s* (New York: Wiley, 1978); James A. Rawley, *Race and Politics: "Bleeding Kansas" and the Coming of the American Civil War* (University of Nebraska Press, 1979).

25. Eric Foner, *Free Soil, Free Labor, Free Men: The Ideology of the Republican Party before the Civil War* (New York: Oxford University Press, 1970); William E. Gienapp, *The Origins of the Republican Party, 1852-1856* (New York: Oxford University Press, 1988); Robert E. McGlone, *John Brown's War Against Slavery* (Cambridge: Cambridge University Press, 2009); Stephen B. Oates, *To Purge This Land With Blood: A Biography of John Brown* (Amherst: University of Massachusetts Press, 1984); Merrill D. Peterson, *John Brown: The Legend Revisited* (University of Virginia Press, 2004).

26. Clement Claiborne Clay, 13 December 1859, *Congressional Globe*, 122.

27. David Emory Shi, *America: A Narrative History* (New York: W.W. Norton and Company, 2019), 649-657.

28. David Herbert Donald, *Lincoln* (New York: Simon and Schuster, 1996); Douglas R. Egerton, *Year of Meteors: Stephen Douglas, Abraham Lincoln, and the Election that Brought on the Civil War* (New York: Bloomsbury Press, 2010); Eric Foner, *The Fiery Trial: Abraham Lincoln and American Slavery* (New York: W.W. Norton and Company, 2010); Harold Holzer, *Lincoln President-Elect: Abraham Lincoln and the Great Secession Winter, 1860-1861* (New York: Simon and Schuster, 2009); James M. McPherson, *Battle Cry of Freedom: The Civil War Era* (New York: Oxford University Press, 2003); Ronald C. White Jr., *A. Lincoln: A Biography* (New York: Random House Trade Paperbacks, 2010).

29. Davis to Constituents, December 14, 1860, *The Papers of Jefferson Davis*, vol. 6, *1856-1860* (Baton Rouge: Louisiana State University Press, 1989), 377.

30. Davis to Constituents, December 14, 1860, *The Papers of Jefferson Davis*, vol. 6, *1856-1860*, 377.

31. Lacy Ford, *The Origins of Southern Radicalism;* George M. Frederickson, *The Black*

Image in the White Mind: The Debate on Afro-American Character and Destiny (New York: Harper and Row, 1972); Eugene D. Genovese, *The Political Economy of Slavery: Studies in the Economy and Society of the Slave South* (New York: Pantheon, 1965); Steven Hahn, *The Roots of Southern Populism: Yeoman Farmers and the Transformation of the Southern Countryside, 1850–1890* (New York: Oxford University Press, 1983); Michael P. Johnson, *Towards a Patriarchal Republic: The Secession of Georgia* (Baton Rouge: Louisiana State University, 1977); Stephanie McCurry, *Masters of Small Worlds: Yeoman Households, Gender Relations, and the Political Culture of the Antebellum South Carolina Low Country* (New York: Oxford University Press, 1997); James Oakes, *The Ruling Race: A History of American Slaveholders* (New York: Alfred A. Knopf, 1982); J. Mills Thornton III, *Politics and Power in a Slave Society: Alabama, 1800–1860* (Baton Rouge: Louisiana State University, 1978).

32. Dan T. Carter, *When the War Was Over: The Failure of Self-Reconstruction in the South, 1865–1867* (Baton Rouge: Louisiana State University Press, 1985); Eric Foner, *Reconstruction: America's Unfinished Revolution, 1863–1877* (New York: 1988); Thomas Holt, *Black Over White: Negro Political Leadership in South Carolina During Reconstruction* (Urbana: University of Illinois Press, 1977).

33. Ira Berlin, *Slaves No More: Three Essays on Emancipation and the Civil War* (New York: Cambridge University Press, 1992); Douglas A. Blackmon, *Slavery by Another Name: The Re-Enslavement of Black Americans from the Civil War to World War II* (New York: Doubleday, 2008); Eric Foner, *Nothing But Freedom: Emancipation and Its Legacy* (Baton Rouge: Louisiana State University, 1983); Leon F. Litwack, *Been in the Storm So Long: The Aftermath of Slavery* (New York: Alfred A. Knopf, 1979); Susan Eve O'Donovan, *Becoming Free in the Cotton South* (Cambridge, MA: Harvard University Press, 2010); Roger L. Ransom and Richard Sutch, *One Kind of Freedom: The Economic Consequences of Emancipation* (New York: Cambridge University Press, 1977).

34. Benjamin G. Humphreys, *Report of the Joint Committee on Reconstruction*, Part 3, (Washington: Government Printing Office, 1866), 182.

35. Carter, *When the War Was Over.*

36. Richard Taylor, *Destruction and Reconstruction: Personal Experiences of the Late War* (New York: D. Appleton and Company, 1879), 249.

37. Taylor, *Destruction and Reconstruction*, 238.

38. Kidada E. Williams, *They Left Great Marks on Me: African American Testimonies of Racial Violence from Emancipation to World War I* (New York: New York University Press, 2022; Amy Louise Wood, *Lynching and Spectacle: Witnessing Racial Violence in America, 1890 to 1940* (Chapel Hill: University Of North Carolina Press, 2009).

39. Michael L. Benedict, *A Compromise of Principle: Congressional Republicans and Reconstruction, 1863–1869* (New York: Norton, 1974); William Gillette, *Retreat from Reconstruction, 1869–1879* (Baton Rouge: Louisiana State University Press, 1979); Michael Perman, *The Road to Redemption: Southern Politics, 1869–1879* (Chapel Hill: University of North Carolina Press, 1984); George C. Rable, *But There Was No Peace: The Role of Violence in the Politics of Reconstruction* (Athens: University of Georgia Press, 1984); Mark Summers, *Railroads, Reconstruction, and the Gospel of Prosperity: Aid Under the Radical Republicans, 1865–1877* (Princeton, NJ: Princeton University Press, 1984); Hans L. Trefousse, *The Radical Republicans: Lincoln's Vanguard for Racial Justice* (New York: Alfred A. Knopf, 1969).

40. William Ivy Hair, *Bourbonism and Agrarian Protest: Louisiana Politics, 1877–1900* (Baton Rouge: Louisiana State University Press, 1969); J. Morgan Kousser, *The Shaping of*

Southern Politics: Suffrage Restriction and the Establishment of the One-Party South, 1880–1910 (New Haven: Yale University Press, 1974); Michael Perman, *Struggle for Mastery: Disenfranchisement in the South, 1888–1908* (Chapel Hill: University of North Carolina Press, 2000); Howard N. Rabinowitz, *Race Relations in the Urban South, 1865–1890* (Athens: University of Georgia Press, 1996); Joel Williamson, *A Rage for Order: Black-White Relations in the American South Since Emancipation* (New York: Oxford University Press, 1986).

41. Philip A. Bruce, The Plantation Negro as a Freeman: Observations on His Character, Conditions, and Prospects in Virginia (New York: G.P. Putnam's Sons, 1889), 83.

42. Jane Dailey, *White Fright: The Sexual Panic at the Heart of America's Racist History* (New York: Basic Books, 2020); Crystal N. Feimster, *Southern Horrors: Women and the Politics of Rape and Lynching* (Cambridge, MA: Harvard University Press, 2009); Glenda Elizabeth Gilmore, *Gender and Jim Crow: Women and the Politics of White Supremacy in North Carolina, 1896–1920* (Chapel Hill: University of North Carolina Press, 1996); Sarah Haley, *No Mercy Here: Gender, Punishment, and the Making of Jim Crow Modernity* (Chapel Hill: University of North Carolina Press, 2016); Leon F. Litwack, *North of Slavery: The Negro in the Free States, 1790–1860* (Chicago: The University of Chicago Press, 1961); Khalil Gibran Muhammad, *The Condemnation of Blackness: Race Crime and the Making of Modern Urban America* (Cambridge, MA: Harvard University Press, 2011); Thomas J. Sugrue, *Sweet Land of Liberty: The Forgotten Struggle for Civil Rights in the North* (Random House Trade Paperbacks, 2009).

43. For the two most known and earliest opponents of the myths that undergirded twentieth century racism, see: Franz Boas, *Race, Language, and Culture* (Chicago: University of Chicago Press, 1995); Gunnar Myrdal, Arnold M. Rose, and Richard Sterner. *An American Dilemma: The Negro Problem and Modern Democracy*, vols. 1 and 2 (New York: Harper & Brothers, 1944).

44. Robert Penn Warren, "The Briar Patch," in *I'll Take My Stand: The South and the Agrarian Tradition* (Baton Rouge: Louisiana State University Press, 1977), 264.

45. Wallace Best, *Passionately Human, No Less Divine: Religion and Black Culture in Chicago* (Princeton, NJ: Princeton University Press, 2005); John Brueggemann, "Racial Considerations and Social Policy in the 1930s," *Social Science History* 26 (Spring 2002): 139–177; Glenda Elizabeth Gilmore, *Defying Dixie: The Radical Roots of Civil Rights, 1919–1950* (New York: W.W. Norton and Company, 2009); James R. Grossman, *Land of Hope: Chicago, Black Southerners, and the Great Migration* (Chicago: University of Chicago Press, 1991); Nicholas Lemann, *The Promised Land: The Great Migration and How it Changed America* (New York: Vintage, 1992); Patricia Sullivan, *Lift Every Voice: The NAACP and the Making of the Civil Rights Movement* (New York: The New Press, 2010); Isabel Wilkerson, *The Warmth of Other Suns: The Epic Story of America's Great Migration* (New York: Random House, 2020).

46. For the Byrnes quote, see: James F. Byrnes to S. W. Copeland, 8 November 1938, Box 12, "Miscellaneous 1938-C" Folder, James F. Byrnes Collection, Strom Thurmond Institute, Clemson University, Clemson, South Carolina (hereafter cited as Byrnes MSS).

47. William H. Chafe, Raymond Gavins, and Robert Korstad, eds., *Remembering Jim Crow: African Americans Tell about Life in the Segregated South* (New York: New Press 2001); Claudrena N. Harold, *New Negro Politics in the Jim Crow South* (Athens: University of Georgia Press, 2016); Robin D. G. Kelley, *Hammer and Hoe: Alabama Communism during the Great Depression* (Chapel Hill: University of North Carolina Press, 1990); Jared Roll, *Spirit of Rebellion: Labor and Religion in the New Cotton South* (Urbana: University of

Illinois Press, 2010); Ward, *Defending White Supremacy;* Nan Elizabeth Woodruff, *American Congo: The African American Freedom Struggle in the Delta* (Cambridge, MA: Harvard University Press, 2003).

48. Ellison D. Smith, 12 May 1944, *Congressional Record*, 4402.

49. Walter George, May 10, 1944, *Congressional Record*, 4251.

50. Thomas Borstelmann, *The Cold War and the Color Line: American Race Relations in the Global Arena* (Cambridge, MA: Harvard University Press, 2001); Jennifer E. Brooks, *Defining the Peace: World War II Veterans, Race, and the Remaking of Southern Political Tradition* (Chapel Hill: University of North Carolina Press, 2004); Chamberlain, *Victory at Home;* Mary L. Dudziak, *Cold War Civil Rights: Race and the Image of American Democracy* (Princeton, NJ: Princeton University Press, 2000); Kari A. Frederickson, *The Dixiecrat Revolt and the End of the Solid South, 1932–1968* (Chapel Hill: University of North Carolina Press, 2001); Neil R. McMillen, *Remaking Dixie: The Impact of World War II on the American South* (Jackson: University Press of Mississippi, 1997); Gail Williams O'Brien, *The Color of the Law: Race, Violence, and Justice in the Post-World War II South* (Chapel Hill: University of North Carolina Press, 2004).

51. Bilbo to B. D. Carter, Folder 7, Box 1066, Bilbo MSS.

52. Richard Russell to Fred L. White, 18 June 1964, Folder 5, Box 38, Russell MSS.

53. Joseph Crespino, *In Search of Another Country: Mississippi and the Conservative Counterrevolution* (Princeton, NJ: Princeton University Press, 2009); Keith M. Finley, *Delaying the Dream: Southern Senators and the Fight Against Civil Rights* (Baton Rouge: Louisiana State University Press, 2008); George Lewis, *Massive Resistance: The White Response to the Civil Rights Movement* (New York: Oxford University Press, 2006); Jason Sokol, *There Goes My Everything: White Southerners in the Age of Civil Rights, 1945–1975* (New York: Vintage Books, 2007); Anders Walker, *The Ghost of Jim Crow: How Southern Moderates Used* Brown v. Board of Education *to Stall Civil Rights* (New York: Oxford University Press, 2009); Jason Morgan Ward, *Defending White Democracy: The Making of the Segregationist Movement and the Remaking of Racial Politics, 1936–1965* (Chapel Hill: University of North Carolina Press, 2011); Clive Webb, *Rabble Rousers: The American Far Right in the Civil Rights Era* (Athens: University of Georgia Press, 2010).

54. John Sparkman to Earl T. Rogers, June 19, 1963, ACC 6689#3, 18-E-3, John Sparkman Collection, W.S. Hoole Special Collections Library (hereafter cited as Sparkman MSS).

55. Numan V. Bartley, *The New South, 1945–1980* (Baton Rouge: Louisiana State University Press, 1995); Dan T. Carter, *The Politics of Rage: George Wallace, The Origins of the New Conservatism, and the Transformation of American Politics* (New York: Simon and Schuster, 1995); Boris Heersink and Jeffrey Jenkins, *Republican Party Politics and the American South, 1865–1968* (New York: Cambridge University Press, 2020); Matthew D. Lassiter, *The Silent Majority: Suburban Politics in the Sunbelt South* (Princeton, NJ: Princeton University Press, 2006); Robert Mickey, *Paths Out of Dixie: The Democratization of Authoritarian Enclaves in America's Deep South, 1944–1972* (Princeton, NJ: Princeton University Press, 2015).

2. THE ESSENTIAL MYTHOLOGY

1. Benedict Anderson, *Imagined Communities: Reflections on the Origin and Spread of Nationalism* (Verso, 2006); Barbara Allen and Thomas J. Schelereth, *Sense of Place: Amer-*

ican Regional Cultures (The University of Kentucky Press, 1992); W. Fitzhugh Brundage, *Where These Memories Grow: History, Memory, and Southern Identity* (Chapel Hill: University of North Carolina Press, 2000); James C. Cobb, *Away Down South: A History of Southern Identity* (New York: Oxford University Press, 2005); Joseph A. Conforti, *Imagining New England: Explorations of Regional Identity from the Pilgrims to the Mid-Twentieth Century* (Chapel Hill: University of North Carolina Press, 2000); Gaines M. Foster, *Ghost of the Confederacy: Defeat, the Lost Cause and the Emergence of the New South, 1865-1913* (New York: Oxford University Press, 1988).

2. Nehemiah Adams, *A South-Side View of Slavery; Or Three Months at the South in 1854*, Third Edition (Port Washington: Kennikat Press, 1969), 18.

3. Adams, *A South-Side View*, 171.

4. J. H. Hammond, "Slavery in the Light of Political Science," *Cotton is King and Pro-slavery Arguments: Comprising the Writings of Hammond, Harper, Christy, Stringfellow, Hodge, Bledsoe, and Cartwright, on This Important Subject*, E. N. Elliott, ed. (Augusta: Pritchard, Abbott, and Loomis,1860), 656.

5. W. Gilmore Simms, "The Morals of Slavery," *The Pro-Slavery Argument as Maintained by the Most Distinguished Writers of the Southern States: Containing the Several Essays, on the subject, of Chancellor Harper, Governor Hammond, Dr. Simms, and Professor Dew* (Philadelphia: Lippincott, Grambo, and Co., 1853), 217.

6. Z. Kingsley *A Treatise on the Patriarchal, or Co-Operative, System of Society as It Exists in Some Governments, and Colonies in America: And in the United States, under the Name of Slavery, with Its Necessity and Advantages.* (publisher not identified, 1829), 16.

7. Albert Taylor Bledsoe, *An Essay on Liberty and Slavery* (Philadelphia: J.P. Lippincott and Co., 1856), 289.

8. Thomas R. Dew, *Review of the Debate in the Virginia Legislature of 1831 and 1832* (Richmond: T. W. White, 1832), 113.

9. Calvin Schermerhorn, *Money over Mastery, Family over Freedom: Slavery in the Antebellum Upper South* (Baltimore: Johns Hopkins University Press, 2011); Stephanie E. Smallwood, *Saltwater Slavery: A Middle Passage from Africa to American Diaspora* (Cambridge, MA: Harvard University Press, 2007); Jeffrey Robert Young, *Domesticating Slavery: The Master Class in Georgia and South Carolina, 1670-1837* (Chapel Hill: University of North Carolina Press, 1999).

10. William Harper, *Memoir on Slavery Read Before the Society for the Advancement of Learning of South Carolina At Its Annual Meeting at Columbia, 1837* (Charleston: James and Burges, 1838), 41. Matthew Estes, echoed Harper's comments, observing that those who treat their "Slaves with unnecessary harshness, may expect the disapprobation of the public." Estes, *A defense of Negro Slavery as it Exists in the United States* (Montgomery, Press of the Alabama Journal, 1846), 125, 131.

11. Estes, *A Defense of Negro Slavery*, 84.

12. Estes, *A Defense*, 133.

13. Hammond, *Cotton is King*, 656.

14. Hammond, *Cotton is King*, 651. Even with this broadening of restrictions, the spirit of paternalism allegedly remained as a benevolent force elevating both black and white. According to Kingsley, the interracial "affection" forged by paternalism "created confidence which becomes reciprocal, and is attended with the most beneficial consequences to both." Kinglsey, *A Treatise on the Patriarchal*, 16.

15. Hammond, *Cotton is King*, 656. Hammond was not alone in his economic determin-

ist message. Matthew Estes, for example, commented "the Master knows from experience that the efficiency and usefulness of his Slaves will depend in a great measure upon the treatment which they receive from him." Estes, *A Defense*, 126.

16. Edward E. Baptist, The *Half Has Never Been Told: Slavery and the Making of American Capitalism* (New York: Basic Books, 2017); Sven Beckert and Seth Rockman, *Slavery's Capitalism: A New History of American Economic Development* (Philadelphia: University of Pennsylvania Press, 2018); Caitlin Rosenthal, *Accounting for Slavery: Masters and Management* (Boston: Harvard University Press, 2018); Joshua D. Rothman, *Flush Times and Fever Dreams: A Story of Capitalism and Slavery in the Age of Jackson* (Athens: University of Georgia Press, 2014); Calvin Schermerhorn, *The Business of Slavery and the Rise of American Capitalism, 1815–1860* (New Haven: Yale University Press, 2015).

17. Bledsoe, *An Essay on Liberty*, 54.

18. Walter Johnson, *Soul by Soul: Life Inside the Antebellum Slave Market* (Cambridge, MA: Harvard University Press, 1999); The research of Elizabeth Fox and Eugene Genovese clearly underscores how utilizing terms such as "hypocrisy" when dealing with Old South paternalism obfuscates the importance of the concept to the region. Although their emphasis on "self-deception" is not without flaw, it represents an interesting take on the issue. Eugene and Elizabeth Fox Genovese, *Fatal Self-Deception: Slaveholding Paternalism in the Old South* (New York: Cambridge University Press, 2011); Eugene Genovese, *The Mind of the Master Class: History and Faith in the Southern Slaveholder's Worldview* (Boston: Cambridge University Press, 2005).

19. A. P. Butler, *Nebraska and Kansas. Speech of Hon. A. P. Butler, of S.C., in the United States Senate, February 24 and 25, 1854* (Washington: Government Printing Office, 1854), 9.

20. John C. Calhoun, "Speech on the Oregon Bill," 27 September 1849, *Union and Liberty: The Political Philosophy of John C. Calhoun*, edited by Ross M. Lence (Liberty Fund, Inc., Indianapolis, 1992).

21. George Fitzhugh, "Southern Thought," *DeBow's Review*, vol. 23 (October 1857): 276.

22. James H. Hammond, 4 March 1858, *Congressional Globe*, 961–962.

23. Hammond, 4 March 1858, *Congressional Globe*, 962.

24. Hammond, 4 March 1858, *Congressional Globe*, 962.

25. Butler, *Nebraska and Kansas*, 3.

26. Davis, 8 December 1859, *Congressional Globe*, 63.

27. Pinckney, 14 February 1820, *History of Congress*, 1324.

28. Hammond, *Cotton is King*, 663.

29. Stephen V. Ash, *When the Yankees Came: Conflict and Chaos in the Occupied South, 1861–1865* (Chapel Hill: University of North Carolina Press, 1995); Glenn David Brasher, *The Peninsula Campaign and the Necessity of Emancipation: African Americans and the Fight For Freedom* (Chapel Hill: University of North Carolina Press, 2013); Andrew F. Lang, *In the Wake of War: Military Occupation, Emancipation, and Civil War America* (Baton Rouge: Louisiana State University Press, 2017).

30. Mark Summers, *Railroads, Reconstruction, and the Gospel of Prosperity: Aid Under the Radical Republicans, 1865–1877* (Princeton, NJ: Princeton University Press, 1984).

31. Philip A. Bruce, *The Plantation Negro as Freeman: Observations on His Character, Condition, and Prospects in Virginia* (Williamstown, MA: Connor House Publishers, 1970).

32. Edward L. Ayers, *The Promise of the New South: Life After Reconstruction* (New York: Oxford University Press, 1993); C. Vann Woodward, *Origins of the New South, 1877–1913*, Revised Edition (Baton Rouge: Louisiana State University Press, 1971).

Notes to Pages 63–68   197

33. Blair L. M. Kelley, *Right to Ride: Streetcar Boycotts and African American Citizenship in the Era of Plessy v. Ferguson* (Chapel Hill: University of North Carolina Press, 2010); Paul Ortiz, *Emancipation Betrayed: The Hidden History of Black Organizing and White Violence in Florida from Reconstruction to the Bloody Election of 1920* (Berkeley: University of California Press, 2005); Samuel Kelton Roberts Jr., *Infectious Fear: Politics, Disease, and the Health Effects of Segregation* (Chapel Hill: University of North Carolina Press, 2009); Heather Andrea Williams, *Help Me Find My People: The African American Search for Family Lost in Slavery* (Chapel Hill: University of North Carolina Press, 2012)

34. Frederick Ludwig Hoffman, *Race Traitors and Tendencies of the American Negro* (New York: Macmillan, 1896), 311.

35. Hoffman, *Race Traitors*, 312.

36. Cash, The Mind of the South, 165-175.

37. Bledsoe, *An Essay on Liberty*, 289.

38. Bruce, *The Plantation Negro as Freeman*, 44.

39. Eric Arensen, *Waterfront Workers of New Orleans: Race, Class, and Politics* (Urbana, University of Illinois Press, 1994); Michelle Brattain, *The Politics of Whiteness: Race, Workers, and Culture in the Modern South* (Princeton, NJ: Princeton University Press, 2001); James C. Cobb, *The Selling of the South: The Southern Crusade for Industrial Development, 1936-1980* (Baton Rouge: Louisiana State University Press, 1982); Gilbert C. Fite, *Cotton Fields No More: Southern Agriculture, 1865-1980* (Lexington: University Press of Kentucky, 1984); Earl Lewis, *In Their Own Interests: Race, Class, and Power in Twentieth-Century Norfolk, Virginia* (Berkeley: University of California Press, 1991); Matthew J. Mancini, *One Dies, Get Another: Convict Leasing in the American South, 1866-1928* (Columbia: University of South Carolina Press, 1996); Jared Roll, *Spirit of Rebellion: Labor and Religion in the New Cotton South* (Urbana: University of Illinois Press, 2010); Mark Schultz, *The Rural Face of White Supremacy: Beyond Jim Crow* (Urbana: University of Illinois Press, 2005); Gavin Wright, *Sharing the Prize: The Economics of the Civil Rights Revolution in the American South* (Cambridge, MA: Harvard University Press, 2013).

40. Thomas Dixon Jr., *The Leopard's Spots: A Romance of the White Man's Burden, 1865-1900* (New York: A Wessels Company, 1906), 311.

41. Allen Ellender to R. B. Chandler, 11 August 1952, Folder: Legislation-Civil Rights-1952, Box 649, Allen Ellender Collection, Ellender Library (hereafter cited as Ellender MSS).

42. Russell Long to A. L. Casselman, 20 August 1963, Box 558, Folder 26, Russell Long Collection, Hill Memorial Library (hereafter cited as Long MSS); see also Lister Hill to J. Carrlton, 10 March 1938, Folder 9, Box 95, Lister Hill Collection, W.S. Hoole Special Collections Library (hereafter cited as Hill MSS).

43. James Byrnes to Wingate Waring, 23 April 1936, Folder: Legislation 1933-1941—Antilynching 1937, Box 42, James Byrnes Collection, Strom Thurmond Institute.

44. Tom Connally to Jesse Daniel Ames, 27 January 1940, Folder: Hearings Anti-Lynching, Box 126, Thomas Connally Collection, Library of Congress.

45. Claude Pepper diary entry 28 August 1944, Folder 1, Box 2, Series 439, Claude Pepper Collection, Claude Pepper Library (hereafter cited as Pepper MSS).

46. Ervin to Harry M. Karawan, 27 March 1956, Folder #1122, Box 15, Sam Ervin Collection, Southern Historical Collection (hereafter cited as Ervin MSS).

47. Kimberley Phillips Boehm. *War! What Is It Good For?: Black Freedom Struggles and the U.S. Military From World War II to Iraq*, John Hope Franklin Series in African American History and Culture (Chapel Hill: The University of North Carolina Press, 2012); Jen-

nifer Delton, "Laboured Protest: Black Civil Rights in New York City and Detroit during the New Deal and Second World War" *American Historical Review* 125, no. 4 (October 1, 2020): 1437–38; Françoise N. Hamlin, *Crossroads at Clarksdale: The Black Freedom Struggle in the Mississippi Delta after World War II*. The John Hope Franklin Series in African American History and Culture (Chapel Hill: University of North Carolina Press, 2012); Kevin M. Kruse and Stephen Tuck, *Fog of War: The Second World War and the Civil Rights Movement* (New York: Oxford University Press, 2012); Mary Elizabeth B. Murphy, *Jim Crow Capital: Women and Black Freedom Struggles in Washington, D.C., 1920–1945* (Chapel Hill: University of North Carolina Press, 2019); Steven White, *World War II and American Racial Politics: Public Opinion, the Presidency, and Civil Rights Advocacy* (Cambridge: Cambridge University Press, 2019).

48. George McClellan, 24 January 1946, *Congressional Record*, 335; see also Olin Johnston to R. Carl Griffith, 16 February 1948, Box 13, Folder: "Legislation 1948 Civil Rights, General," Olin Johnston Collection, South Caroliniana Library (hereafter cited as Johnston MSS).

49. Connally, 17 November 1937, *Congressional Record*, 65.

50. Charles Wallace Collins, *Whither the Solid South: A Study in Politics and Race Relations* (New Orleans: Pelican Publishing Company, 1947), 40.

51. Ellender to Mother M. Columba, 16 March 1949, Folder: "Civil Rights, 1949," Box 603, Ellender MSS.

52. Long to Bobby Queyrouze, 31 July 1952, Box 17, Folder 1, Long MSS.

53. Russell to Joe Ackerman Jr., 2 October 1957, Box 133, Folder 1, Russell MSS.

54. Russell, 27 February 1960, *CR*, 3699.

55. J. William Fulbright to H. Charles Johnston, 28 October 1957, Series 66:3, Box 8, Folder 3, J. William Fulbright Collection, Mullins Library (hereafter cited as Fulbright MSS).

56. Fulbright to Bob E. Rice, 27 May 1961, Series 64:3, Folder 14, Box 9, Fulbright MSS.

57. Steve Estes, *I Am a Man!: Race, Manhood, and the Civil Rights Movement* (Chapel Hill: University of North Carolina Press, 1999); Adam Fairclough, *To Redeem the Soul of America: The Southern Christian Leadership Conference and Martin Luther King Jr* (Athens: University of Georgia Press, 1987); Lynne B. Feldman, *A Sense of Place: Birmingham's Black Middle-Class Community, 1890–1930* (Tuscaloosa: University of Alabama Press, 1992); William P. Jones, *The March on Washington: Jobs, Freedom, and the Forgotten History of Civil Rights* (New York: W.W. Norton, 2013); Robert Korstad, *Civil Rights Unionism: Tobacco Workers and the Struggle for Democracy in the Mid-Twentieth Century South* (Chapel Hill: University of North Carolina Press, 2003); Emily Epstein Landau, *Spectacular Wickedness: Sex, Race, and Memory in Storyville, New Orleans* (Baton Rouge: Louisiana State University Press, 2013); Barbara Ransby, *Ella Baker and the Black Freedom Movement: A Radical Democratic Vision* (Chapel Hill: University of North Carolina Press, 2003); Mary G. Rolinson, *Grassroots Garveyism: The Universal Negro Improvement Association in the Rural South, 1920–1927* (Chapel Hill: University of North Carolina Press, 2007); Rebecca Sharpless, *Cooking in Other Women's Kitchens: Domestic Workers in the South, 1865–1960* (Chapel Hill: University of North Carolina Press, 2010); Monica M. White, *Freedom Farmers: Agricultural Resistance and the Black Freedom Movement* (Chapel Hill: University of North Carolina Press, 2018).

58. Kris Drocher, *Raising Racists: The Socialization of White Children in the Jim Crow*

South (Lexington: University Press of Kentucky, 2011); McRae, *Mothers of Massive Resistance*, 41–85.

59. Fulbright to H. Alex Smith, 3 August 1956, BCN 84, Folder 26, Fulbright MSS.

60. Tower, 9 June 1964, *Congressional Record*, 14503.

61. Tower, Congressional Record, 14503.

62. Tower, *Congressional Record*, 14503.

63. Gore, 25 April 1964, *Congressional Record*, 9083.

64. G. Avery Lee, *Messages From the Second Annual Conference on Human Relations* (Forest Hills Baptist Church Raleigh, North Carolina: March 5-6, 1963), 3.

65. G. Avery Lee, *Some Quiet Thoughts on a Turbulent Issue* (Nashville: Christian Life Commission, 1956).

66. *Southern Baptist Convention Annual*, 1954, 404.

67. Mark Newman, *Getting Right With God: Southern Baptists and Desegregation, 1945-1995* (Tuscaloosa: University of Alabama Press, 2001).

68. Ellender to H.A. Ghislain, 2 February 1946, Folder: "Education and Labor #2 FEPC," Box 1280, Ellender MSS.

69. Ellender to Reuben T. Douglas, 3 June 1954, Folder: "Legislation-Civil Rights-1954," Box 668, Ellender MSS.

70. Ellender to Anderson Washington, 8 March 1956, Folder: "Legislation-Civil Rights-1956," Box 688, Ellender MSS.

71. Russell, 27 February 1960, *Congressional Record*, 3698.

72. Aniko Bodroghkozy, *Equal Time: Television and the Civil Rights Movement* (Urbana University of Illinois Press, 2012); Allison Graham, *Framing the South: Hollywood, Television, and Race During the Civil Rights Struggle* (Baltimore: Johns Hopkins University Press, 2001); Kay Mills, *Changing Channels: The Civil Rights Case That Transformed Television* (Jackson: University Press of Mississippi, 2004); Sasha Torres, *Black, White, and in Color: Television and Black Civil Rights* (Princeton, NJ: Princeton University Press, 2003).

3. THE LINK AND THE ALBATROSS

1. Estes, *A Defense of Slavery*, 49.

2. William Harper, *Memoir on Slavery Read Before The Society for the Advancement of Learning of South Carolina At Its Annual Meeting at Columbia, 1837* (Charleston: James and Burges, 1838), 38.

3. James Henry Hammond, *Gov. Hammond's Letters on Southern Slavery: Addressed to Thomas Clarkson, the English Abolitionist* (Charleston: Walker and Burke Printers, 1845), 20.

4. Thomas Hobbes, *Leviathan*, ed., J. C. A. Gaskin (New York: Oxford University Press, 1998), 84.

5. Simms, *Pro-Slavery Arguments*, 222.

6. Estes, *A Defense of Negro Slavery*, 50.

7. E. N. Elliott, "Slavery in the Light of International Law," *Cotton is King*, 731.

8. Edmond Ruffin, *The Diary of Edmund Ruffin, vol. 1*, 18 July 1857, 90.

9. A myriad of studies debunk the racial narrative of contentedness and docility found in the South, including: William L. Andrews, *Slavery and Class in the American South: A Generation of Slave Narrative Testimony, 1840-1865* (New York: Oxford University Press,

2019); John W. Blassingame, *The Slave Community: Plantation Life in the Antebellum South* (New York: Oxford University Press, 1972); Stephanie M. H. Camp, *Closer to Freedom: Enslaved Women and Everyday Resistance in the Plantation South* (Chapel Hill: University of North Carolina Press, 2004); Richard J. Follett, *The Sugar Masters: Planters and Slaves in Louisiana's Cane World, 1820–1860* (Baton Rouge: Louisiana State University Press, 2005); John Hope Franklin and Loren Schweninger, *Runaway Slaves: Rebels on the Plantation* (New York: Oxford University Press, 1999); Michael A. Gomez, *Exchanging Our Country Marks: The Transformation of African Identities in the Colonial and Antebellum South* (Chapel Hill: University of North Carolina Press, 1998); Frederick C. Knight, *Working the Diaspora: The Impact of African Labor on the Anglo-American World, 1650–1850* (New York: New York University Press, 2010); Philip D. Morgan, *Slave Counterpoint: Black Culture in the Eighteenth-Century Chesapeake and Lowcountry* (Chapel Hill: University of North Carolina Press, 1998); Michael Mullin, *Africa in America: Slave Acculturation and Resistance in the American South and British Caribbean, 1736–1831* (Urbana: University of Illinois Press, 1992); Daniel Rasmussen, *American Uprising: The Untold Story of America's Largest Slave Revolt* (New York: Harper Collins, 2011); Betty Wood, *Women's Work, Men's Work: The Informal Slave Economies of Lowcountry Georgia* (Athens: University of Georgia Press, 1995).

10. Estes, *A Defense of Negro Slavery*, 74.
11. Sims, "The Morals of Slavery," *The Pro-Slavery Argument*, 243.
12. Thomas Dew, *The Proslavery Argument*, 333.
13. William J. Grayson, *The Hireling and the Slave, Chicora, and Other Poems* (Charleston: McCarter and Company, 1856) vii.
14. Grayson, *The Hireling and the Slave*, x.
15. Bledsoe, *An Essay on Liberty and Slavery*, 299.
16. George Fitzhugh, "Southern Thought," *DeBow's Review*, 1857, 293.
17. James Hammond, *Gov. Hammond's Letters*, 18–20.
18. Hammond, 4 March 1858, *Congressional Globe*, 962.
19. Dew, *The Pro-Slavery Arguments*, 460. For additional information on the curse of Ham, see: David M. Goldenberg, *The Curse of Ham: Race and Slavery in Early Judaism, Christianity, and Islam* (Princeton: Princeton University Press, 2003) and Stephen R. Haynes, *Noah's Curse: The Biblical Justification for American Slavery* (New York: Oxford University Press, 2002).
20. Harper, *Memoir on Slavery*, 11.
21. Thornton Stringfellow, "Statistical View of Slavery," *Cotton is King*, 543.
22. Edward A. Pollard, *Black Diamonds Gathered in the Darkey Homes of the South* (New York: Pudney and Russell, 1859), 81.
23. J. B. Thrasher, *Slavery: A Divine Institution* (Port Gibson, MS: Southern Reveille Book and Job Office, 1861), 20.
24. Thrasher, *Slavery*, 20.
25. Stringfellow, "Statistical View of Slavery," *Cotton is King*, 546.
26. Charles Hodge, "The Bible Argument on Slavery," *Cotton is King*, 873.
27. Dew, "Professor Dew on Slavery," *The Pro-Slavery Argument*, 333.
28. Estes, *A Defense of Negro Slavery*, 96.
29. Estes, *A Defense of Negro Slavery*, 183.
30. Thrasher, *Slavery*, 21.
31. Sims, "The Morals of Slavery," *The Pro-Slavery Argument*, 243.

32. Elliott, "Slavery in the Light of International Law," *Cotton is King*, 737.
33. Davis, 8 December 1859, *Congressional Globe*, 63.
34. Dew, "Professor Dew on Slavery," *The Pro-Slavery Argument*, 410.
35. Harper, "Slavery in the Light of Social Ethics," *Cotton is King*, 619.
36. Estes, *A Defense*, 57.
37. *Southern Quarterly*, February 1857, 292.
38. Sims, "The Morals of Slavery," *The Proslavery Argument*, 213.
39. S.A. Cartwright, "Slavery in Light of Ethnology," *Cotton is King*, 701.
40. Dew, "Professor Dew on Slavery," *The Proslavery Argument*, 429-430.
41. Elliott, "Slavery in Light of International Law," *Cotton is King*, 737.
42. For recent scholarly treatment on the experience of free blacks prior to the Civil War, see: Sylvanie A. Diouf, *Slavery's Exiles: The Story of the American Maroons* (New York: New York University Press, 2014); Erica Armstrong Dunbar, *A Fragile Freedom: African American Women and Emancipation in the Antebellum City* (New Haven: Yale University Press, 2011); Steven Hahn, *The Political Worlds of Slavery and Freedom* (Cambridge, MA: Harvard University Press, 2009); James Oliver Horton and Lois E. Horton, *In Hope of Liberty: Culture, Community, and Protest Among Northern Free Blacks, 1700-1860* (New York: Oxford University Press, 1997); Jane G. Landers, ed., *Against the Odds: Free Blacks in the Slave Societies of the Americas* (London: Frank Cass, 1996); Cheryl Janifer LaRoche, *Free Black Communities and the Underground Railroad: The Geography of Resistance* (Urbana: University of Illinois Press, 2013); Richard S. Newman and James Mueller, eds., *Antislavery and Abolition in Philadelphia: Emancipation and the Long Struggle for Racial Justice in the City of Brotherly Love* (Baton Rouge: Louisiana State University Press, 2011); Rita Roberts, *Evangelicalism and the Politics of Reform in Northern Black Thought, 1776-1863* (Baton Rouge: Louisiana State University Press, 2010); Julie Winch, *Between Slavery and Freedom: Free People of Color in America from Settlement to the Civil War* (Lantham, MD: Rowman & Littlefield, 2014).
43. Harper, "Slavery in Light of Social Ethics," *Cotton is King*, 593.
44. For another example that emphasizes Black inferiority, see: Chancellor Harper, "Slavery in Light of Social Ethics," *Cotton is King*, 593. For some of the literature on the abolitionist movement, see: Eric Foner, *Gateway to Freedom: The Hidden History of the Underground Railroad* (New York: W.W. Norton, 2016); Kelly Carter Jackson, *Force and Freedom: Black Abolitionists and the Politics of Violence* (Philadelphia: University of Pennsylvania Press, 2019); Patrick Rael, *Black Identity and Black Protest in the Antebellum North* (Chapel Hill: University of North Carolina Press, 2002); Manisha Sinha, *The Slave's Cause: A History of Abolition* (New Haven: Yale University Press, 2016).
45. Samuel A. Cartwright, "The Education, Labor, and Wealth of the South," *Cotton is King*, 884.
46. Josiah Priest, *Bible Defence of Slavery : or the Origin, History, and Fortunes of the Negro Race* (Louisville: J.F. Brennan, 1851), 255.
47. Hammond, "Slavery in Light of Political Science," *Cotton is King*, 645.
48. Mary Boykin Chesnut, C. Vann Woodward, and Elisabeth Muhlenfeld. *The Original Civil War Diaries of Mary Boykin Chesnut* (New York: Oxford University Press, 1984).
49. Bruce, *The Plantation Negro as Freeman*, 83.
50. A wide array of sources address various aspects of the link between race and gender in the American South, including: Daina Ramey Berry and Leslie M. Harris., eds., *Sexuality and Slavery: Reclaiming Intimate Histories in the Americas* (Athens: University of

Georgia Press, 2018); Victoria E. Bynum, *Unruly Women: The Politics of Social and Sexual Control in the Old South* (Chapel Hill: University of North Carolina Press, 1992); Feimster, *Southern Horrors;* Craig Thompson Friend and Lorri Glover, eds., *Southern Manhood: Perspectives on Masculinity in the Old South* (Athens: University of Georgia Press, 2004); Annette Gordon-Read, *The Hemingses of Monticello: An American Family* (New York: W.W. Norton, 2008); Martha Elizabeth Hodes, *White Women, Black Men: Illicit Sex in the Nineteenth-Century South* (New Haven: Yale University Press, 1997); Sally G. McMillen, *Southern Women: Black and White in the Old South* (Arlington Heights: Harlan Davidson, 1992); Jennifer L. Morgan, *Laboring Women: Reproduction and Gender in New World Slavery* (Philadelphia: University of Pennsylvania Press, 2004); Brenda E. Stevenson, "What's Love Got to Do With It? Concubinage and Enslaved Black Women and Girls in the Antebellum South," *Journal of African American History* 98 (Winter 2013): 99–125.

    51. Dwight Lowell Dumond, ed., *Southern Editorials on Secession* (New York: The Century Company, 1931), 223.

    52. Drew Gilpin Faust, *Mothers of Invention: Women of the Slaveholding South in the American Civil War* (New York: Vintage Books, 1997); Stephanie McCurry, *Confederate Reckoning: Power and Politics in the Civil War South* (Cambridge, MA: Harvard University Press, 2010); LeeAnn Whites and Alecia P. Long, ed., *Occupied Women: Gender, Military Occupation, and the American Civil War* (Baton Rouge: Louisiana State University Press, 2009).

    53. Jane Turner Censer, *The Reconstruction of White Southern Womanhood, 1865–1895* (Baton Rouge; Louisiana State University Press, 2003); Claude A. Clegg III, *Troubled Ground: A Tale of Murder, Lynching, and Reckoning in the New South* (Urbana: University of Illinois Press, 2010); David Fort Godshalk, *Veiled Visions: The 1906 Atlanta Race Riot and the Reshaping of American Race Relations* (Chapel Hill: University of North Carolina Press, 2005); Jacquelyn Dowd Hall, *Revolt Against Chivalry: Jessie Daniel Ames and the Women's Campaign Against Lynching* (New York: Columbia University Press, 1979); J. Joseph Huthmacher, *Senator Robert F. Wagner and the Rise of Urban Liberalism* (Cambridge, MA: Harvard University Press, 1968); Leon Litwack, *Trouble in Mind: Black Southerners in the Age of Jim Crow* (New York: Alfred A. Knopf, 1998); George C. Rable "The South and the Politics of Anti-Lynching Legislation, 1920–1940," *The Journal of Southern History* 51 (May 1985): 201–220; Hannah Rosen, *Terror in the Heart of Freedom: Citizenship, Sexual Violence, and the Meaning of Race in the Postemancipation South* (Chapel Hill: University of North Carolina Press, 2009); George B. Tindall, *The Emergence of the New South, 1913–1945* (Baton Rouge: Louisiana State University Press, 1967), 550–555; Williams, *They Left Great Marks on Me;* Joel Williamson, "Wounds Not Scars: Lynching the National Conscience and the American Historian," *The Journal of American History* 83 (March 1997): 1221–1253; Wood, *Lynching and Spectacle;* Robert L. Zangrando, *The NAACP Crusade Against Lynching, 1909–1950* (Philadelphia: Temple University Press, 1980).

    54. Ayers, *Promise of the New South;* Jane Dailey, Glenda Elizabeth Gilmore, and Bryant Simon, ed., *Jumpin' Jim Crow: Southern Politics from Civil War to Civil Rights* (Princeton, NJ: Princeton University Press, 2000); Hale, *Making Whiteness;* Stephen Kantrowitz, *Ben Tillman and the Reconstruction of White Supremacy* (Chapel Hill: University of North Carolina Press, 2000); Tindall, *The Emergence of the New South;* Woodward, *Origins of the New South;* Woodward, *The Strange Career of Jim Crow.*

    55. Theodore G. Bilbo, *Take Your Choice: Separation or Mongrelization* (Poplarville, MS: Dream House Publishing Co., 1947), 54; Theodore Bilbo to Quincy Ewing, 18 Janu-

ary 1938, Box 332, Folder: "January 18 1938 B," Theodore Bilbo Collection, McCain Library (hereafter cited as Bilbo MSS).

56. Bilbo to William S. McNair, 28 June 1943, Box 1066, Folder 8, Bilbo MSS.

57. Bilbo, *Take Your Choice*, 54.

58. Bilbo to Ernest E. Taylor, 22 May 1944, Folder 2, Box 1067, Bilbo MSS.

59. For scholarship emphasizing the importance of the Great Depression and New Deal in shaping regional race relations, see: Gilmore, *Defying Dixie*; Ira Katznelson, *When Affirmative Action was White: An Untold History of Racial Inequality in Twentieth-Century America* (New York: W.W. Norton, 2005); Korstad, *Civil Rights Unionism*; Paul V. Murphy, *The Rebuke of History: Southern Agrarians and American Conservative Thought* (Chapel Hill: University of North Carolina Press, 2001); Patterson, *Congressional Conservatism*; Patricia Sullivan, *Days of Hope: Race and Democracy in the New Deal Era* (Chapel Hill: University of North Carolina Press, 1996); Schultz, *The Rural Face of White Supremacy*; Gavin Wright, *Old South, New South: Revolutions in the Southern Economy Since the Civil War* (New York: Basic Books, 1986).

60. Long, 2 March 1960, *Congressional Record*, 4162.

61. Long, 2 March 1960, *Congressional Record*, 4162.

62. Ervin to C. W. Houston, 18 September 1956, Folder # 1126, Box 15, Ervin MSS.

63. Ervin to C. W. Houston, 18 September 1956.

64. Ervin, 16 February 1960, *Congressional Record*, 2601.

65. Robert Byrd, 1 May 1964, *Congressional Record*, 9825.

66. Pamphlet, B. J. Gaillot Jr., "God Gave The Law of Segregation to Moses on Mount Sinai," 1960, 1–3, 15. Found in Box 2, Folder 6, Plaquemines Parish—Rod Lincoln Collection, Center for Southeast Louisiana Studies, Southeastern Louisiana University.

67. *The Citizens' Council*, April–May 1961, 4.

68. Herman E. Talmadge, *You and Segregation* (Birmingham: Vulcan Press Incorporated, 1955), 49.

69. Talmadge, 3 March 1960, *Congressional Record*, 4299; see also: Thurmond, 28 April 1964, *Congressional Record*, 9283.

70. Holland, 3 March 1960, *Congressional Record*, 4380.

71. Holland, 3 March 1960, *Congressional Record*, 4380.

72. *The Citizens' Council*, February 1956, 3.

73. Albert Gore to constituent, 28 August 1957, Folder: Judiciary-Civil Rights-1957, Box 53, Gore Collection, Albert Gore Research Center (hereafter cited as Gore MSS).

74. Harry Byrd, "Statement 1 November 1955 on Segregation," Box 409, Harry Byrd Collection, Alderman Library (hereafter cited as Byrd MSS).

75. Byrd to James Kilpatrick, 8 October 1958, Box 245, "Kilpatrick, James J.," Byrd MSS.

76. Russell to W. C. Wright, 24 February 1960, Box 65, Folder 5, Russell MSS.

77. Russell, 16 March 1960, *Congressional Record*, 5721.

78. Ellender, 18 June 1964, *Congressional Record*, 14277.

79. Ellender, 18 June 1964, *Congressional Record*, 14277.

80. Long, 18 May 1964, *Congressional Record*, 11234.

81. Long, 18 May 1964, *Congressional Record*, 11234.

82. Thurmond, 14 April 1964, *Congressional Record*, 7903.

83. *The Citizens' Council*, August 1960, 3.

84. Johnston, 19 June 1964, Box 128, Folder: "Media Script 1964," Johnston MSS.

85. Long to Stephen B. Lemann, 26 June 1957, Box 22, Folder 25, Long MSS.

86. Long, 3 April 1964, *Congressional Record*, 6820; see also Long, 24 March 1964, *Congressional Record*, 6073.
87. Russell, 16 March 1964, *Congressional Record*, 5346.
88. Ervin to H. Shelton Smith, 11 April 1956, Folder 1125, Box 15, Ervin MSS.
89. Byrd, Public Statement, 25 July 1956, Folder: "Statement—July 26, 1956 on the so-called Civil Rights Legislation," Box 410, Byrd MSS.
90. Russell, 14 April 1964, *Congressional Record*, 7878.
91. Anthony P. Dunbar, *Against the Grain: Southern Radicals and Prophets, 1929–1959* (Charlottesville: University Press of Virginia, 1981); John Egerton, *Speak Now Against the Day: The Generation Before the Civil Rights Movement in the South* (Chapel Hill: University of North Carolina Press 1995); John T. Kneebone, *Southern Liberal Journalists and the Issue of Race, 1920–1944* (Chapel Hill: University of North Carolina Press 1996); Jennifer Ritterhouse, *Discovering the South: One Man's Travels through a Changing America in the 1930s* (Chapel Hill: University of North Carolina Press, 2017); Morton Sosna, *In Search of the Silent South: Southern Liberals and the Race Issue* (New York: Columbia University Press, 1977).
92. Russell, 18 June 1964, *Congressional Record*, 14299.

4. THE CONNECTING THREAD

1. Richard R. Beeman, *Plain, Honest Men: The Making of the American Constitution* (New York: Random House Trade Paperbacks, 2010); William J. Cooper, *Liberty and Slavery: Southern Politics to 1860* (New York: Alfred A. Knopf, 1983); Max Edling, *A Revolution in Favor of Government: Origins of the U.S. Constitution and the Making of the American State* (Oxford: Oxford University Press, 2008); Ellis, *Founding Brothers;* Pauline Maier, *Ratification: The People Debate the Constitution, 1787–1788* (New York: Simon & Schuster, 2014); Drew McCoy, *The Last of the Fathers: James Madison and the Republican Legacy* (New York: Cambridge University Press, 1989); Forrest McDonald, *Novus Ordo Seclorum: The Intellectual Origins of the Constitution* (Lawrence: University Press of Kansas, 1987); J. G. A. Pocock, *The Machiavellian Moment: Florentine Republican Thought and the Atlantic Republican Tradition* (Princeton, NJ: Princeton University Press, 1975); Rakove, *Original Meanings;* Gordon Wood, *The Creation of the American Republic, 1776–1787* (Chapel Hill: University of North Carolina Press, 1969); Wood, *The Radicalism of the American Revolution* (New York: Alfred A. Knopf, 1992).
2. Allan Kulikoff, *The Agrarian Origins of American Capitalism* (Charlottesville: University Press of Virginia, 1996); Angela Lakwete, *Inventing the Cotton Gin: Machine and Myth in Antebellum America* (Baltimore, MD: Johns Hopkins University Press, 2005).
3. William W. Freehling, "The Founding Fathers and Slavery." *The American Historical Review* 77, no. 1 (1972): 81–93.
4. Morgan, *American Slavery*.
5. Dew, *Review of the Debate*, 112.
6. Dew, *Review of the Debate*, 112-113.
7. George Fitzhugh, *Cannibals All! Or Slaves Without Masters* (Cambridge: Belknap Press, 1960), 201.
8. Dew, *Review of the Debate*, 113.
9. Robert Y. Hayne, 25 January 1830, *Register of Debates*, 48.

10. Quote taken from John Calhoun's "A Disquisition on Government" found in: Ross M. Lence, ed., *Union and Liberty: The Political Philosophy of John Calhoun* (Indianapolis: The Liberty Fund, 1992), 42.

11. John Calhoun, "A Disquisition on Government," *Union and Liberty*, 42.

12. Dew, *A Defense of Negro Slavery*, 223.

13. William Trescott, 4 July 1860, "The National Anniversary," *Southern Quarterly Review* (reprint), vol. 18, 1850 (New York: AMS Press, Inc, 1965), 180.

14. Robert Y. Hayne, 25 January 1830, *Register of Debates*, 48.

15. Davis, Resolutions on the Relations of the States, February 2, 1860, *The Papers of Jefferson Davis*, vol. 6, 273.

16. Bledsoe, *An Essay on Liberty and Slavery*, 382.

17. Dew, *Review of the Debate*, 66. See also: Sven Beckert, *Empire of Cotton: A Global History* (Cambridge, MA: Harvard University Press, 2013); Robin Blackburn, *The American Crucible: Slavery, Emancipation, and Human Rights* (New York: Verso, 2011); Johnson, *River of Dark Dreams*.

18. Fitzhugh, *Cannibals All!*, 190.

19. Fitzhugh, *Cannibals All!*, 254.

20. Hammond, "Slavery in the Light of Political Science," *Cotton is King*, 684.

21. William Kauffman Scarborough, *The Diary of Edmund Ruffin*, vol. 1, *Toward Independence, October 1856 - April 1861* (Baton Rouge: Louisiana State University Press, 1972), 229.

22. H. W. Brands, *Heirs of the Founders: The Epic Rivalry of Henry Clay, John Calhoun and Daniel Webster, the Second Generation of American Giants* (New York: Doubleday 2019); Margaret L. Coit, *John C. Calhoun: American Portrait* (Norwalk, CT: Easton Press, 1993); Richard E. Ellis, *The Union at Risk: Jacksonian Democracy, States' Rights and the Nullification Crisis* (New York: Oxford University Press, 1989); William W. Freehling, *Prelude to Civil War: The Nullification Controversy in South Carolina, 1816-1836* (New York: Oxford University, Press, 1995); John Niven, *John C. Calhoun and the Price of Union: A Biography* (Baton Rouge: Louisiana State University Press, 1993); Harry L. Watson, *Liberty and Power: The Politics of Jacksonian America* (New York: Hill and Wang, 2006).

23. Calhoun, "Discourse on the Constitution and Government of the United States," *Union and Liberty*, 268.

24. John C. Calhoun, "Exposition and Protest," *Union and Liberty*, 311–365.

25. Calhoun, 4 March 1850, *Congressional Globe*, 452.

26. Calhoun, "Speech on the Admission of California," 4 March 1850, *Union and Liberty*, 599.

27. Calhoun, "Speech on the Admission of California," 274

28. Calhoun, "Speech on the Admission of California," 586.

29. Calhoun, "A Disquisition on Government," *Union and Liberty*, 35.

30. Calhoun, "A Discourse on the Constitution and Government," *Union and Liberty*, 133.

31. Calhoun, "A Discourse on the Constitution," 275.

32. Calhoun, "A Discourse on the Constitution," 275–276.

33. Calhoun, "A Discourse on the Constitution, 277.

34. Calhoun, 4 March 1860, *Congressional Globe*, 455.

35. Edmund Ruffin, 18 November 1859, *Diary*, 357; see also: Eric H. Walthers, *The Fire-Eaters* (Baton Rouge: Louisiana State University Press, 1992).

36. Anthony J. Badger, ed., *New Deal/New South* (Fayetteville: University of Arkansas Press, 2007); Roger Biles, *The South and the New Deal* (Lexington: University of Kentucky Press, 1994); James Cobb, *Away Down South: A History of Southern Identity* (New York: Oxford University Press, 2005); Alison Collis Greene, *No Depression in Heaven: The Great Depression, the New Deal, and the Transformation of Religion in the Delta* (New York: Oxford University Press, 2016); William E. Leuchtenburg, *The White House Looks South: Franklin D. Roosevelt, Harry S. Truman, Lyndon B. Johnson* (Baton Rouge: Louisiana State University Press, 2005); William A. Link, *The Paradox of Southern Progressivism, 1880–1930* (Chapel Hill: University of North Carolina Press, 1992); Natalie J. Ring, *The Problem South: Region, Empire, and the New Liberal State, 1880–1930* (Athens University of Georgia Press, 2012); Jennifer Ritterhouse, *Growing Up Jim Crow: How Black and White Southern Children Learned Race* (Chapel Hill: University of North Carolina Press, 2006); Jeannie M. Whayne, *A New Plantation South: Land, Labor, and Federal Favor in Twentieth-Century Arkansas* (Charlottesville: University Press of Virginia, 1996); Lee L. Willis, *Southern Prohibition: Race, Reform, and Public Life in Middle Florida, 1821–1920* (Athens: University of Georgia Press, 2011).

37. Russell, 26 January 1938, *Congressional Record*, 1100.
38. Bilbo, 21 January 1938, *Congressional Record*, 881.
39. Bailey, 18 November 1937, *Congressional Record*, 113.
40. Byrnes, 11 January 1938, *Congressional Record*, 310.
41. Bilbo, 14 November 1942, *Congressional Record*, 8840.
42. Doxey, 18 November 1942, *Congressional Record*, 8945.
43. Russell, 17 November 1942, *Congressional Record*, 8903.
44. Doxey, 18 November 1942, *Congressional Record*, 8933.
45. Hill, 21 November 1942, *Congressional Record*, 9044.
46. Smith, 21 November 1942, *Congressional Record*, 9043.
47. Bilbo, 12 November 1943, *Congressional Record*, 9441.
48. Connally, 9 May 1944, *Congressional Record*, 4183.
49. Smith, 12 May 1944, *Congressional Record*, 4402.
50. Robertson, 2 August 1948, *Congressional Record*, 9621.
51. Hill, 28 January, 1946, *Congressional Record*, 455.

52. Byrd to Merle Way, 22 February 1961, Folder: Constituent Correspondence-1961-February, Box 306, Byrd MSS.

53. Ellender to E. F. Pawsat, 19 January 1953. Folder: Legislation-Civil Rights—1953, Box 660, Ellender MSS.

54. Ervin to P. W. Gaither, 16 July 1963, Folder #3823, Box 85, Ervin MSS.

55. Herman Talmadge speech before Richmond Kiwanis Club, 29 April 1957. Folder 3, Box 303, Talmadge MSS.

56. Thurmond to James Timmerman, 10 July 1961, Folder: Civil Rights 3 (Race Relations), Box 3 (1961), Thurmond MSS.

57. Thurmond to C. E. Tollison, 24 August 1962, Folder: CR 3; Folder I, Box 3 (1962), Thurmond MSS.

58. Thurmond to Thomas R. Waring, 4 September 1957. Folder: Legislation: Civil Rights Filibuster, Folder 1, 1957 Box 4, Thurmond MSS.

59. Hill, 23 March 1964, *Congressional Record*, 5956.
60. Tower, 13 April 1964, *Congressional Record*, 7776.
61. Ervin, 8 April 1964, *Congressional Record*, 7224.

62. Johnston, 21 March 1964, *Congressional Record*, 6045.
63. Eastland, 21 March 1964, *Congressional Record*, 5865.
64. Long, 13 March 1964, *Congressional Record*, 5220.
65. John Tower, 19 March 1964, *Congressional Record*, 5725.
66. Hill, 20 April 1964, *Congressional Record*, 8444.
67. Byrd, 20 May 1964, *Congressional Record*, 11522.
68. Long, 14 April 1964, *Congressional Record*, 7907.
69. George McClellan, 11 May 1965, *Congressional Record*, 10524.
70. Hill, 9 March 1964, *Congressional Record*, 4759.
71. Bilbo, 2 February 1938, *Congressional Record*, 1388.
72. Russell, 14 April 1964, *Congressional Record*, 7879. Others such as Alabama's John Sparkman emphasized that busing provisions should be included in the bill so that it was something other than a sectional proposal (Sparkman, 21 April 1964, *Congressional Record*, 8616).
73. Eastland, 22 March 1965, *Congressional Record*, 5871.
74. Ervin, 23 April 1965, *Congressional Record*, 8352.
75. Robertson, 28 April 1965, *Congressional Record*, 8826.
76. Thurmond, 3 May 1965, *Congressional Record*, 9236.
77. Stennis, 4 May 1965, *Congressional Record*, 9335.
78. Holland, 7 May 1965, *Congressional Record*, 9938.
79. Eastland, 20 May 1965, *Congressional Record*, 11089.

5. THE DIFFERENCE THIS TIME

1. Daina Ramey Berry, *The Price for Their Pound of Flesh: The Value of the Enslaved, from Womb to Grave, in the Building of a Nation* (New York: Random House, 2018); Robert William Fogel and Stanley Engerman, *Time on the Cross: The Economics of American Negro Slavery*, 2 vols. (Boston: Little, Brown, 1974); Joshua D. Rothman, The *Ledger and the Chain: How Domestic Slave Traders Shaped America* (Basic Books, 2021); Calvin Schermerhorn, *The Business of Slavery and the Rise of American Capitalism, 1815–1860* (New Haven: Yale University Press, 2015); Samuel H. Williamson & Louis P. Cain, "Measuring Slavery in 2020 Dollars," MeasuringWorth, 2021.URL: www.measuringworth.com/slavery.php; Gavin Wright, *Slavery and American Economic Development* (Baton Rouge: Louisiana State University Press, 2006).

2. Blackmon, *Slavery by Another Name;* Mary Ellen Curtin, *Black Prisoners and Their World: Alabama, 1865–1900* (Charlottesville: University Press of Virginia, 2000); Alex Lichtenstein, *Twice the Work of Free Labor: The Political Economy of Convict Labor in the New South* (New York: Verso, 1996); Mancini, *One Dies, Get Another;* David M. Oschinsky, *Worse Than Slavery: Parchman Farm and the Ordeal of Jim Crow Justice* (New York: Free Press, 1996).

3. Jules Abels, *Man of Fire: John Brown and the Cause of Liberty* (New York: The Macmillan Company, 1971); Paul Finkelman, *His Soul Goes Marching On: Responses to John Brown and the Harpers Ferry Raid* (Charlottesville: University Press of Virginia, 1995); Tony Horwitz, *Midnight Rising: John Brown and the Raid That Sparked the Civil War* (Detroit, MI: Gale/Cengage, 2012); Stephen B. Oates, *To Purge This Land With Blood: A Biography of John Brown*; David S. Reynolds, *John Brown, Abolitionist: The Man Who Killed*

Slavery, Sparked the Civil War, and Seeded Civil Rights (New York: Alfred A. Knopf, 2006); *Times Picayune*, 26 October 1869, 4.

4. New York Democratic Vigilance Association, *Rise and Progress of the Bloody Outbreak at Harpers Ferry* (New York, 1859), 18, 4.

5. *Times-Picayune*, 8 November 1859, 1.

6. *Times-Picayune*, 16 November 1859, 1

7. *New York Times*, 27 October 1859, 4.

8. *New York Times*, 21 November 1859, 4

9. Allan Nevins, *The Emergence of Lincoln*, vol. 2 (New York: Charles Scribner's Sons, 1950) 98-101; Oates, *To Purge this Land*, 308-356.

10. *Times Picayune*, 4 December 1859, 5. See also: "What Shall the South Do?," Wilmington *Daily Herald*, December 5, 1859, *Civil War Era NC*, https://cwnc.omeka.chass.ncsu.edu/items/show/11, accessed January 27, 2022.

11. *Times Picayune*, 8 December 1859, 9.

12. Nevins, *The Emergence of Lincoln*, 102-112; Oates, *To Purge this Land*, 320-324; Potter, *The Impending Crisis*, 380-384.

13. R. R. Butler, *Speech of Hon. R. R. Butler, Representative from Carter and Johnson Counties, in the House of Representatives, Upon the Resolutions Introduced by Mr. Bayless, in Reference to the Harper's Ferry Insurrection* (Nashville, Tennessee, 1859), 1-2.

14. *Frederick Douglass Papers*, 17 February 1860, 2.

15. New Orleans, *Daily Crescent*, 20 December 1860, 1.

16. Iverson, 6 December 1859, *Congressional Globe*, 15.

17. *New York Times*, 5 December 1859, 4.

18. Clay, December 13, 1859, *Congressional Globe*, 125.

19. "The Position of the Cotton States," Louisville, *Daily Courier*, 20 December 1860, in *Southern Editorials on Secession*, ed. Dwight Lowell Dumond (New York: The Century Co., 1931), 359.

20. *Daily True Delta*, 23 November 1860, 4.

21. *Daily True Delta*, 5 December 1860, 2.

22. See: "The Election Returns," *Richmond Semi-Weekly Examiner*, 9 November 1860 and "A Few Reflections on Secession," *The Daily Herald*, 9 November 1860, in *Southern Editorials*, 223-228. See also: Dwight Dumond, *The Secession Movement, 1860-1861* (New York: Macmillan, 1931); Douglas R. Egerton, *Year of Meteors: Stephen Douglas, Abraham Lincoln, and the Election That Brought on the Civil War* (New York: Bloomsbury Press, 2014); James A. Fuller, *The Election of 1860 Reconsidered* (Kent, OH: The Kent State University Press, 2012); Michael S. Green, *Lincoln and The Election of 1860* (Carbondale: Southern Illinois University Press, 2020); Michael Fitzgibbon Holt, *The Election of 1860: "A Campaign Fraught with Consequences"* (Lawrence: University Press of Kansas, 2017); Harold Holzer, *Lincoln President-Elect: Abraham Lincoln and the Great Secession Winter 1860-1861* (New York: Simon & Schuster, 2009).

23. Dumond, *Southern Editorials*, 228.

24. *Times-Picayune*, 18 December 1860, 9.

25. Clingman, 4 December 1860, *Congressional Globe*, 3.

26. *Times-Picayune*, 18 December 1860, 9.

27. *Daily True Delta*, 30 December 1860, 2.

28. Walter L. Buenger, *Secession and the Union in Texas* (Austin: University of Texas Press, 2013); Steven A. Channing, *Crisis of Fear: Secession in South Carolina* (New York:

Norton, 1974); Charles B. Dew, *Apostles of Disunion: Southern Secession Commissioners and the Causes of the Civil War* (Charlottesville: University of Virginia Press, 2016); William W. Freehling and Craig M. Simpson, *Secession Debated: Georgia's Showdown in 1860* (New York: Oxford University Press, 1992); Jon L. Wakelyn, *Southern Pamphlets on Secession, November 1860–April 1861* (Chapel Hill: University of North Carolina Press, 2009).

29. *Times-Picayune*, 18 December 1860, 9
30. *Daily True Delta*, 30 December 1860, 2.
31. Thomas Clingman, 4 December 1960, *Congressional Globe*, 5.
32. Jefferson Davis, 10 December 1860, *Congressional Globe*, 30.
33. *Daily True Delta*, 1 January 1861, 4.
34. Iverson, 13 December 1860, *Congressional Globe*, 49–50.
35. *Times-Picayune*, 13 January 1861, 1.
36. Davis, 14 December 1860, To Our Constituents, *The Papers of Jefferson Davis, vol. 6* (Baton Rouge: Louisiana State University Press, 2014), 377.
37. Iverson, 5 December 1860, *Congressional Globe*, 11.
38. Davis, 21 January 1861, *Congressional Globe*, 487.
39. Davis, *Congressional Globe*, 487.
40. Mallory, 21 January 1861, *Congressional Globe*, 486.
41. *Daily True Delta*, 22 February 1861, 6.
42. Davis, 18 February 1861, Inaugural Address, *The Papers of Jefferson Davis*, vol. 7, 49.
43. David Detzerm, *Dissonance: The Turbulent Days between Fort Sumter and Bull Run* (Orlando: Harvest Books, 2007); Harry V. Jaffa and Allen C. Guelzo, *A New Birth of Freedom: Abraham Lincoln and the Coming of the Civil War* (New York: Rowman & Littlefield, 2018); James M. McPherson, *Abraham Lincoln* (Oxford: Oxford University Press, 2009).
44. Gregory P. Downs, *Declaration of Dependence: The Long Reconstruction of Popular Politics in the South, 1861–1908* (Chapel Hill: University of North Carolina Press, 2011); Downs, *After Appomattox: Military Occupation and the Ends of War* (Cambridge, MA: Harvard University Press, 2015); James K. Hogue, *Uncivil War: Five New Orleans Street Battles and the Rise of Radical Reconstruction* (Baton Rouge: Louisiana State University Press, 2006); Heather Cox Richardson, *The Death of Reconstruction: Race, Labor, and Politics in the Post-Civil War North, 1865–1901* (Cambridge, MA: Harvard University Press, 2001); Richardson, *West from Appomattox: The Reconstruction of America after the Civil War* (New Haven: Yale University Press, 2007); Richard White, *The Republic for Which It Stands: The United States during Reconstruction and the Gilded Age, 1865–1896* (New York: Oxford University Press, 2017).
45. Hill, 11 May 1944, *Congressional Record*, 4321.
46. Byrd to Cecil Graves, 15 December 1953, Box 199, Folder: "G-Miscellaneous," Byrd MSS.
47. Johnston to G. P. Hill, 9 July 1954, Folder: "Legislation 1954, Civil Rights School Segregation," Box 40, Johnston MSS.
48. Ervin to J. H. Burke, 23 August 1954, Folder #279, Box 4, Ervin MSS; CE: Sam Ervin to Frances Lacey, 15 June 1954, Folder 278, Box 4, Ervin MSS.
49. Gore to James D. McDuffie, 23 July 1954, B 46, Folder: "Judiciary-Civil Rights 1of 1," Gore MSS.
50. Ellender to Reuben T. Douglas, 3 June 1954, Folder: "Legislation-Civil Rights-1954," Box 668, Ellender MSS.
51. Michael J. Klarman, *From Jim Crow to Civil Rights: The Supreme Court and the*

Struggle for Racial Equality (New York: Oxford University Press, 2006); Richard Kluger, *Simple Justice: The History of Brown v. Board of Education and Black America's Struggle for Equality* (New York: Alfred A. Knopf, 2011); Mark Tushnet, *Making Civil Rights Law: Thurgood Marshall and the Supreme Court, 1936–1961* (New York: Oxford University Press, 1996); Williams, *Eyes on the Prize*, 29–34.

52. Numan V. Bartley, *The Rise of Massive Resistance: Race and Politics in the South During the 1950's* (Baton Rouge: Louisiana State University Press, 1999); David L. Chappell, *A Stone of Hope: Prophetic Religion and the Death of Jim Crow* (Chapel Hill: University of North Carolina Press, 2004); Pete Daniel, *Lost Revolutions: The South in the 1950s* (Chapel Hill: University of North Carolina Press, 2000); Brian J. Daugherity and Charles C. Bolton, *With All Deliberate Speed Implementing Brown v. Board of Education* (Fayetteville: University of Arkansas Press, 2011); Matthew D. Lassiter and Andrew B. Lewis, *The Moderates' Dilemma: Massive Resistance to School Desegregation in Virginia* (Charlottesville: University Press of Virginia, 1998); Elizabeth Gillespie McRae, *Mothers of Massive Resistance: White Women and the Politics of White Supremacy* (New York: Oxford University Press, 2020).

53. Thurmond to Felix Morley, 3 February 1956, Folder: "Segregation Folder 1," Box 12, Thurmond MSS.

54. John Kyle Day, *The Southern Manifesto: Massive Resistance and the Fight To Preserve Segregation* (Jackson: University of Mississippi Press, 2014); Finley, *Delaying the Dream*, 142–154

55. For the text of the Manifesto see: *Congressional Record*, 12 March 1956, 4169.

56. Fulbright to Thad N. Marsh, 17 Marsh 1956, Folder 1 Series 71, Box 10, Fulbright MSS.

57. Ervin to Fred B. Helms, 13 March 1956, Folder 1120, Box 15, Ervin MSS.

58. See Joseph Crespino, *Strom Thurmond's America* (New York: Hill and Wang, 2013); John Kyle Day, *The Southern Manifesto: Massive Resistance and the Fight to Preserve Segregation* (Jackson: University Press of Mississippi, 2017); Finley, *Delaying the Dream*.

59. Gore to Waddy Currin, 5 January 1957, Special Series 20, Drawers 31–32, Folder: "Segregation," Gore MSS.

60. Gore to Russell M. D. Bruce, 29 March 1956, Special Series 20, Drawers 31–32, Folder: "Segregation," Gore MSS.

61. Ellender to Frank Voelker, 28 February 1956, Folder: "Legislation-Civil Rights-1956," Box 668, Ellender MSS.

62. Ellender to Frank Voelker, 28 February 1956, Folder: "Legislation-Civil Rights-1956," Box 668, Ellender MSS.

63. Christopher Myers Asch, *The Senator and the Sharecropper: The Freedom Struggles of James O. Eastland and Fannie Lou Hammer* (Chapel Hill: University of North Carolina Press, 2011); Stephen E. Berrey, *The Jim Crow Routine: Everyday Performances of Race, Civil Rights, and Segregation in Mississippi* (Chapel Hill: University of North Carolina Press, 2015); Lance Hill, *The Deacons for Defense: Armed Resistance and the Civil Rights Movement* (Chapel Hill: University of North Carolina Press, 2004); J. Todd Moye, *Let the People Decide: Black Freedom and White Resistance Movements in Sunflower County, Mississippi, 1945–1986* (Chapel Hill: University of North Carolina Press, 2004); Stanley Nelson, *Klan of Devils: The Murder of a Black Louisiana Deputy Sheriff* (Baton Rouge: Louisiana State University Press, 2021).

64. Newspaper, *Citizens' Council*, May 1956, 2.

65. Newspaper, *Citizens' Council*, February 1959, 2.

66. Byrd, "Statement 25 September 1957 on Sending Federal Troops into Arkansas to Enforce School Integration," Box 410, Byrd MSS.

67. Pamphlet, Jack Ricau, "Integration: Threat to Freedom and How to Defeat It," 1957, 3, Box 2, Folder 6, Plaquemines Parish—Rod Lincoln Collection.

68. Borstelmann, *The Cold War and the Color Line;* Dudziak, *Cold War Civil Rights;* Brenda Gayle Plummer, *Rising Wind: Black Americans and U.S. Foreign Affairs, 1936-1960* (Chapel Hill: University of North Carolina Press, 1996); Jeff R. Woods, *Black Struggle, Red Scare: Segregation and Anti-Communism in the South, 1948-1968* (Baton Rouge: Louisiana State University Press, 2003).

69. *The Citizens' Council,* May 1956, 2. See also: *The Citizens' Council:* October 1957, 2; September 1958, 4; November 1958, 2; May 1959, 2; July–August 1961, 4.

70. C. E. Vetter to John Rarick, 17 December 1965, Box 99, Folder 420, John Rarick Collection, Center for Southeast Louisiana Studies.

71. Russell to W. T. Duncan, 29 January 1938, Folder 4, Box 2 Russell MSS.

72. Russell to May Gee, 23 June 1964, Folder 3, Box 8, Russell MSS.

73. Russell to Earnest Trapnell, 27 July 1964, Folder 1, Box 36, Russell MSS.

74. Russell to Guy Hornsby, 25 July 1964, Folder 1, Box 36, Russell MSS.

75. Russell to D. R. Bryan, 19 June 1964, Folder 4, Box 38, Russell MSS.

76. Sparkman to J. A. Norris, 2 June 1964, 66A, 89, Box 35, (no folder in box), Sparkman MSS.

77. Byrd to W. F. Barclay, Folder: July Constituent Correspondence, Box 347, Byrd MSS.

78. Hill to William I. Byrd, 23 June 1964, Box 496, Folder 162, Hill MSS.

79. Ervin to C. L. Miller, 23 June 1964, Folder 4438, Box 100, Ervin MSS.

80. Thurmond to R. L. Prince, 24 June 1964, Box 6, Folder: "Civil Rights 1, Folder 23," Thurmond MSS.

81. Maarten Zwiers, *Senator James Eastland: Mississippi's Jim Crow Democracy* (Baton Rouge: Louisiana State University, 2015).

82. Cohadas, *Strom Thurmond and the Politics of Southern Change;* Crespino, *Strom Thurmond's America;* Finley, *Delaying the Dream,* 182-188; 266-269.

CONCLUSION

1. William Lowndes Yancey, *Speech of the Hon. William L. Yancey, of Alabama: Delivered in the National Democratic Convention, Charleston, April 28th, 1860. With the Protest of the Alabama Delegation* (Charleston, SC, 1860), 7.

2. Fulbright to Alvey Edwards, 22 March 1954, BCN 19, 14A, Fulbright MSS.

3. Russell to Walter Smith, 10 July 1964, Box 36, Folder 8, Russell MSS.

4. See Kruse, *White Flight;* McRae, *Mothers of Massive Resistance;* and Lassiter, *The Silent Majority.*

5. Kruse, *White Flight.* See also Keith Finley, "White Flight and the Alteration of the Southern Political Narrative: Louisiana's Sixth District Elects a Congressman, 1966," *Louisiana History 5,* 61, no. 1 (Winter 2020): 71-106.

BIBLIOGRAPHY

MANUSCRIPT COLLECTIONS

Albert Gore Center, Middle Tennessee State University
    Albert Gore Sr. Senate Papers
Alderman Library, University of Virginia
    Harry F. Byrd Papers
Allen J. Ellender Memorial Library, Nicholls State University
    Allen J. Ellender Papers
Center for Regional Studies, Archives, Southeastern Louisiana University
    AFL-CIO Collection
    Hebert Collection
    James H. Morrison Collection
    John R. Rarick Collection
    Plaquemines Parish—Rod Lincoln Collection
Claude Pepper Library, Florida State University
    Claude D. Pepper Papers
    Spessard L. Holland Papers
Hill Memorial Library, Louisiana State University
    Overton Brooks Papers
    Russell B. Long Papers
Robert Mann Collection
Library of Congress, Washington, D.C.
    Thomas Connally Papers
Lyndon Baines Johnson Presidential Library
    Lyndon B. Johnson Papers
        House of Representatives Papers
        LBJ Archives: Congressional Files
        LBJ Archives: Famous Names

LBJ Archives: Selected Names
Pre-Presidential Confidential Files
Senate Papers
Oral History Collection
McCain Library, University of Southern Mississippi
Theodore G. Bilbo Papers
Mullins Library, University of Arkansas J. William Fulbright Papers
Richard B. Russell Library, University of Georgia
Richard B. Russell Papers
Herman E. Talmadge Papers
South Caroliniana Library, University of South Carolina
Olin Johnston Papers
Southern Historical Collection, University of North Carolina
Sam J. Ervin Papers
Strom Thurmond Institute, Clemson University
James F. Byrnes Papers J. Strom Thurmond Papers
W.S. Hoole Special Collections Library, University of Alabama
Lister Hill Papers
John Sparkman Papers

GOVERNMENT PUBLICATIONS

Congressional Globe
Congressional Record
History of Congress

SELECTED PROSLAVERY AND
SEGREGATIONIST LITERATURE

Adams, Nehemiah. *A South-Side View of Slavery; or Three Months at the South in 1854.* Port Washington: Kennikat Press, 1969.
Bilbo, Theodore G. *Take Your Choice: Separation or Mongrelization.* Poplarville: Dream House Publishing Company, 1947.
Bledsoe, Albert Taylor. *An Essay on Liberty and Slavery.* Philadelphia: J.P. Lippincott and Co., 1856.
Bruce, Philip Alexander. *The Plantation Negro as Freeman: Observations on His Character, Condition, and Prospects in Virginia.* New York: G. P. Putnam's Sons, 1889.
Butler, Roderick Randum. *Speech of Hon. R. R. Butler, Representative from Carter and Johnson Counties, in the House of Representatives, Upon the Resolutions introduced by Mr. Bayless, in Reference to the Harper's Ferry Insurrection.* Nashville, Tennessee, 1859.

Byrnes, James F. *All in One Lifetime*. New York: Harper, 1958.
Calhoun, John C. and Ross M. Lance, ed. *Union and Liberty: The Political Philosophy of John C. Calhoun*. Liberty Fund, Inc., Indianapolis, 1992.
Connally, Tom. *My Name is Tom Connally*. New York: Thomas Y. Crowell Company, 1952.
Davis, Jefferson, Mary Seaton Dix, and Lynda Lasswell Crist. *The Papers of Jefferson Davis*. vol. 6. Baton Rouge: Louisiana State University Press, 1989.
Dew, Thomas R. *Review of the Debate in the Virginia Legislature of 1831 and 1832*. Richmond: T. W. White, 1832.
Dixon Jr, Thomas. *The Leopard's Spots: A Romance of the White Man's Burden, 1865-1900*. New York: A Wessels Company, 1906.
Dumond, Dwight L, ed. *Southern Editorials on Secession*. New York: The Century Company, 1931.
Elliott, E. N. ed. *Cotton is King and Proslavery Arguments: Comprising the Writings of Hammond, Harper, Christy, Stringfellow, Hodge, Bledsoe, and Cartwright, on This Important Subject*. Augusta: Pritchard, Abbott, and Loomis, 1860.
Estes, Matthew. *A Defense of Negro Slavery as it Exists in the United States*. Montgomery: Press of the Alabama Journal, 1846.
Farrand, Max, ed. *The Records of the Federal Convention of 1787*. vol. 2. New Haven: Yale University Press, 1911.
Fitzhugh, George. *Cannibals All! Or Slaves Without Masters*. Cambridge: Belknap Press, 1960.
———. "Southern Thought." *DeBow's Review*. vol. 23 (October 1857): 276.
Grayson, William J. *The Hireling and the Slave, Chicora, and Other Poems*. Charleston: McCarter and Company, 1856.
Hammond, James Henry. *Gov. Hammond's Letters on Southern Slavery: Addressed to Thomas Clarkson, the English Abolitionist*. Charleston: Walker and Burke Printers, 1845.
Harper, William. *Memoir on Slavery Read Before the Society for the Advancement of Learning of South Carolina at Its Annual Meeting at Columbia, 1837*. Charleston: James and Burges, 1838.
Harper, William, et al. *The Pro-Slavery Argument as Maintained by the Most Distinguished Writers of the Southern States: Containing the Several Essays, on the subject, of Chancellor Harper, Governor Hammond, Dr. Simms, and Professor Dew*. Philadelphia: Lippincott, Grambo, and Co., 1853.
Hoffman, Frederick Ludwig. *Race Traitors and Tendencies of the American Negro*. New York: Macmillan, 1896.
Kingsley, Z. *A Treatise on the Patriarchal, or Co-Operative, System of Society as It Exists in Some Governments, and Colonies in America: And in the United States, under the Name of Slavery, with Its Necessity and Advantages*. [Publisher not identified], 1829.
Lee, G. Avery. *Messages From the Second Annual Conference on Human Relations*. Forest Hills Baptist Church. Raleigh, North Carolina: March 5-6, 1963.

———. *Some Quiet Thoughts on a Turbulent Issue*. Nashville: Christian Life Commission, 1956.

New York Democratic Vigilance Association. *Rise and Progress of the Bloody Outbreak at Harpers Ferry*. New York, 1859.

Pollard, Edward A. *Black Diamonds Gathered in the Darkey Homes of the South*. New York: Pudney and Russell, 1859.

Priest, Josiah. *Bible Defence of Slavery: or the Origin, History, and Fortunes of the Negro Race*. Louisville: J.F. Brennan, 1851.

Ruffin, Edmund, and William Kauffman Scarborough. *The Diary of Edmund Ruffin. vol. 1*. Baton Rouge: Louisiana State University Press, 1990.

Talmadge, Herman E. *You and Segregation*. Birmingham: Vulcan Press Incorporated, 1955.

Taylor, Richard. *Destruction and Reconstruction: Personal Experiences of the Late War*. New York: D. Appleton and Company, 1879.

Thrasher, J. B. *Slavery: A Divine Institution*. Port Gibson, MS: Southern Reveille Book and Job Office, 1861.

Twelve Southerners. *I'll Take My Stand: The South and the Agrarian Tradition*. Baton Rouge: Louisiana State University Press, 1977.

Yancey, William Lowndes. *Speech of the Hon. William L. Yancey, of Alabama: Delivered in the National Democratic Convention, Charleston, April 28th, 1860. With the Protest of the Alabama Delegation*. Charleston, SC, 1860.

Walker, David. *Walker's Appeal in Four Articles*. Boston, 1830.

NEWSPAPERS

Atlanta Constitution
Niles' Weekly Register (Baltimore)
States-Item (Baton Rouge)
Morning Advocate (Baton Rouge)
Dallas Morning News
Citizens' Council (Jackson)
Kansas City Star
Commercial Appeal (Memphis)
Bee (New Orleans)
Daily Crescent (New Orleans)
Daily True Delta (New Orleans)
Debow's Review (New Orleans)
Picayune (New Orleans)
New York Times
Richmond Examiner
Shreveport Journal
Southern Quarterly Review
Washington Post

ARTICLES

Billington, Monroe. "Lyndon Johnson and Blacks: The Early Years." *Journal of Negro History* 62 (January 1977): 26–42.

Brueggemann, John. "Racial Considerations and Social Policy in the 1930s." *Social Science History* 26 (Spring 2002): 139–177.

Bullock, Charles S., III, and David W. Brady. "Party, Constituency, and Roll-Call Voting in the U.S. Senate." *Legislative Studies Quarterly* 8 (February, 1983): 29–43.

"The Committee System—Congress at Work." *Congressional Digest* 34 (February 1955): 47–49, 64.

Coombs, John C. "The Phases of Conversion: A New Chronology for the Rise of Slavery in Early Virginia." *William and Mary Quarterly* 68 (July 2011): 332–60.

Dalfiume, Richard M. "The 'Forgotten Years' of the Negro Revolution." *Journal of American History* 55 (June, 1968): 90–106.

Davidson, Bill. "Lyndon Johnson: Can A Southerner Be Elected President?" *Look* 23 (August 1959): 63–71.

Divine, Robert A. "The Cold War and the Election of 1948." *Journal of American History* 59 (June, 1972): 90–110.

Finkle, Lee. "The Conservative Aims of Militant Rhetoric: Black Protest During World War II." *Journal of American History* 60 (December, 1973): 692–713.

Finley, Keith M. "White Flight and the Alteration of the Southern Political Narrative: Louisiana's Sixth District Elects a Congressman, 1966." *Louisiana History* 5, 61, no. 1 (Winter 2020): 71–106.

Fleisher, Richard. "Explaining the Change in Roll-Call Voting Behavior of Southern Democrats." *Journal of Politics* 55 (May 1993): 327–341.

Freehling, William W. "The Founding Fathers and Slavery." *American Historical Review* 77, no. 1 (1972): 81–93.

Gray, Charles H. "A Scale Analysis of the Voting Records of Senators Kennedy, Johnson, and Goldwater, 1957–1960." *American Political Science Review* 55 (September 1965): 615–621.

Hall, Jacquelyn Dowd. "The Long Civil Rights Movement and the Political Uses of the Past." *Journal of American History* 91 (March 2005): 1233–1263.

Hood, M. V., III, Quentin Kidd, and Irwin L. Morris, "Of Byrd[s] and Bumpers: Using Democratic Senators to Analyze Political Change in the South, 1960–1995." *American Journal of Political Science* 43 (April 1999): 465–487.

Huitt, Ralph K. "Democratic Leadership in the Senate." *American Political Science Review* 55 (June 1961): 333–344.

Kaye, Anthony E. "The Second Slavery: Modernity in the Nineteenth Century South and the Atlantic World." *Journal of Southern History* 75 (August 2009): 627–650.

Klarman, Michael J. "How Brown Changed Race Relations: The Backlash Thesis." *Journal of American History* 81 (June 1994): 81–118.

Meier, August, and John H. Bracey Jr. "The NAACP as a Reform Movement, 1909–1965: To Reach the Conscience of America." *Journal of Southern History* 59 (February 1993): 3–30.

Poole, Keith T. and R. Steven Daniels. "Ideology, Party, and Voting in the U.S. Congress, 1959–1980." *American Political Science Review* 79 (June 1985): 373–399.

Rable, George C. "The South and the Politics of Anti-Lynching Legislation, 1920–1940." *Journal of Southern History* 51 (May 1985): 201–220.
Rockman, Seth. "What Makes the History of Capitalism Newsworthy?" *Journal of the Early Republic* 34 (Fall 2014): 439–466.
Shuman, Howard E. "Senate Rules and the Civil Rights Bill: A Case Study." *American Political Science Review* 51 (December 1957): 955–977.
Sitkoff, Harvard. "Harry Truman and the Election of 1948: The Coming of Age of Civil Rights in American Politics." *Journal of Southern History* 37 (November 1971): 597–616.
Stevenson, Brenda E. "What's Love Got to Do With It? Concubinage and Enslaved Black Women and Girls in the Antebellum South." *Journal of African American History* 98 (Winter 2013): 99–125.
Whitby, Kenny J. and Franklin D. Gilliam Jr. "A Longitudinal Analysis of Competing Explanations for the Transformation of Southern Congressional Politics." *Journal of Politics* 53 (May 1991): 504–518.
Williamson, Joel. "Wounds Not Scars: Lynching the National Conscience and the American Historian." *Journal of American History* 83 (March 1997): 1221–1253.
Wood, Randall B. "Dixie's Dove: J. William Fulbright, the Vietnam War, and the American South." *Journal of Southern History* 60 (August 1994): 533–52.
Wynn, Neil A. "The Impact of the Second World War on the American Negro." *Journal of Negro History* 6 (1971): 42–53.

BOOKS

Abels, Jules. *Man on Fire: John Brown and the Cause of Liberty*. New York: Macmillan, 1971.
Ader, Emile B. *The Dixiecrat Movement: Its Role in Third Party Politics*. Washington: Public Affairs Press, 1955.
Allen, Barbara, and Thomas J. Schelereth. *Sense of Place: American Regional Cultures*. Lexington: University of Kentucky Press, 1992.
Allmendinger, David, Jr. *Nat Turner and the Rising in Southampton County*. Baltimore: Johns Hopkins University Press, 2014.
Ambrose, Stephen. *Eisenhower: Soldier and President*. New York: Simon and Schuster, 1990.
Anderson, Benedict. *Imagined Communities: Reflections on the Origin and Spread of Nationalism*. New York: Verso, 2006.
Andrews, William L. *Slavery and Class in the American South: A Generation of Slave Narrative Testimony, 1840–1865*. New York: Oxford University Press, 2019.
Aptheker, Herbert. *Nat Turner's Slave Rebellion: Together with the Full Text of*

the So-Called "Confessions" of Nat Turner Made in Prison in 1831. New York: Humanities Press, 1966.

Arensen, Eric. *Waterfront Workers of New Orleans: Race, Class, and Politics.* Urbana, University of Illinois Press, 1994.

Asch, Christopher Myers. *The Senator and the Sharecropper: The Freedom Struggles of James O. Eastland and Fannie Lou Hammer.* Chapel Hill: University of North Carolina Press, 2011.

Ashmore, Henry S. *Hearts and Minds: The Anatomy of Racism from Roosevelt to Reagan.* New York: McGraw-Hill, 1982.

Ashworth, John. *Slavery, Capitalism, and Politics in the Antebellum Republic, 1820–1850.* New York: Cambridge University Press, 1995.

Ayers, Edward L. *The Promise of the New South: Life After Reconstruction.* New York: Oxford University Press, 1992.

Ayers, Edward L., et al. *All Over the Map: Rethinking American Regions.* Baltimore: Johns Hopkins University Press, 1996.

Badger, Anthony J. *The New Deal: The Depression Years, 1933–1940.* New York: Hill and Wang, 1988.

———, ed. *New Deal/New South: An Anthony J. Badger Reader.* Fayetteville: University of Arkansas Press, 2007.

Baptist, Edward E. *The Half Has Never Been Told: Slavery and the Making of American Capitalism.* New York: Basic Books, 2017.

Barnard, William D. *Dixiecrats and Democrats: Alabama Politics, 1942–1950.* Tuscaloosa: University of Alabama Press, 1974.

Bartley, Numan V. *The New South, 1945–1980.* Baton Rouge: Louisiana State University Press, 1995.

———. *The Rise of Massive Resistance: Race and Politics in the South During the 1950's.* Baton Rouge: Louisiana State University Press, 1999.

Beals, Melba. *White is A State of Mind: A Memoir.* New York: G.P. Putnam's Sons, 1999.

Beckert, Sven, and Seth Rockman. *Slavery's Capitalism: A New History of American Economic Development.* Philadelphia: University of Pennsylvania Press, 2018.

Becnel, Thomas A. *Senator Allen Ellender of Louisiana: A Biography.* Baton Rouge: Louisiana State University Press, 1995.

Beeman, Richard R. *Plain, Honest Men: The Making of the American Constitution.* New York: Random House, 2010.

Bell, Inge Powell. *CORE and the Strategy of Nonviolence.* New York: Random House, 1968.

Benedict, Michael L. *A Compromise of Principle: Congressional Republicans and Reconstruction, 1863–1869.* New York: Norton, 1974.

Berlin, Ira. *Many Thousands Gone: The First Two Centuries of Slavery in North America.* Cambridge, MA: Belknap Press of Harvard University Press, 1998.

———. *Slaves No More: Three Essays on Emancipation and the Civil War.* New York: Cambridge University Press, 1992.

Berlin, Ira, and Ronald Hoffman, eds. *Slavery and Freedom in the Age of the American Revolution.* Charlottesville: University of Virginia Press, 1983.

Berman, Daniel M. *A Bill Becomes Law: Congress Enacts Civil Rights Legislation.* Second Edition. New York: The MacMillan Co., 1966.

Berman, William C. *The Politics of Civil Rights in the Truman Administration.* Columbus: Ohio State University Press, 1970.

Berrey, Stephen E. *The Jim Crow Routine: Everyday Performances of Race, Civil Rights, and Segregation in Mississippi.* Chapel Hill: University of North Carolina Press, 2015.

Berry, Daina Ramey. *The Price for Their Pound of Flesh: The Value of the Enslaved, from Womb to Grave, in the Building of a Nation.* New York: Random House, 2018.

Berry, Daina Ramey, and Leslie M. Harris., eds. *Sexuality and Slavery: Reclaiming Intimate Histories in the Americas.* Athens: University of Georgia Press, 2018.

Berry, Mary Frances. *Black Resistance/White Law: A History of Constitutional Racism in America.* New York: Appleton-Century-Crofts, 1971.

Best, Wallace. *Passionately Human, No Less Divine: Religion and Black Culture in Chicago.* Princeton, NJ: Princeton University Press, 2005.

Biles, Roger. *The South and the New Deal.* Lexington: University of Kentucky Press, 1994.

Billings, Warren M. *Sir William Berkeley and the Forging of Colonial Virginia.* Baton Rouge: Louisiana State University Press, 2004.

Blackburn, Robin. *The American Crucible: Slavery, Emancipation, and Human Rights.* New York: Verso, 2011.

Blackmon, Douglas A. *Slavery by Another Name: The Re-Enslavement of Black Americans from the Civil War to World War II.* New York: Doubleday, 2008.

Blassingame, John W. *The Slave Community: Plantation Life in the Antebellum South.* New York: Oxford University Press, 1972.

Blum, John Morton. *V Was For Victory: Politics and American Culture During World War II.* New York: Harcourt Brace Jovanovich, 1976.

Blumberg, Rhoda Lois. *Civil Rights: The 1960s Freedom Struggle.* rev. ed. Boston: Twayne Publishers, 1991.

Boas, Franz. *Race, Language, and Culture.* Chicago: University of Chicago Press, 1995.

Bodroghkozy, Aniko. *Equal Time: Television and the Civil Rights Movement.* Urbana: University of Illinois Press, 2012.

Boehm, Kimberley Phillips. *War! What Is It Good For?: Black Freedom Struggles and the U.S. Military From World War II to Iraq.* Chapel Hill: University of North Carolina Press, 2012.

Bone, Hugh A. *Party Committees and National Politics*. Seattle: University of Washington Press, 1960.
Borstelmann, Thomas. *The Cold War and the Color Line: American Race Relations in the Global Arena*. Cambridge, MA: Harvard University Press, 2001.
Brands, H. W. *Heirs of the Founders: The Epic Rivalry of Henry Clay, John Calhoun and Daniel Webster, the Second Generation of American Giants*. New York: Doubleday 2019.
Brattain, Michelle. *The Politics of Whiteness: Race, Workers, and Culture in the Modern South*. Princeton, NJ: Princeton University Press, 2001.
Brauer, Carl M. *John F. Kennedy and the Second Reconstruction*. New York: Columbia University Press, 1977.
Breen, Patrick H. *The Land Shall Be Deluged in Blood: A New History of the Nat Turner Revolt*. New York: Oxford University Press, 2016.
Brinkley, Alan. *The End of Reform: New Deal Liberalism in Depression and War*. New York: Alfred A. Knopf, 1995.
Brooks, Jennifer E. *Defining the Peace: World War II Veterans, Race, and the Remaking of Southern Political Tradition*. Chapel Hill: University of North Carolina Press, 2004.
Brown, Charles H. *Agents of Manifest Destiny: The Lives and Times of the Filibusterers*. Chapel Hill: University of North Carolina Press, 1980.
Brown, Kathleen M. *Good Wives, Nasty Wenches, and Anxious Patriarchs: Gender, Race, and Power in Colonial Virginia*. Chapel Hill, University of North Carolina Press, 1996.
Brown, Walter J. *James F. Byrnes of South Carolina: A Remembrance*. Macon, GA: Watson-Brown Foundation/Mercer University, 1992.
Brundage, W. Fitzhugh. *Where These Memories Grow: History, Memory, and Southern Identity*. Chapel Hill: University of North Carolina Press, 2000.
Buenger, Walter L. *Secession and the Union in Texas*. Austin: University of Texas Press, 2013.
Burdette, Franklin L. *Filibustering in the Senate*. Princeton, NJ: Princeton University Press, 1940.
Burk, Robert. *The Eisenhower Administration and Black Civil Rights*. Knoxville: University of Tennessee Press, 1984.
Burnard, Trevor. *Planters, Merchants and Slaves: Plantation Societies in British America, 1650-1820*. Chicago: University of Chicago Press, 2015.
Bynum, Victoria E. *Unruly Women: The Politics of Social and Sexual Control in the Old South*. Chapel Hill: University of North Carolina Press, 1992.
Byrd, Robert C. *The Senate, 1789-1989: Addresses on the History of the United States Senate*. Washington: Government Printing Office, 1988.
Camp, Stephanie M. H. *Closer to Freedom: Enslaved Women and Everyday Resistance in the Plantation South*. Chapel Hill: University of North Carolina Press, 2004.

Campbell, Ernest Q. *Christians in Racial Crisis: A Study of the Little Rock Ministry.* Washington: Public Affairs Press, 1959.
Carter, Dan T. *The Politics of Race: George Wallace, the Origins of the New Conservatism, and the Transformation of American Politics.* New York: Simon and Schuster, 1995.
———. *When the War Was Over: The Failure of Self-Reconstruction in the South, 1865–1867.* Baton Rouge: Louisiana State University Press, 1985.
Cash, Wilbur J. *The Mind of the South.* New York: Vintage Books, 1991.
Cashman, Sean Dennis. *African-Americans and the Quest for Civil Rights, 1900–1990.* New York: New York University Press, 1991.
Cayton, Andrew R. L. *The Dominion of War: Empire and Liberty in North America, 1500–2000.* New York: Penguin, 2005.
Censer, Jane Turner. *The Reconstruction of White Southern Womanhood, 1865–1895.* Baton Rouge: Louisiana State University Press, 2003.
Chafe, William H., Raymond Gavins, and Robert Korstad, eds. *Remembering Jim Crow: African Americans Tell about Life in the Segregated South.* New York: New Press 2001.
Chamberlain, Charles D. *Victory at Home: Manpower and Race in the American South during World War II.* Athens: University of Georgia Press, 2003.
Channing, Steven A. *Crisis of Fear: Secession in South Carolina.* New York: Norton, 1974.
Chappell, David L. *A Stone of Hope: Prophetic Religion and the Death of Jim Crow.* Chapel Hill: University of North Carolina Press, 2004.
Chesnut, Mary Boykin, C. Vann Woodward, and Elisabeth Muhlenfeld. *The Original Civil War Diaries of Mary Boykin Chesnut.* New York: Oxford University Press, 1984.
Claney, Paul R. *Just a Country Lawyer: A Biography of Senator Sam Ervin.* Bloomington: Indiana University Press, 1974.
Clegg, Claude A., III. *Troubled Ground: A Tale of Murder, Lynching, and Reckoning in the New South.* Urbana: University of Illinois Press, 2010.
Cobb, James C. *Away Down South: A History of Southern Identity.* New York: Oxford University Press, 2005.
———. *The Selling of the South: The Southern Crusade for Industrial Development, 1936–1980.* Baton Rouge: Louisiana State University Press, 1982.
Cobb, James C., and Michael V. Namorato, eds. *The New Deal and the South: Essays.* Jackson: University Press of Mississippi, 1984.
Cohen, Lizabeth. *Making a New Deal: Industrial Workers in Chicago, 1919–1939.* New York: Cambridge University Press, 1990.
Coit, Margaret L. *John C. Calhoun: American Portrait.* Norwalk, CT: Easton Press, 1993.
Collins, Charles Wallace. *Whither the Solid South: A Study in Politics and Race Relations.* New Orleans: Pelican Publishing Company, 1947.

Conforti, Joseph A. *Imagining New England: Explorations of Regional Identity from the Pilgrims to the Mid-Twentieth Century.* Chapel Hill: University of North Carolina Press, 2000.
Conkin, Paul K. *Big Daddy from the Pedernales: Lyndon Baines Johnson.* Boston: Twayne Publishers, 1986.
Cook, Robert. *Sweet Land of Liberty? The African-American Struggle for Civil Rights in the Twentieth Century.* New York: Longman, 1998.
Cooper, William J. *Liberty and Slavery: Southern Politics to 1860.* New York: Alfred Knopf, 1983.
———. *The South and the Politics of Slavery, 1828–1856.* Baton Rouge: Louisiana State University Press, 1978.
Cox, Marcus S. *Segregated Soldiers: Military Training at Historically Black Colleges in the Jim Crow South.* Baton Rouge: Louisiana State University Press 2013.
Crespino, Joseph. *In Search of Another Country: Mississippi and the Conservative Counterrevolution.* Princeton, NJ: Princeton University Press, 2009.
———. *Strom Thurmond's America.* New York: Hill and Wang, 2012.
Crosby, Emilye, ed. *Civil Rights History from the Ground Up: Local Struggles, a National Movement.* Athens: University of Georgia Press, 2011.
Curtin, Mary Ellen. *Black Prisoners and Their World: Alabama, 1865–1900.* Charlottesville: University Press of Virginia, 2000.
Dabney, Dick. *A Good Man: The Life of Senator Sam J. Ervin.* Boston: Houghton Mifflin, 1976.
Dailey, Jane. *White Fright: The Sexual Panic at the Heart of America's Racist History.* New York: Basic Books, 2020.
Dailey, Jane, Glenda Elizabeth Gilmore, and Bryant Simon, ed. *Jumpin' Jim Crow: Southern Politics from Civil War to Civil Rights.* Princeton, NJ: Princeton University Press, 2000.
Dallek, Robert. *Flawed Giant: Lyndon Johnson and His Times, 1961–1973.* New York: Oxford University Press, 1998.
———. *Lone Star Rising: Lyndon Johnson and His Times, 1908–1960.* New York: Oxford University Press, 1991.
Daniel, Pete. *Lost Revolutions: The South in the 1950s.* Chapel Hill: University of North Carolina Press, 2000.
Daugherity, Brian J. and Charles C. Bolton, *With All Deliberate Speed Implementing Brown v. Board of Education.* Fayetteville: University of Arkansas Press, 2011.
Davis, David Brion. *The Problem of Slavery in the Age of Revolution.* Ithaca: Cornell University Press, 1975.
Dawley, Alan. *Struggles for Justice: Moral Responsibility and the Liberal State.* Cambridge, MA: Harvard University Press, 1991.
Day, John Kyle. *The Southern Manifesto: Massive Resistance and the Fight to Preserve Segregation.* Jackson: University of Mississippi Press, 2014.

Deal, J. Douglas. *Race and Class in Colonial Virginia: Indians, Englishmen, and Africans on the Eastern Shore of Virginia during the Seventeenth Century.* New York: Garland Publishing, 1993.

Detzerm, David. *Dissonance: The Turbulent Days between Fort Sumter and Bull Run.* Orlando: Harvest Books, 2007.

Dew, Charles B. *Apostles of Disunion: Southern Secession Commissioners and the Causes of the Civil War.* Charlottesville: University of Virginia Press, 2016.

Diamond, Robert A., ed. *Congressional Quarterly's Guide to U.S. Elections.* Washington: Congressional Quarterly, Inc., 1975.

Dierenfield, Bruce J. *Keeper of the Rules: Congressman Howard W. Smith of Virginia.* Charlottesville: University Press of Virginia, 1987.

Diouf, Sylvanie A. *Slavery's Exiles: The Story of the American Maroons.* New York: New York University Press, 2014.

Donald, David H. *Lincoln.* New York: Simon and Schuster, 1996.

Downs, Gregory P. *After Appomattox: Military Occupation and the Ends of War.* Cambridge, MA: Harvard University Press, 2015.

———. *Declaration of Dependence: The Long Reconstruction of Popular Politics in the South, 1861–1908.* Chapel Hill: University of North Carolina Press, 2011.

Dray, Philip. *At the Hands of Persons Unknown: The Lynching of Black America.* New York: Random House, 2002.

Drocher, Kris. *Raising Racists: The Socialization of White Children in the Jim Crow South.* Lexington: University Press of Kentucky, 2011.

Drury, Allen. *A Senate Journal, 1943–1945.* New York: McGraw Hill, 1963.

Dudziak, Mary L. *Cold War Civil Rights: Race and the Image of American Democracy.* Princeton, NJ: Princeton University Press, 2000.

Dugger, Ronnie. *The Politician: The Drive for Power from the Frontier to Master of the Senate.* New York: Norton, 1982.

Dulles, Foster Rhea. *The Civil Rights Commission, 1957–1965.* East Lansing: Michigan State University Press, 1968.

———. *Labor In America: A History.* New York: Thomas Y. Crowell Company, 1966.

Dumond, Dwight. *The Secession Movement, 1860–1861.* New York: Macmillan, 1931.

Dunbar, Anthony P. *Against the Grain: Southern Radicals and Prophets, 1929–1959.* Charlottesville: University Press of Virginia, 1981.

Dunbar, Erica Armstrong. *A Fragile Freedom: African American Women and Emancipation in the Antebellum City.* New Haven: Yale University Press, 2011.

DuVal, Kathleen. *Independence Lost: Lives on the Edge of the American Revolution.* New York: Random House, 2015.

Edling, Max. *A Revolution in Favor of Government: Origins of the U.S. Constitution and the Making of the American State.* New York: Oxford University Press, 2008).

Egerton, Douglas R. *Year of Meteors: Stephen Douglas, Abraham Lincoln, and the Election that Brought on the Civil War.* New York: Bloomsbury Press, 2010.

Egerton, John. *Speak Now against the Day: The Generation Before the Civil Rights Movement in the South.* Chapel Hill: University of North Carolina Press, 1995.

Eisenhower, Dwight D. *The White House Years: Waging Peace, 1956–1961.* Garden City: Doubleday and Company, 1956.

Ellis, Joseph J. *Founding Brothers: The Revolutionary Generation.* New York: Vintage Books, 2002.

Ellis, Richard E. *The Union at Risk: Jacksonian Democracy, States' Rights and the Nullification Crisis.* New York: Oxford University Press, 1989.

Eltis, David. *The Rise of African Slavery in the Americas.* New York: Cambridge University Press, 2000.

Estes, Steve. *I Am a Man!: Race, Manhood, and the Civil Rights Movement.* Chapel Hill: University of North Carolina Press, 1999.

Etcheson, Nicole. *Bleeding Kansas: Contested Liberty in the Civil War Era.* University of Kansas Press, 2006.

Evans, Rowland, and Robert Novak. *Lyndon Johnson: The Exercise of Power.* New York: The New American Library, 1966.

Fairclough, Adam. *Better Day Coming: Blacks and Equality, 1890–2000.* New York: Viking, 2001.

———. *To Redeem the Soul of America: The Southern Christian Leadership Conference and Martin Luther King Jr.* Athens: University of Georgia Press, 1987.

Faragher, John Mack, ed. *Rereading Frederick Jackson Turner: "The Significance of the Frontier in American History" and other Essays.* New Haven: Yale University Press, 1999.

Farmer, James. *An Autobiography of the Civil Rights Movement.* New York: Arbor Press, 1985.

Faust, Drew, ed. *The Ideology of Slavery: Proslavery Thought in the Antebellum South, 1830–1860.* Baton Rouge: Louisiana State University Press, 1981.

———. *Mothers of Invention: Women of the Slaveholding South in the American Civil War.* New York: Vintage Books, 1997.

Fehrenbacher, Don E. *The Slaveholding Republic: An Account of the United States Government's Relations to Slavery.* New York: Oxford University Press, 2002.

Feimster, Crystal N. *Southern Horrors: Women and the Politics of Rape and Lynching.* Cambridge, MA: Harvard University Press, 2009.

Feldman, Lynne B. *A Sense of Place: Birmingham's Black Middle-Class Community, 1890–1930.* Tuscaloosa: University of Alabama Press, 1992.

Finkelman, Paul. *His Soul Goes Marching On: Responses to John Brown and the Harpers Ferry Raid.* Charlottesville: University Press of Virginia, 1995.

———. *Slavery and the Founders: Race and Liberty in the Age of Jefferson.* New York: M.E. Sharpe, 2001.

Finley, Keith M. *Delaying the Dream: Southern Senators and the Fight Against Civil Rights, 1938-1965.* Baton Rouge: Louisiana State University Press, 2008.

Fite, Gilbert C. *Cotton Fields No More: Southern Agriculture, 1865-1980.* Lexington: University Press of Kentucky, 1984.

Fogel, Robert William, and Stanley Engerman. *Time on the Cross: The Economics of American Negro Slavery.* Boston: Little, Brown, 1974.

Follett, Richard J. *The Sugar Masters: Planters and Slaves in Louisiana's Cane World, 1820-1860.* Baton Rouge: Louisiana State University Press, 2005.

Foner, Eric. *The Fiery Trial: Abraham Lincoln and American Slavery.* New York: W.W. Norton, 2010.

———. *Free Soil, Free Labor, Free Men: The Ideology of the Republican Party Before the Civil War.* New York: Oxford University Press, 1970.

———. *Gateway to Freedom: The Hidden History of the Underground Railroad.* New York: W.W. Norton, 2016.

———. *Nothing But Freedom: Emancipation and Its Legacy.* Baton Rouge: Louisiana State University, 1983.

———. *Reconstruction: America's Unfinished Revolution, 1863-1877.* New York: Harper Collins, 1988.

Forbes, Matthew Pierce. *The Missouri Compromise and Its Aftermath: Slavery and the Meaning of America.* Chapel Hill: University of North Carolina Press, 2009.

Ford, Lacy K. *Deliver Us from Evil: The Slavery Question in the Old South.* New York: Oxford University Press, 2009.

———. *Origins of Southern Radicalism: The South Carolina Upcountry, 1800-1860.* New York: Oxford University Press, 1991.

Foster, Gaines M. *Ghosts of the Confederacy: Defeat, the Lost Cause, and the Emergence of the New South.* New York: Oxford University Press, 1987.

Franklin, John Hope, and Loren Schweninger. *Runaway Slaves: Rebels on the Plantation.* New York: Oxford University Press, 1999.

Frederickson, George M. *The Black Image in the White Mind: The Debate on Afro-American Character and Destiny.* New York: Harper and Row, 1972.

Frederickson, Kari A. *The Dixiecrat Revolt and the End of the Solid South, 1932-1968.* Chapel Hill: University of North Carolina Press, 2001.

Freehling, William W. *Prelude to Civil War: The Nullification Controversy in South Carolina, 1816-1836.* New York: Oxford University Press, 1995.

Freehling, William W., and Craig M. Simpson, *Secession Debated: Georgia's Showdown in 1860.* New York: Oxford University Press, 1992.

Frey, Sylvia R. *Water from the Rock: Black Resistance in a Revolutionary Age.* Prince-ton, NJ: Princeton University Press, 1991.

Freyer, Tony Allen. *The Little Rock Crisis: A Constitutional Interpretation.* Westport: Greenwood Press, 1984.

Friedel, Frank. *F.D.R. and the South.* Baton Rouge: Louisiana State University Press, 1965.

Friend, Craig Thompson, and Lorri Glover, eds. *Southern Manhood: Perspectives on Masculinity in the Old South.* Athens: University of Georgia Press, 2004.

Fuller, James A. *The Election of 1860 Reconsidered.* Kent, OH: The Kent State University Press, 2012.

Games, Allison. *Migration and the Origins of the English Atlantic World.* Cambridge, MA: Harvard University Press, 1999.

Garfinkel, Herbert. *When Negroes March: The March on Washington Movement in the Organizational Politics of the FEPC.* New York: Atheneum, 1969.

Garrison, Tim Alan. *The Legal Ideology of Removal: The Southern Judiciary and the Sovereignty of Native American Nations.* Athens: University of Georgia Press, 2002.

Garson, Robert A. *The Democratic Party and the Politics of Sectionalism, 1941–1948.* Baton Rouge: Louisiana State University Press, 1974.

Gaston, Paul. *The New South Creed: A Study in Southern Mythmaking.* New York: Alfred A. Knopf, 1970.

Genovese, Eugene D. *The Mind of the Master Class: History and Faith in the Southern Slaveholder's Worldview.* Boston: Cambridge University Press, 2005.

———. *The Political Economy of Slavery: Studies in the Economy and Society of the Slave South.* New York: Pantheon, 1965.

Genovese, Eugene D., and Elizabeth Fox Genovese. *Fatal Self-Deception: Slaveholding Paternalism in the Old South.* New York: Cambridge University Press, 2011.

Gienapp, William E. *The Origins of the Republican Party, 1852–1856.* New York: Oxford University Press, 1988.

Gillette, William. *Retreat from Reconstruction, 1869–1879.* Baton Rouge: Louisiana State University Press, 1979.

Gilmore, Glenda E. *Defying Dixie: The Radical Roots of Civil Rights, 1919–1950.* New York: W.W. Norton, 2009.

———. *Gender and Jim Crow: Women and the Politics of White Supremacy in North Carolina, 1896–1920.* Chapel Hill: University of North Carolina Press, 1996.

Godshalk, David Fort. *Veiled Visions: The 1906 Atlanta Race Riot and the Reshaping of American Race Relations.* Chapel Hill: University of North Carolina Press, 2005.

Goldenberg, David M. *The Curse of Ham: Race and Slavery in Early Judaism, Christianity, and Islam.* Princeton: Princeton University Press, 2003.

Goldman, Eric F. *The Tragedy of Lyndon Johnson.* New York: Alfred A. Knopf, 1969.

Goldsmith, John A. *Colleagues: Richard B. Russell and His Apprentice, Lyndon B. Johnson.* Washington: Seven Locks Press, 1993.

Gomez, Michael A. *Exchanging Our Country Marks: The Transformation of African Identities in the Colonial and Antebellum South.* Chapel Hill: University of North Carolina Press, 1998.

Gordon-Read, Annette. *The Hemingses of Monticello: An American Family.* New York: W.W. Norton, 2008.

Gore, Albert. *Let the Glory Out: My South and Its Politics.* New York: Viking Press, 1972.

Gorman, Joseph B. *Kefauver: A Political Biography.* New York: Oxford University Press, 1971.

Graham, Allison. *Framing the South : Hollywood, Television, and Race During the Civil Rights Struggle.* Baltimore: Johns Hopkins University Press, 2001.

Green, A. Wigfall. *The Man: Bilbo.* Baton Rouge: Louisiana State University Press, 1963.

Green, Michael S. *Lincoln and The Election of 1860.* Carbondale: Southern Illinois University Press, 2020.

Greenberg, Kenneth S. *Nat Turner: A Slave Rebellion in History and Memory.* New York: Oxford University Press, 2004.

Greene, Alison Collis. *No Depression in Heaven: The Great Depression, the New Deal, and the Transformation of Religion in the Delta.* New York: Oxford University Press, 2016.

Grossman, James. *Land of Hope: Chicago, Black Southerners, and the Great Migration.* Chicago: University of Chicago Press, 1989.

Guasco, Michael. *Slaves and Englishmen: Human Bondage in the Early Modern Atlantic World.* Philadelphia: University of Pennsylvania Press, 2014.

Hahn, Steven. *The Political Worlds of Slavery and Freedom.* Cambridge, MA: Harvard University Press, 2009.

———. *The Roots of Southern Populism: Yeoman Farmers and the Transformation of the Southern Countryside, 1850–1890.* New York: Oxford University Press, 1983.

Hair, William Ivy. *Bourbonism and Agrarian Protest: Louisiana Politics, 1877–1900.* Baton Rouge: Louisiana State University Press, 1969.

Hale, Grace Elizabeth. *Making Whiteness: The Culture of Segregation in the South, 1890–1940.* New York: Vintage Books, 1999.

Haley, Sarah. *No Mercy Here: Gender, Punishment, and the Making of Jim Crow Modernity.* Chapel Hill: University of North Carolina Press, 2016.

Hall, Jacquelyn Dowd. *Revolt Against Chivalry: Jessie Daniel Ames and the Women's Campaign Against Lynching.* New York: Columbia University Press, 1979.

Hamlin, Françoise N. *Crossroads at Clarksdale: The Black Freedom Struggle in the Mississippi Delta after World War II.* Chapel Hill: University of North Carolina Press, 2012.

Hammond, John Craig. *Slavery, Freedom, and Expansion in the Early American West.* Charlottesville: University of Virginia Press, 2007.

Harold, Claudrena N. *New Negro Politics in the Jim Crow South.* Athens: University of Georgia Press, 2016.

Haynes, George H. *The Senate of the United States: Its History and Practice.* New York: Russell and Russell, 1960.
Haynes, Stephen R. *Noah's Curse: The Biblical Justification of American Slavery.* New York: Oxford University Press, 2002.
Hays, Brooks. *A Southern Moderate Speaks.* Chapel Hill: University of North Carolina Press, 1959.
Heersink, Boris, and Jeffrey Jenkins. *Republican Party Politics and the American South, 1865–1968.* New York: Cambridge University Press, 2020.
Hill, Lance. *The Deacons for Defense: Armed Resistance and the Civil Rights Movement.* Chapel Hill: University of North Carolina Press, 2004.
Hodes, Martha Elizabeth. *White Women, Black Men: Illicit Sex in the Nineteenth-Century South.* New Haven: Yale University Press, 1997.
Hogue, James K. *Uncivil War: Five New Orleans Street Battles and the Rise of Radical Reconstruction.* Baton Rouge: Louisiana State University Press, 2006.
Holt, Michael. *The Election of 1860: "A Campaign Fraught with Consequences.* Lawrence: University Press of Kansas, 2017.
———. *The Fate of Their Country: Politicians, Slavery Extension, and the Coming of the Civil War.* New York: Hill and Wang, 2005.
———. *The Political Crisis of the 1850s.* New York: Wiley, 1978.
Holt, Sharon Ann. *Making Freedom Pay: Race, Violence, and the American South after the Civil War.* Chicago: University of Chicago Press, 2013.
Holt, Thomas. *Black Over White: Negro Political Leadership in South Carolina During Reconstruction.* Urbana: University of Illinois Press, 1977.
Holzer, Harold. *Lincoln President-Elect: Abraham Lincoln and the Great Secession Winter, 1860–1861.* New York: Simon and Schuster 2009.
Horne, Gerald. *The Counter-Revolution of 1776: Slave Resistance and the Origins of the United States.* New York: New York University Press, 2014.
———. *The Deepest South: The United States, Brazil, and the African Slave Trade.* New York: New York University Press, 2007.
Horton, James Oliver, and Lois E. Horton. *In Hope of Liberty: Culture, Community, and Protest Among Northern Free Blacks, 1700–1860.* New York: Oxford University Press, 1997.
Horwitz, Tony. *Midnight Rising: John Brown and the Raid That Sparked the Civil War.* Detroit: Gale/Cengage, 2012.
Huthmacher, J. Joseph. *Senator Robert F. Wagner and the Rise of Urban Liberalism.* Cambridge, MA: Harvard University Press, 1968.
Hyde, Samuel C., Jr. *Pistols and Politics: Feuds, Factions, and the Struggle for Order in Louisiana's Florida Parishes, 1810–1935.* 2nd ed. Baton Rouge: Louisiana State University Press, 2018.
Jackson, Kelly Carter. *Force and Freedom: Black Abolitionists and the Politics of Violence.* Philadelphia: University of Pennsylvania Press, 2019.

Jaffa, Harry V. and Allen C. Guelzo. *A New Birth of Freedom: Abraham Lincoln and the Coming of the Civil War.* New York: Rowman & Littlefield, 2018.
Johnson, Lyndon B. *The Vantage Point: Perspectives of the Presidency, 1963–1969.* New York: Holt, Rinehart, and Winston, 1971.
Johnson, Michael P. *Towards a Patriarchal Republic: The Secession of Georgia.* Baton Rouge: Louisiana State University, 1977.
Johnson, Sam Houston. *My Brother Lyndon.* New York: Cowles Book Company, Inc., 1969.
Johnson, Walter. *River of Dark Dreams: Slavery and Empire in the Cotton Kingdom.* Cambridge, MA: Harvard University Press, 2013.
———. *Soul by Soul: Life Inside the Antebellum Slave Market.* Cambridge, MA: Harvard University Press, 1999.
Johnston, Erle. *I Rolled with Ross: A Political Portrait.* Baton Rouge: Moran Publishing Corporation, 1980.
Jones, William P. *The March on Washington: Jobs, Freedom, and the Forgotten History of Civil Rights.* New York: W.W. Norton, 2013.
Jordan, Winthrop D. *White over Black: American Attitudes toward the Negro, 1550–1812.* Chapel Hill: University of North Carolina Press, 1968.
Kantrowitz, Stephen. *Ben Tillman and the Reconstruction of White Supremacy.* Chapel Hill: University of North Carolina Press, 2000.
Karabell, Zachary. *The Last Campaign: How Truman Won the 1948 Election.* New York: Alfred A. Knopf, 2000.
Karp, Matthew. *This Vast Southern Empire: Slaveholders at the Helm of American Foreign Policy.* Cambridge, MA: Harvard University Press, 2016.
Katznelson, Ira. *When Affirmative Action Was White: An Untold History of Racial Inequality in Twentieth-Century America.* New York: W.W. Norton, 2005.
Kearns, Doris. *Lyndon Johnson and the American Dream.* New York: Harper and Row, 1968.
Kelley, Blair L. M. *Right to Ride: Streetcar Boycotts and African American Citizenship in the Era of Plessy v. Ferguson.* Chapel Hill: University of North Carolina Press, 2010.
Kelley, Robin D. G. *Hammer and Hoe: Alabama Communism during the Great Depression.* Chapel Hill: University of North Carolina Press, 1990.
Key, V. O. *Southern Politics in State and Nation.* New York: Alfred A. Knopf, 1949.
Kirby, John B. *Black Americans in the Roosevelt Era: Liberalism and Race.* Knoxville: University of Tennessee Press, 1980.
Kirk, John A. *Redefining the Color Line: Black Activism in Little Rock Arkansas, 1940–1970.* Gainesville: University Press of Florida, 2002.
Klarman, Michael J. *From Jim Crow to Civil Rights: The Supreme Court and the Struggle for Racial Equality.* New York: Oxford University Press, 2006.
Kluger, Richard. *Simple Justice: The History of Brown v. Board of Education and Black America's Struggle for Equality.* New York: Alfred A. Knopf, 1976.

Kneebone, John T. *Southern Liberal Journalists and the Issue of Race, 1920–1944.* Chapel Hill: University of North Carolina Press 1996.
Knight, Frederick C. *Working the Diaspora: The Impact of African Labor on the Anglo-American World, 1650–1850.* New York: New York University Press, 2010.
Korstad, Robert. *Civil Rights Unionism: Tobacco Workers and the Struggle for Democracy in the Mid-Twentieth Century South.* Chapel Hill: University of North Carolina Press, 2003.
Kousser, J. Morgan. *The Shaping of Southern Politics: Suffrage Restriction and the Establishment of the One-Party South, 1880–1910.* New Haven: Yale University Press, 1974.
Kruse, Kevin M. *White Flight: Atlanta and the Making of Modern Conservatism.* Princeton, NJ: Princeton University Press, 2013.
Kruse, Kevin M., and Stephen Tuck. *Fog of War: The Second World War and the Civil Rights Movement.* New York: Oxford University Press, 2012.
Kulikoff, Allan. *The Agrarian Origins of American Capitalism.* Charlottesville: University Press of Virginia, 1996.
———. *Tobacco and Slaves: The Development of Southern Cultures in the Chesapeake, 1680–1800.* Chapel Hill: University of North Carolina Press, 1986.
Lakwete, Angela. *Inventing the Cotton Gin: Machine and Myth in Antebellum America.* Baltimore, MD: Johns Hopkins University Press, 2005.
Landau, Emily Epstein. *Spectacular Wickedness: Sex, Race, and Memory in Storyville, New Orleans.* Baton Rouge: Louisiana State University Press, 2013.
Landers, Jane G., ed. *Against the Odds: Free Blacks in the Slave Societies of the Americas.* London: Frank Cass, 1996.
LaRoche, Cheryl Janifer. *Free Black Communities and the Underground Railroad: The Geography of Resistance.* Urbana: University of Illinois Press, 2013.
Lassiter, Matthew D., and Andrew B. Lewis, *The Moderates' Dilemma: Massive Resistance to School Desegregation in Virginia.* Charlottesville: University Press of Virginia, 1998.
Laue, James H. *Direct Action and Desegregation, 1960–1962: Toward a Theory of the Rationalization of Protest.* New York: Carlson Publishing, Inc., 1989.
Lawson, Steven F. *Black Ballots: Voting Rights in the South, 1944–1969.* New York: Columbia University Press, 1976.
———. *In Pursuit of Power: Civil Rights and Black Politics in America Since 1941.* Philadelphia: Temple University Press, 1991.
———. *Running for Freedom: Civil Rights and Black Politics in America Since 1941,* 2nd Ed. New York: McGraw-Hill, 1997.
Lemann, Nicholas. *The Promised Land: The Great Black Migration and How It Changed America.* New York: Alfred A. Knopf, 1991.
Leuchtenberg, William E. *Franklin D. Roosevelt and the New Deal, 1932–1940.* New York: Harper and Row, 1963.

———. *The White House Looks South: Franklin D. Roosevelt, Harry S. Truman, Lyndon B. Johnson*. Baton Rouge: Louisiana State University Press, 2005.

Lewis, Earl. *In Their Own Interests, Race, Class, and Power in Twentieth-Century Norfolk, Virginia*. Berkeley: University of California Press, 1991.

Lichtenstein, Alex. *Twice the Work of Free Labor: The Political Economy of Convict Labor in the New South*. New York: Verso, 1996.

Link, William A. *The Paradox of Southern Progressivism, 1880–1930*. Chapel Hill: University of North Carolina Press, 1992.

Litwack, Leon F. *Been in the Storm So Long: The Aftermath of Slavery*. New York: Alfred A. Knopf, 1979.

———. *Trouble in Mind: Black Southerners in the Age of Jim Crow*. New York: Alfred A. Knopf, 1998.

Loevy, Robert D., ed. *The Civil Rights Act of 1964: The Passage of the Law that Ended Racial Segregation*. Albany: State University of New York Press, 1997.

Loveland, Anne C. *Southern Evangelicals and the Social Order, 1800–1860*. Baton Rouge: Louisiana State University Press, 1980.

Maier, Pauline. *Ratification: The People Debate the Constitution, 1787–1788*. New York: Simon & Schuster, 2014.

Mancall, Peter C., ed. *The Atlantic World and Virginia, 1550–1624*. Chapel Hill: University of North Carolina Press, 2008.

Mancini, Matthew J. *One Dies, Get Another: Convict Leasing in the American South, 1866–1928*. Columbia: University of South Carolina Press, 1996.

Mann, Robert. *The Walls of Jericho: Lyndon Johnson, Hubert Humphrey, Richard Russell, and the Struggle for Civil Rights*. New York: Harcourt Brace and Company, 1996.

Marable, Manning. *Race, Reform, and Rebellion: The Second Reconstruction in Black America, 1945–1990*. 2nd ed. Jackson: University Press of Mississippi, 1991.

Mason, Matthew. *Slavery and Politics in the Early American Republic*. Chapel Hill: University of North Carolina Press, 2008.

Mathews, Donald G. *Religion in the Old South*. Chicago: University of Chicago Press, 1977.

Matthews, Donald R. *U.S. Senators and Their World*. New York: Alfred A. Knopf, 1960.

Matusow, Allen J. *The Unraveling of America: A History of Liberalism in the 1960s*. New York: Harper and Row, 1984.

Maxwell, Angie. *The Indicted South: Public Criticism, Southern Inferiority, and the Politics of Whiteness*. Chapel Hill: The University of North Carolina Press, 2014.

Mayer, Henry. *All on Fire: William Lloyd Garrison and the Abolition of Slavery*. New York: St. Martin's Press, 1998.

McCoy, Donald R., and Richard T. Ruetten. *Quest and Response: Minority Rights and the Truman Administration*. Lawrence: University Press of Kansas, 1973.

McCoy, Drew. *The Last of the Fathers: James Madison and the Republican Legacy*. New York: Cambridge University Press, 1989.
McCurry, Stephanie. *Confederate Reckoning: Power and Politics in the Civil War South*. Cambridge, MA: Harvard University Press, 2010.
———. *Masters of Small Worlds: Yeoman Households, Gender Relations, and the Political Culture of the Antebellum South Carolina Low Country*. New York: Oxford University Press, 1997.
McDonald, Forrest. *Novus Ordo Seclorum: The Intellectual Origins of the Constitution*. Lawrence: University Press of Kansas, 1987.
McDonnell, Michael A. *The Politics of War: Race, Class, and Conflict in Revolutionary Virginia*. Chapel Hill: University of North Carolina Press, 2007.
McGlone, Robert E. *John Brown's War against Slavery*. Cambridge: Cambridge University Press, 2009.
McMillen, Neil R. *The Citizens' Councils: Organized Resistance to the Second Reconstruction, 1954–1964*. Chicago: University of Illinois Press, 1974.
———. *Remaking Dixie: The Impact of World War II on the American South*. Jackson: University Press of Mississippi, 1997.
McMillen, Sally G. *Southern Women: Black and White in the Old South*. Arlington Heights: Harlan Davidson, 1992.
McPherson, James M. *Abraham Lincoln*. New York: Oxford University Press, 2009.
———. *Battle Cry of Freedom: The Civil War Era*. New York: Oxford University Press, 2003.
McRae, Elizabeth Gillespie. *Mothers of Massive Resistance: White Women and the Politics of White Supremacy*. New York: Oxford University Press, 2020.
Meier, August and Elliott Rudwick. *CORE: A Study in the Civil Rights Movement, 1942–1968*. New York: Oxford University Press, 1973.
Merrill, Walter M. *The Letters of William Lloyd Garrison. vol. 1, I Will Be Heard! 1822–1835*. Cambridge: Belknap Press, 1971.
Metcalf, George R. *From Little Rock to Boston: The History of School Desegregation*. Westport: Greenwood Press, 1983.
Mickey, Robert. *Paths Out of Dixie: The Democratization of Authoritarian Enclaves in America's Deep South, 1944–1972*. Princeton, NJ: Princeton University Press, 2015.
Miller, William. *Fishbait: The Memoirs of the Congressional Doorkeeper*. Englewood Cliffs, NJ: Prentice-Hall, 1977.
Mills, Kay. *Changing Channels: The Civil Rights Case That Transformed Television*. Jackson: University Press of Mississippi, 2004.
Moore, John R. *Senator Josiah Bailey of North Carolina: A Political Biography*. Durham, NC: Duke University Press, 1968.
Morgan, Chester M. *Redneck Liberal: Theodore G. Bilbo and the New Deal*. Baton Rouge: Louisiana State University Press, 1985.
Morgan, Edmund S. *American Slavery, American Freedom: The Ordeal of Colonial Virginia*. New York: Norton, 1975.

Morgan, Jennifer L. *Laboring Women: Reproduction and Gender in New World Slavery*. Philadelphia: University of Pennsylvania Press, 2004.
Morgan, Kenneth. *Slavery and Servitude in Colonial North America: A Short History*. New York: New York University Press, 2001.
Morgan, Philip D. *Slave Counterpoint: Black Culture in the Eighteenth-Century Chesapeake and Lowcountry*. Chapel Hill: University of North Carolina Press, 1998.
Morgan, Ted. *FDR: A Biography*. New York: Simon and Schuster, 1985.
Morris, Thomas D. *Southern Slavery and the Law, 1619-1860*. Chapel Hill: University of North Carolina Press, 1996.
Morrison, Michael A. *Slavery and the American West: The Eclipse of Manifest Destiny*. Chapel Hill: University of North Carolina Press, 1999.
Moye, J. Todd. *Let the People Decide: Black Freedom and White Resistance Movements in Sunflower County, Mississippi, 1945-1986*. Chapel Hill: University of North Carolina Press, 2004.
Muhammad, Khalil Gibran. *The Condemnation of Blackness: Race Crime and the Making of Modern Urban America*. Cambridge, MA: Harvard University Press, 2011.
Mullin, Michael. *Africa in America: Slave Acculturation and Resistance in the American South and British Caribbean, 1736-1831*. Urbana: University of Illinois Press, 1992.
Murphy, Paul V. *The Rebuke of History: Southern Agrarians and American Conservative Thought*. Chapel Hill: University of North Carolina Press, 2001.
Myrdal, Gunnar, Arnold M. Rose, and Richard Sterner. *An American Dilemma: The Negro Problem and Modern Democracy. vols. 1 and 2*. New York: Harper & Brothers, 1944.
Nash, Gary B. *Red, White, and Black: The Peoples of Early America*. Englewood Cliffs, NJ: Prentice-Hall, 1982.
Nelson, Stanley. *Klan of Devils: The Murder of a Black Louisiana Deputy Sheriff*. Baton Rouge: Louisiana State University Press, 2021.
Nevins, Allan. *The Emergence of Lincoln. vol. 2*. New York: Charles Scribner's Sons, 1950.
Newby, I. A. *Jim Crow's Defense: Anti-Negro Thought in America, 1900-1930*. Baton Rouge: Louisiana State University Press, 1965.
Newman, Mark. *Getting Right with God: Southern Baptists and Desegregation, 1945-1995*. Tuscaloosa: University Of Alabama Press, 2001.
Newman, Richard S., and James Mueller, eds. *Antislavery and Abolition in Philadelphia: Emancipation and the Long Struggle for Racial Justice in the City of Brotherly Love*. Baton Rouge: Louisiana State University Press, 2011.
Newman, Simon P. *A New World of Labor: The Development of Planation Slavery in the British Atlantic*. Philadelphia: University of Pennsylvania Press, 2013.
Niven, John. *John C. Calhoun and the Price of Union: A Biography*. Baton Rouge: Louisiana State University Press, 1993.

Oakes, James. *The Ruling Race: A History of American Slaveholders.* New York: Alfred A. Knopf, 1982.
Oates, Stephen B. *The Fires of Jubilee: Nat Turner's Fierce Rebellion.* New York: Harper Perennial, 1990.
———. *To Purge This Land With Blood: A Biography of John Brown.* Amherst: University of Massachusetts Press, 1984.
O'Brien, Gail Williams. *The Color of the Law: Race, Violence, and Justice in the Post-World War II South.* Chapel Hill: University of North Carolina Press, 2004.
O'Donovan, Susan Eve. *Becoming Free in the Cotton South.* Cambridge, MA: Harvard University Press, 2010.
Ortiz, Paul. *Emancipation Betrayed: The Hidden History of Black Organizing and White Violence in Florida from Reconstruction to the Bloody Election of 1920.* Berkeley: University of California Press, 2005.
Oschinsky, David M. *Worse Than Slavery: Parchman Farm and the Ordeal of Jim Crow Justice.* New York: Free Press, 1996.
Parent, Anthony S., Jr. *Foul Means: The Formation of a Slave Society in Virginia, 1660–1740.* Chapel Hill: University of North Carolina Press, 2003.
Parkinson, Robert G. *The Common Cause: Creating Race and Nation in the American Revolution.* Chapel Hill: University of North Carolina Press, 2016.
Patterson, James T. *Congressional Conservatism and the New Deal: The Growth of the Conservative Coalition in Congress, 1933–1939.* Lexington: University Press of Kentucky, 1967.
Peck, James. *Freedom Ride.* New York: Simon and Schuster, 1962.
Pepper, Claude D. *Pepper: Eyewitness to a Century.* New York: Harcourt, Brace, Jovanovich, 1987.
Perman, Michael. *Pursuit of Unity: A Political History of the American South.* Chapel Hill: University of North Carolina Press, 2009.
———. *The Road to Redemption: Southern Politics, 1869–1879.* Chapel Hill: University of North Carolina Press, 1984.
———. *The Southern Political Tradition.* Baton Rouge: Louisiana State University Press, 2012.
———. *Struggle for Mastery: Disfranchisement in the South, 1888–1908.* Chapel Hill: University of North Carolina Press, 2001
Peterson, Merrill D. *John Brown: The Legend Revisited.* Charlottesville: University of Virginia Press, 2004.
Phipps, Joe. *Summer Stock: Behind the Scenes with LBJ in '48: Recollections of a Political Drama.* Fort Worth: Texas Christian University Press, 1992.
Plummer, Brenda Gayle. *Rising Wind: Black Americans and U.S. Foreign Affairs, 1936–1960.* Chapel Hill: University of North Carolina Press, 1996.
Pocock, J. G. A. *The Machiavellian Moment: Florentine Republican Thought and the Atlantic Republican Tradition.* Princeton, NJ: Princeton University Press, 1975.

Potter, David. *The Impending Crisis, 1848–1861*. New York: Harper & Row, 1976.
Powledge, Fred. *Free at Last? The Civil Rights Movement and the People Who Made It*. Boston: Little, Brown, and Co., 1991.
Rabinowitz, Howard N. *Race Relations in the Urban South, 1865–1890*. Athens: University of Georgia Press, 1996.
Rable, George C. *But There Was No Peace: The Role of Violence in the Politics of Reconstruction*. Athens: University of Georgia Press, 1984.
Rael, Patrick. *Black Identity and Black Protest in the Antebellum North*. Chapel Hill: University of North Carolina Press, 2002.
Rakove, John N. *Original Meanings: Politics and Ideas in the Making of the Constitution*. New York: Alfred A. Knopf, 1996.
Ransby, Barbara. *Ella Baker and the Black Freedom Movement: A Radical Democratic Vision*. Chapel Hill: University of North Carolina Press, 2003.
Ransom, Roger L. and Richard Sutch. *One Kind of Freedom: The Economic Consequences of Emancipation*. New York: Cambridge University Press, 1977.
Rasmussen, Daniel. *American Uprising: The Untold Story of America's Largest Slave Revolt*. New York: Harper Collins, 2011.
Rawley, James A. *Race and Politics: "Bleeding Kansas" and the Coming of the American Civil War*. Lincoln: University of Nebraska Press, 1979.
Reed, Merl E. *Seedtime for the Modern Civil Rights Movement: The President's Committee on Fair Employment Practice, 1941–1946*. Baton Rouge: Louisiana State University Press, 1991.
Reed, Roy. *Faubus: The Life and Times of an American Prodigal*. Fayetteville: University of Arkansas Press, 1997.
Reynolds, David S. *John Brown, Abolitionist: The Man Who Killed Slavery, Sparked the Civil War, and Seeded Civil Rights*. New York: Alfred A. Knopf, 2006.
Rice, James D. *Tales from a Revolution: Bacon's Rebellion and the Transformation of Early America*. New York: Oxford University Press, 2013.
Richardson, Heather Cox. *The Death of Reconstruction: Race, Labor, and Politics in the Post-Civil War North, 1865–1901*. Cambridge, MA: Harvard University Press, 2001.
———. *West from Appomattox: The Reconstruction of America after the Civil War*. New Haven: Yale University Press, 2007.
Riddick, Floyd M. *Senate Procedure: Precedents and Practices*. Washington: Government Printing Office, 1981.
Ring, Natalie J. *The Problem South: Region, Empire, and the New Liberal State, 1880–1930*. Athens University of Georgia Press, 2012.
Ritterhouse, Jennifer. *Discovering the South: One Man's Travels Through a Changing America in the 1930s*. Chapel Hill: University of North Carolina Press, 2017.
———. *Growing Up Jim Crow: How Black and White Southern Children Learned Race*. Chapel Hill: University of North Carolina Press, 2006.

Roberts, Justin. *Slavery and the Enlightenment in British North America, 1650–1820*. Chicago: University of Chicago Press, 2015.

Roberts, Rita. *Evangelicalism and the Politics of Reform in Northern Black Thought, 1776–1863*. Baton Rouge: Louisiana State University Press, 2010.

Roberts, Samuel Kelton Jr. *Infectious Fear: Politics, Disease, and the Health Effects of Segregation*. Chapel Hill: University of North Carolina Press, 2009.

Rohrbough, Malcolm J. *Trans-Appalachian Frontier: Peoples, Societies, and Institutions, 1775–1850*. 3rd ed. Bloomington: Indiana University Press, 2008.

Rolinson, Mary G. *Grassroots Garveyism: The Universal Negro Improvement Association in the Rural South, 1920–1927*. Chapel Hill: University of North Carolina Press, 2007.

Roll, Jared. *Spirit of Rebellion: Labor and Religion in the New Cotton South*. Urbana: University of Illinois Press, 2010.

Rorabaugh, W. J. *Kennedy and the Promise of the Sixties*. New York: Cambridge University Press, 2002.

Rosen, Hannah. *Terror in the Heart of Freedom: Citizenship, Sexual Violence, and the Meaning of Race in the Postemancipation South*. Chapel Hill: University of North Carolina Press, 2009.

Rosenthal, Caitlin. *Accounting for Slavery: Masters and Management*. Boston: Harvard University Press, 2018.

Ross, James D., Jr. *The Rise and Fall of the Southern Tenant Farmers Union in Arkansas*. Knoxville: University of Tennessee Press, 2018.

Rothman, Adam. *Slave Country: American Expansion and the Origins of the Deep South*. Cambridge, MA: Harvard University Press, 2007.

Rothman, Joshua D. *Flush Times and Fever Dreams: A Story of Capitalism and Slavery in the Age of Jackson*. Athens: University of Georgia Press, 2014.

———. *The Ledger and the Chain: How Domestic Slave Traders Shaped America*. New York: Basic Books, 2021.

Salmond, John A. *"My Mind Set on Freedom": A History of the Civil Rights Movement, 1954–1968*. Chicago: Ivan R. Dee, 1997.

Schermerhorn, Calvin. *The Business of Slavery and the Rise of American Capitalism, 1815–1860*. New Haven: Yale University Press, 2015.

———. *Money over Mastery, Family over Freedom: Slavery in the Antebellum Upper South*. Baltimore: Johns Hopkins University Press, 2011.

Schultz, Mark. *The Rural Face of White Supremacy: Beyond Jim Crow*. Urbana: University of Illinois Press, 2005.

Sharpless, Rebecca. *Cooking in Other Women's Kitchens: Domestic Workers in the South, 1865–1960*. Chapel Hill: University of North Carolina Press, 2010.

Shaw, Jenny. *Everyday Life in the Early English Caribbean: Irish, Africans, and the Construction of Difference*. Athens: University of Georgia Press, 2013.

Sherrill, Robert. *Gothic Politics in the Deep South: Stars of the New Confederacy*. New York: Ballantine Books, 1968.

Silkey, Sarah L. *Black Woman Reformer: Ida B. Wells, Lynching, and Transatlantic Activism*. Athens: University of Georgia Press, 2015.

Sinha, Manisha. *The Slave's Cause: A History of Abolition*. New Haven: Yale University Press, 2016.

Sitkoff, Harvard. *A New Deal for Blacks: The Emergence of Civil Rights as a National Issue—The Depression Decade*. New York: Oxford University Press, 1978.

Smallwood, Stephanie E. *Saltwater Slavery: A Middle Passage from Africa to American Diaspora*. Cambridge, MA: Harvard University Press, 2007.

Smith, H. Shelton. *In His Image but . . . : Racism in Southern Religion, 1780–1910*. Durham, NC: Duke University Press, 1972.

Snyder, Christina. *Slavery in Indian Country: The Changing Face of Captivity in Early America*. Cambridge, MA: Harvard University Press, 2010.

Sokol, Jason. *There Goes My Everything: White Southerners in the Age of Civil Rights, 1945–1975*. New York: Vintage Books, 2007.

Sosna, Morton. *In Search of the Silent South: Southern Liberals and the Race Issue*. New York: Columbia University Press, 1977.

Spitzberg, Irving J., Jr. *Racial Politics in Little Rock, 1954–1964*. New York: Garland Publishers, 1987.

Steinberg, Alfred. *Sam Johnson's Boy: A Close-Up of the President from Texas*. New York: MacMillan, 1968.

Steptoe, Tyina L. *Houston Bound: Culture and Color in a Jim Crow City*. Berkeley: University of California Press, 2015.

Stewart, James B. *Holy Warriors: The Abolitionists and American Slavery*. New York: Hill & Wang, 1976.

Sugrue, Thomas J. *Sweet Land of Liberty: The Forgotten Struggle for Civil Rights in the North*. New York: Random House, 2009.

Sullivan, Patricia. *Days of Hope: Race and Democracy in the New Deal Era*. Chapel Hill: University of North Carolina Press, 1996.

Summers, Mark. *Railroads, Reconstruction, and the Gospel of Prosperity: Aid Under the Radical Republicans, 1865–1877*. Princeton, NJ: Princeton University Press, 1984.

Tadman, Michael. *Speculators and Slaves: Masters, Traders, and Slaves in the Old South*. Madison: University of Wisconsin Press, 1989.

Talmadge, Herman E. *Talmadge: A Political Legacy, A Politician's Life*. Atlanta: Peachtree, 1987.

Thornton, J. Mills, III. *Politics and Power in a Slave Society: Alabama, 1800–1860*. Baton Rouge: Louisiana State University, 1978.

Tindall, George B. *The Emergence of the New South, 1913–1945*. Baton Rouge: Louisiana State University Press, 1967.

Tomich, Dale. *Atlantic Transformations: Empire Politics and Slavery during the Nineteenth Century*. Albany: State University of New York Press, 2020.

———. *Through the Prism of Slavery: Labor, Capital, and World Economy*. Lanham, MD: Rowman & Littlefield, 2004.

Torres, Sasha. *Black, White, and in Color: Television and Black Civil Rights.* Princeton, NJ: Princeton University Press, 2003.
Tower, John G. *Consequences: A Personal and Political Memoir.* Boston: Little, Brown, 1991.
Trefousse, Hans L. *The Radical Republicans: Lincoln's Vanguard for Racial Justice.* New York: Alfred A. Knopf, 1969.
Truman, Harry S. *Memoirs of Harry S. Truman: Years of Trial and Hope.* New York: Doubleday, 1956.
Tushnet, Mark. *Making Civil Rights Law: Thurgood Marshall and the Supreme Court, 1936–1961.* New York: Oxford University Press, 1996.
Unger, Irwin, and Debi Unger. *LBJ: A Life.* New York: Wiley, 1999.
Van Cleve, George William. *A Slaveholders' Union: Slavery, Politics, and the Constitution in the Early American Republic.* Chicago: University of Chicago Press, 2010.
Von Atta, John R. *Wolf by the Ears: The Missouri Crisis, 1819–1821.* Baltimore: Johns Hopkins University Press, 2015.
Wakelyn, Jon L. *Southern Pamphlets on Secession, November 1860–April 1861.* Chapel Hill: University of North Carolina Press, 2009.
Waldstreicher, David. *Slavery's Constitution: From Revolution to Ratification.* New York: Hill and Wang, 2010.
Walker, Anders. *The Ghost of Jim Crow: How Southern Moderates Used* Brown v. Board of Education *to Stall Civil Rights.* New York: Oxford University Press, 2009.
Walker, David. *Walker's Appeal in Four Articles.* Boston, 1830.
Walsh, Lorena S. *Motives of Honor, Pleasure, and Profit: Plantation Management in the Colonial Chesapeake, 1607–1763.* Chapel Hill: University of North Carolina Press, 2010.
Walther, Eric H. *The Fire-Eaters.* Baton Rouge: Louisiana State University Press, 1992.
Ward, Jason Morgan. *Defending White Democracy: The Making of the Segregationist Movement and the Remaking of Racial Politics, 1936–1965.* Chapel Hill: University of North Carolina Press, 2011.
Wareing, John. *Indentures Migration and the Servant Trade from London to America, 1618–1718: "There is a Great Want of Servants."* New York: Oxford University Press, 2017.
Watson, Harry L. *Liberty and Power: The Politics of Jacksonian America.* New York: Hill and Wang, 2006.
Webb, Clive. *Rabble Rousers: The American Far Right in the Civil Rights Era.* Athens: University of Georgia Press, 2010.
Weiss, Nancy J. *Farewell to the Party of Lincoln: Black Politics in the Age of FDR.* Princeton, NJ: Princeton University Press, 1983.
Whalen, Charles, and Barbara Whalen. *The Longest Debate: A Legislative History of the 1964 Civil Rights Act.* Cabin John, MD: Seven Locks Press, 1985.

Whayne, Jeannie M. *A New Plantation South: Land, Labor, and Federal Favor in Twentieth-Century Arkansas.* Charlottesville: University Press of Virginia, 1996.

White, Monica M. *Freedom Farmers: Agricultural Resistance and the Black Freedom Movement.* Chapel Hill: University of North Carolina Press, 2018.

White, Richard. *The Republic for Which It Stands: The United States during Reconstruction and the Gilded Age, 1865-1896.* New York: Oxford University Press, 2017.

White, Ronald C., Jr. *A. Lincoln: A Biography.* New York: Random House, 2010.

White, Steven. *World War II and American Racial Politics: Public Opinion, the Presidency, and Civil Rights Advocacy.* Cambridge: Cambridge University Press, 2019.

White, William S. *Citadel: The Story of the United States Senate.* New York: Harper Collins, 1956.

Whites, LeeAnn, and Alecia P. Long, ed. *Occupied Women: Gender, Military Occupation, and the American Civil War.* Baton Rouge: Louisiana State University Press, 2009.

Wicker, Tom. *JFK and LBJ: The Influence of Personality Upon Politics.* Chicago: Ivan R. Dee, 1968.

Wilkerson, Isabel. *The Warmth of Other Suns: The Epic Story of America's Great Migration.* New York: Random House, 2020.

Wilkinson, J. Harvie, III. *From Brown to Bakke: The Supreme Court and School Integration, 1954-1978.* New York: Oxford University Press, 1979.

Williams, Eric. *Capitalism and Slavery.* Chapel Hill: University of North Carolina Press, 1944.

Williams, Heather Andrea. *Help Me Find My People: The African American Search for Family Lost in Slavery.* Chapel Hill: University of North Carolina Press, 2012.

Williams, Juan. *Eyes on the Prize: America's Civil Rights Years, 1954-1965.* New York: Viking Press, 1987.

Williams, Kidada E. *They Left Great Marks on Me: African American Testimonies of Racial Violence from Emancipation to World War I.* New York: New York University Press, 2022.

Williamson, Joel. *A Rage for Order: Black-White Relations in the American South Since Emancipation.* New York: Oxford University Press, 1986.

Willis, Lee L. *Southern Prohibition: Race, Reform, and Public Life in Middle Florida, 1821-1920.* Athens: University of Georgia Press, 2011.

Winch, Julia. *Between Slavery and Freedom: Free People of Color in America from Settlement to the Civil War.* Lanham, MD: Rowman & Littlefield, 2014.

Wolters, Ronald. *The Burdens of Brown: Thirty Years of School Desegregation.* Knoxville: University Press of Tennessee, 1984.

Wood, Amy Louise. *Lynching and Spectacle: Witnessing Racial Violence in America, 1890 to 1940.* Chapel Hill: University Of North Carolina Press, 2009.

Wood, Betty. *Women's Work, Men's Work: The Informal Slave Economies of Low-country Georgia*. Athens: University of Georgia Press, 1995.

Wood, Gordon. *The Creation of the American Republic, 1776–1787*. Chapel Hill: University of North Carolina Press, 1969.

———. *The Radicalism of the American Revolution*. New York: Alfred A. Knopf, 1992.

Wood, Peter H. *Black Majority: Negroes in Colonial South Carolina from 1670 through the Stono Rebellion*. New York: Alfred A. Knopf, 1974.

Woodruff, Nan Elizabeth. *American Congo: The African American Freedom Struggle in the Delta*. Cambridge, MA: Harvard University Press, 2003.

Woods, Jeff R. *Black Struggle, Red Scare: Segregation and Anti-Communism in the South, 1948–1968*. Baton Rouge: Louisiana State University Press, 2003.

Woodward, C. Vann. *American Counterpoint: Slavery and Racism in the North-South Dialogue*. Boston: Little, Brown and Company, 1971.

———, *Origins of the New South, 1877–1913*. Baton Rouge: Louisiana University Press, 1971.

———. *The Strange Career of Jim Crow*. 3rd ed. New York: Oxford University Press, 1974.

Woodworth, Steven E. *Manifest Destinies: America's Westward Expansion and the Road to the Civil War*. New York: Alfred A. Knopf, 2010.

Work, Monroe N., ed. *Negro Year Book: An Annual Encyclopedia of the Negro, 1937–1938*. Tuskegee, AL: Negro Yearbook Publishing Company/Tuskegee Institute, 1937.

Wright, Gavin. *Old South, New South: Revolutions in the Southern Economy Since the Civil War*. New York: Basic Books, 1986.

———. *Sharing the Prize: The Economics of the Civil Rights Revolution in the American South*. Cambridge, MA: Harvard University Press, 2013.

———. *Slavery and American Economic Development*. Baton Rouge: Louisiana State University Press, 2006.

Yarnell, Allen. *Democrats and Progressives: The 1948 Presidential Election as a Test of Postwar Liberalism*. Berkeley: University of California Press, 1974.

Young, Jeffrey Robert. *Domesticating Slavery: The Master Class in Georgia and South Carolina, 1670–1837*. Chapel Hill: University of North Carolina Press, 1999.

Zangrando, Robert L. *The NAACP Crusade Against Lynching, 1909–1950*. Philadelphia: Temple University Press, 1980.

Zwiers, Maarten. *Senator James Eastland: Mississippi's Jim Crow Democrat*. Baton Rouge: Louisiana State University Press, 2015.

INDEX

1860 presidential election, 13–14, 30–31, 95, 108, 118, 147, 152–57, 162

Abolitionism, 9, 43, 58, 66, 145; and the 1860 presidential election, 31, 95; and Brown's Raid, 19, 29–30, 146–53; and the Constitution, 22–23, 121–31; in the early nineteenth century, 51–55, 113; the emergence of, 6; and Nehemiah Adams, 49; the political threat of, 12–13, 60, 75–76, 83, 85, 88, 90–95, 117–18, 119–20, 152–57; and the Turner Rebellion, 24–26, 53; and westward expansion, 26–29; and William L. Garrison, 23–24
Adams, Nehemiah, 48–49
Africa(ns), 21, 53, 58, 80–92, 95, 102
African Americans, 1, 4–5, 9, 11–12, 81–82, 179, 181, 183; from 1877 to 1945, 62–67, 98–105, 128, 132, 160; in the antebellum South, 24, 29–30, 49–50, 53, 57–60, 83, 88–95, 115, 119, 154; during Civil War and Reconstruction, 33–38, 60–62, 96–97, 146–47; post WWII, 46–47, 68–71, 74–78, 106–11, 133, 141–43, 169
Alabama, 4; and Andrew Moore, 152; and the Birmingham protest, 78; and Clement Clay, 152; and the Confederate capital, 156; and Freedom Rides, 70; and John Sparkman, 46, 173 and Lister Hill, 138–40, 173
Amalgamation, 93–95, 103–7
American Revolution, 18–19, 23–25, 32, 113–14, 117, 138–40
American Slavery, American Freedom (Morgan), 115
Antislavery movement: and 1850s manifestations of, 90, 92, 95, 123–24, 127; Abraham Lincoln, 153; and Brown's Raid, 29–32, 150; in the Colonial and Revolutionary eras, 19, 23, 25; early nineteenth-century manifestations of, 52–53, 60; expansion of, 21
Arbery, Ahamoud, 1
Arkansas: and George McClellan, 68, 139; integration of, 70, 168, 175; and Orval Faubus, 168; and William J. Fulbright, 68, 72, 165
Army of Northern Virginia, 111
Articles of Confederation, 19
Atlanta, GA, 2

Bacon's Rebellion, 17–18
Bailey, Josiah, 131
Barnett, Ross, 168

Beecher, Henry Ward, 149
Berkeley, William, 18
Bible, 12, 85, 101, 120
Bilbo, Theodore G.: and antilynching laws, 131, 140; and poll taxes, 132–33; and *Take Your Choice*, 99; and WWII, 43
Billings, MT, 109
Birmingham, AL: protests, 78, 169
Black Belt, 4
Black Codes, 34–35, 37, 97
"Black Republican," 119, 148, 154
Bledsoe, Albert T.: and the Constitution, 119; and threats of emancipation, 64; and paternalism, 50, 56; and upliftment, 83
Bourbons, 38, 97
Boston, MA, 49
Breckinridge, John, 30
Britain, 18–19, 139
Brown v. Board of Education, 2, 5, 13–14, 43–44, 70, 75, 103–4, 160–66, 170, 172, 174–75, 180–83
Brown II, 13, 162–64
Brown, John, 13–14, 29–30, 44, 147–52
Bruce, Philip, 64
Butler, A. P., 28, 57–59
Butler, Roderick Randum, 150
Byrd, Harry F.: and Civil Rights Act of 1964, 139, 173; and government, 110, 135; and massive resistance, 161–63, 169; and race, 105–6
Byrd, Robert, 101
Byrnes, James F.: and antilynching, 66, 131; and anti-South sentiment, 41

Calhoun, John C., 155; comments on slavery by, 57; concurrent majority/ dual presidency, 13, 120–27; and *Exposition and Protest*, 37; and liberty, 116; referenced in civil rights debate, 135–36, 181; and slippery slope, 131
Canaanites, 85, 101

Capitalism, 18, 25–27, 54–55
Cartwright, Samuel A., 93
Cash, Wilbur, 11, 46
Charlotte, NC, 2
Chesnut, Mary, 94
Christian Life Commission, 75
Christianity: and *Brown v. Board*, 75; and Martin Luther King, Jr., 170; and paternalism and, 56, 81; and upliftment and, 81, 85–87; and William L. Garrison, 23
Citizens' Council, 103–4, 107, 168, 170–71
Citizens' Council of Greater New Orleans, 171
Civil Rights Act of 1875, 37
Civil Rights Act of 1957, 175
Civil Rights Act of 1960, 77
Civil Rights Act of 1964, 45–46, 108–9, 137–40, 172–75, 181
Civil Rights Cases (1883), 37
Civil War, 150; and impact on race relations, 9–11, 34, 36–39, 64, 98, 127–29, 146–47, 183; and military conflict, 2, 5–6, 158; and memory of, 15, 45–46, 70, 111, 134, 160, 163, 166, 172; and slavery, 59–60, 62, 66
Clay, Clement, 152
Clingman, Thomas, 153, 155
Cold War, 43, 169
Compromise of 1850, 27, 122–23
Compromise of 1877, 36, 97
Concurrent majority, 13, 124–27
Connally, Tom, 66, 68
Connor, Eugene "Bull," 78
Confederacy of Six Nations, 125
Confederate States of America, 6, 15, 31, 36, 60–61, 147, 153–60, 172
Conservatism, 8, 16, 36–37, 128, 149
Constitution, 5, 12–16, 181–83; and antebellum interpretations of, 27, 29; and civil rights debate reference to, 8, 134–38, 140–43, 172–73; and poll taxes, 42, 132–34; secession and, 31–32, 154, 158–59; segregation and, 37,

44–45, 75, 78, 104, 163, 166; slavery and, 19–22, 59, 92, 112–30, 181–83
Cotton, 17, 25–26, 55, 115
Cotton gin, 17, 115
Crittenden Compromise, 156

Daily Courier (Louisville), 152
Daily Crescent (New Orleans), 151, 153
Davis, Jefferson: as president of the Confederate States of America, 158; as senator, 31, 58–59, 90, 118, 155–59
Declaration of Independence, 139, 184
De jure segregation, 15, 41, 43, 172
Dees, James P., 102
Deliver Us from Evil (Ford), 25
Democratic Party: and antebellum era, 28; and Bourbons, 38, 97, 146, 159–60; and civil rights in the twentieth century, 46, 139, 165; and election of 1860, 30; and Reconstruction, 61; and the Solid South, 73
Dew, Thomas R.: and God and slavery, 85; and liberty and slavery, 115–16; and paternalism, 50–51; and the Turner Rebellion, 51; and upliftment, 83
Double V Campaign, 42
Douglass, Frederick, 151
Douglas, Stephen, 30
Doxey, Wall, 132
Dual presidency, 124–26

Early National Period, 114, 118
Early Republic, 113
Eastland, James, 174; and the Civil Rights Act of 1964, 137–38; and the Voting Rights Act of 1965, 141–43
Eisenhower, Dwight, 169
Ellender, Allen: and *Brown v. Board*, 162, 166–67; and the Constitution, 135; and race, 65, 69, 76–77, 106
Elliott, E. N., 82
Ellsworth, John, 20
Emancipation Proclamation, 4, 96

Episcopal, 102
Ervin, Sam: and *Brown v. Board*, 161; and the Civil Rights Act of 1964, 137, 173–74; and the Constitution, 135, 142; and race, 101, 109; and Southern Manifesto, 164–65
Estes, Matthew: and the abolitionist movement, 52–53; and the constitution, 116; and perceptions of race, 80, 82, 88; and proslavery arguments, 25
Exposition and Protest (Calhoun), 37, 121

Faubus, Orval, 168
FEPC, 134
Fifteenth Amendment, 61, 105, 142
Filibuster, 14; and the Civil Rights Act of 1957, 175; and the Civil Rights Act of 1960, 77; and the Civil Rights Act of 1964, 139, 141, 172–75; and *Pursuit of Unity*, 3; and the Wagner-Van Nuys Antilynching Bill, 131
Fire-eaters, 31, 60, 82, 120, 127, 150, 159, 162, 164
First Emancipation, 19
Fitzhugh, George: and liberty and slavery, 57; and paternalism, 115; and slippery slope, 119–20, 130
Ford, Lacy, 25
Florida: and the Civil War, 158–59; Claude Pepper, 67, 104; Spessard Holland, 103, 143; Stephen Mallory, 157; Zephanian Kingsley, 50
Floyd, George, 1
Floyd, John, 24
Fort Pickens, 158
Fort Sumter, 159
Founding Fathers: and the Constitution, 19–20, 48, 112–13; and proslavery use, 12–13, 112–17, 120, 125; and prosegregation use, 13, 37, 43, 113–14, 130, 133, 138–39, 141
Fourteenth Amendment, 37, 61, 105

Franklin, Benjamin, 19
Freedmen, 5, 7, 33–36, 61–64, 90, 97, 146
Free soil movement, 29, 92, 98
Freedom Rides, 70
Fugitive slaves, 27, 153, 158
Fulbright, J. William: and Freedom Rides (1961), 70; and Little Rock, 70, 72; and moderation of, 72; and Southern Manifesto, 165, 181

Gabriel's Rebellion, 53
Garrison, William L., 23–24, 29, 49, 75
Genesis, 85
George III, 125
George, Walter: and the Constitution, 42; and poll taxes, 42; Southern Manifesto, 164
Georgia: and Alfred Iverson, 151, 157; and Herman Talmadge, 102, 135; and Richard Russell, 13, 45, 69, 77, 105–6, 109, 131, 140, 164, 171–72, 182; and Savannah, 49; and Walter George, 42, 164
Gore, Albert, Sr.: and *Brown v. Board*, 161–62; and civil rights, 73, 104; Southern Manifesto, 165–66
Graham, Frank, 104
Grayson, William J., 83
Great Depression, 129–30
Great Migration, 40–41
Great Society, 130

Ham, the curse of, 85, 101–2
Hammond, James Henry: and capitalism, 53–56; and the Constitution, 120; and content slaves, 49–50, 84; and miscegenation, 94; and Mudsill class, 57–60; and slave revolts, 53–54; and upliftment, 81, 84
Harpers Ferry, 13, 29–30, 44, 147–48
Harper, William: and Christianity and slavery, 85; and perceptions of the enslaved, 92; and slave treatment, 51–52; and upliftment, 80

Hayne, Robert Y.: and the Constitution, 117–18; and liberty and slavery, 116
Helena, MT, 109
Hill, Lister: and the Civil Rights Act of 1964, 138–40, 173; and FEPC, 134
Hobbes, Thomas, 81
Hodge, Charles, 87–88
Hoffman, Frederick, 63
Holland, Spessard, 103, 143
House of Representatives 21–22, 38
Humphreys, Benjamin G.: and Reconstruction race relations, 34

Imperialism, 8–9, 22, 26–27, 33, 85, 89, 127
Indentured servants, 17–19
Individual rights: and coded narrative and segregation, 8, 11, 47, 74, 128–29, 132, 134–35, 140–41; and the constitution, 21–22; and post–Jim Crow outlook, 15–16, 73, 183; slavery and, 26, 117
Interposition, 14, 45, 121, 163, 165–68, 174
Irrepressible conflict, 148, 150
Iverson, Alfred, 151, 156–57

Jackson, Andrew, 124
Jefferson, Thomas: and the Constitution, 119; and Kentucky and Virginia Resolutions, 37; and memory of, 139; and Missouri controversy, 22, 27
Jim Crow. *See* Segregation
Johnson, Andrew, 35–36
Johnson, Lyndon B.: and Great Society, 130; and Southern Manifesto, 165
Johnston, Olin: and *Brown v. Board*, 161–62; and the Civil Rights Act of 1964, 108, 137

Kansas-Nebraska Act, 28, 57, 119
Kentucky and Virginia Resolutions, 37
King Cotton, 115
King, Martin Luther, Jr., 169–70

Index

Kingsley, Zephaniah, Jr., 50
Kruse, Kevin, 182–83
Ku Klux Klan, 97

Lee, George Avery, 74–75
Lee, Robert E., 111, 172
Liberator, The, 23–24
Lincoln, Abraham: and the 1860 presidential election, 13–14, 30–31, 95–96, 108, 147, 152–55, 163; and Emancipation Proclamation, 4, 96; inauguration of, 157–58, 162; and Republican Party, 31, 46, 154–55; and slavery, 30–31; and war, 158–59
Literacy tests, 38, 133
Little Rock Central High School, 70, 169
Long, Russell: and the Civil Rights Act of 1964, 108–9, 138–39; perceptions of the South, 69; and race, 66, 100, 106–7
Lost Cause, 15, 45, 86, 111, 171–72
Louisiana, 2: and Allen Ellender, 65–66, 69, 76, 106, 135, 166; and Citizens' Council, 171; Protestantism, 74–75; Russell Long, 66, 69, 100, 106–7, 108, 139; Thomas Moore, 152
Louisiana Purchase, 22
Lynching, 41–42, 66–67, 97, 104, 131–32, 140, 160, 171, 178

Madison, James, 37, 140
Mallory, Stephen, 157
Manifest Destiny, 27, 85
Market Revolution, 26
Mason-Dixon Line, 17, 30, 39, 62, 75–76, 91–92, 98, 103, 109, 117–18, 123, 140, 149, 155, 183
Massachusetts, 23, 48
Massive resistance, 8, 14, 44, 105, 107, 162–75, 180–83
McClellan, George: and Civil Rights Act of 1964, 139; perceptions of race, 68
McWillie, William: and Compromise of 1850, 28

Memoir on Slavery (Harper), 85
Mexican War, 27, 52
Mind of the South (Cash), 46
Miscegenation, 93–95, 103–7
Mississippi: and Benjamin G. Humphreys, 34; and J. B. Thrasher, 87; and James Eastland, 137, 141–42, 174; and Jefferson Davis, 31, 90, 155; and John Pettus, 152; and John Stennis, 143, 164; and Ross Barnett, 168; and Theodore Bilbo, 43, 99, 131–32, 133; and Wall Doxey, 132; and William McWillie, 28; and vagrancy laws, 34
Missouri Compromise, 22, 26–27, 59, 123
"modern racial ideology," 8, 40
Montana, 109
Montgomery, AL, 156
Moore, Andrew, 152
Moore, Thomas, 152
Mordan, Edmund, 115
Mudsill theory, 57–58, 62, 84, 116–16

NAACP, 41, 66, 131
Natural law/rights, 15, 61, 101, 103, 120
New Deal, 14, 42, 46, 129, 136
New South, 3, 6–7, 9, 37, 44, 63–66, 70, 130, 167, 171
New York, NY, 58, 148–49
New York Democratic Vigilance Association, 148
New York Times, The, 149
Nixon, Richard, 8, 135
Noah, 85
North Carolina: Frank Graham, 104; James P. Dees, 102; Josiah Bailey, 131; Sam Ervin, 101, 135, 161, 164, 173; Thomas Clingman, 153–54; and Republican Party presence in, 38; and Secession and, 159
Nullification, 45, 121–22, 124, 163, 165

Obama, Barack, 2
Old South, 3, 6–7, 9, 13–14, 36–37, 45,

Old South (*continued*)
63–67, 70, 72, 78, 94, 111, 133, 135, 162–65, 167, 169, 171, 178
Old Testament, 85
Onuf, Peter, 21

Paternalism, 10, 51, 53–56, 63–66
Pepper, Claude: and antilynching, 67; and moderation of, 104
Perman, Michael, 3
Perpetual union, 127, 129, 157–58
Pettus, John, 152
Philadelphia, PA, 20, 59, 118
Phillips, Wendell, 149
Pinckney, Charles, 22, 55, 59
Plain folk, 32
Planter, 18, 32, 34, 50, 58, 145–46, 159
Plessy v. Ferguson, 37, 98–99
Poll tax, 38, 42, 132–34, 160
Pollard, Edward, 86–87
Popular sovereignty, 27, 30
Populist Party, 38
Presbyterian, 88
Priest, Josiah, 93
Princeton Theological Seminary, 87
Progressive period, 128
Property rights: and abolitionists, 95, 128; African Americans and, 34, 87; and coded narrative, 8, 73, 134–35, 138, 140–41; and the Constitution, 12, 21–23, 118–19, 123; and fugitive slaves, 27; and influence on secession, 30, 156; postsegregation, 16, 47, 183; and slavery, 18, 91
Proto-Dorian-convention, 11
Pursuit of Unity (Perman), 3

Race consciousness, 102–3
Racialist ideology, 10–11, 39, 41, 63, 80, 104, 108
Reconstruction, 2, 5–7, 36–37, 38, 61–63, 97–98, 108, 111, 146, 159–60, 173
Radical Republicans, 35–37, 61, 97
Republican ideology, 19–20, 22, 32, 112, 117, 125

Republican Party, 180, 182; and Abraham Lincoln, 6, 30, 147, 152–54; and antislavery sentiment, 6, 29–30, 92; and "Black Republicanism," 119, 148, 151–59; and Brown's Raid, 148–49, 152; and John Tower, 72–73; and populists, 39; and Reconstruction, 35–37, 61, 146, 159; and Southern Strategy, 72–73; and territorial expansion, 29–30, 92, 156; and twentieth-century southern hatred of, 46
Retrogression, 11, 38, 70, 89, 92–99
Richmond Examiner, 95
Robertson, A. Willis, 134, 142
Roman Republic, 125
Roosevelt, Franklin, 129
Ruffin, Edmund, 82, 120, 127
Russell, Richard B.: and antilynching, 131; and the Civil Rights Act of 1960, 77; and the Civil Rights Act of 1964, 45, 109–11, 140–41, 181–82; and the Constitution, 13, 182; and Lost Cause, 173; and poll taxes, 132–33; and race, 69–70, 105–9; and slippery slope, 130–32, 171–72; and Southern Manifesto, 164
Rutledge, John, 20

San Domingue, 24
Savannah, GA, 49
Savage ideal, 46
School of Civilization, 11, 63, 66, 70, 106
Secession, 6, 9, 13, 22, 29, 30–35, 44–35 60, 78, 97, 117, 127, 146, 152, 155–59, 162–63, 167–68, 180, 183
Second slavery, 25
Segregation, 3–5, 7, 9–12, 14–16, 17, 48, 50, 85, 112–14, 146–47, 178–83; and the constitution, 127–41; in the early twentieth century, 41–43, 65–68; and Emergence of, 36–40, 61–65, 98–99; post-*Brown*, 43–47, 69–79, 146–47, 160–62, 164, 167–76; and racism, 99–111

Senate, 72, 104, 182; and balance of slave and free state in, 26; and Civil Rights Act of 1964, 172–75; Constitution and, 21–22; and prosegregation comments in, 69, 100, 131, 140; and proslavery comments in, 57–58, 122, 155–57; and seniority in, 38; and Southern Manifesto, 164–66
"separate but equal," 37, 45, 64, 65, 68, 147
Siege mentality, 7, 9, 123, 126, 181, 184
Silent majority, 169–70
Simms, William Gilmore, 49, 81
Sit-in movement, 77
Slavery, 3, 5–10, 12–16, 34, 37–38, 40, 47, 61–64, 72, 75, 79, 101, 105–11, 170, 178, 181, 183; and alleged Social value of, 56–60; as cause of Civil War, 29–33, 146, 148, 150–59, 163, 170; in the Colonial era, 17–19; and the Constitution, 19–22, 112–20, 122–29, 135; and racial inferiority of, 48–56, 80–99; and revolts, 23–25, 53; and westward expansion, 22–23, 26–29
Slippery slope: civil rights reforms and, 128–29, 133, 138, 160; described, 120; and John C. Calhoun, 122, 124; and Richard Russell, 171; and Strom Thurmond, 136
Smith, Ellison "Cotton Ed," 42, 132
Smith v. Allwright (1944), 160
Social Darwinism, 62, 99
South Carolina, 2; and A. P. Butler, 28, 57; and Charles Pinckney, 22, 59; and in the Colonial era, 18; and Edmund Ruffin, 120; and Ellison "Cotton Ed" Smith, 42, 132; and Fort Sumter, 155; and James Byrnes, 41, 66, 131; and James H. Hammond, 49, 54, 58; and John C. Calhoun, 13, 57, 116, 120–25; and John Rutledge, 20; and Olin Johnston, 108, 137, 161; and Robert Y. Hayne, 116; and Secession of, 152, 154–55; and South Carolina Society for the Advancement of Learning, 80;

and Strom Thurmond, 163, 174; and vagrancy laws, 34; and William G. Simms, 49; and William Harper, 51
South Carolina Society for the Advancement of Learning, 80
Southern Baptist Convention, 75
Southern Manifesto, 163–66, 169, 181
Southern strategy, 8, 73, 135
"Southern way of life," 7, 17, 25, 36, 37, 77, 128, 160, 180
Sparkman, John, 46, 173
Spencer, Herbert, 62
States' rights, 6, 16, 37, 44, 127, 129, 132–33, 163, 180
Stephens, Alexander, 156
Stennis, John, 143, 164
Stringfellow, Thornton, 86–87
Stowe, Harriet Beecher, 49, 57
Suburban, 15–16, 134, 141, 176, 182–83
Supreme Court, 114; and *Brown v. Board*, 70, 160–61, 166; and Christian Life Commission, 75; and *Plessy v. Ferguson*, 128; and *Smith v. Allwright*, 160

Take Your Choice (Bilbo), 99
Talmadge, Herman: and the Constitution and, 135; as Georgia's governor, 164; race and, 102–3
Tariff, 118, 121–22
Television, 42, 77–78, 179
Texas: and John Tower, 72–73, 137; and Lyndon Johnson, 165; and Tom Connally, 66, 68
Textile industry, 26, 55
Taylor, Breonna, 1
Taylor, Richard, 36
Tennessee: and Albert Gore, 73, 104, 161, 165–66; and Republican Party in, 38; and Roderick Random Butler, 150–51
Thirteenth Amendment, 111
Thrasher, J. B., 87, 89
Thurmond, Strom: and the Civil Rights Act of 1957, 175; and Civil Rights Act of 1964, 174–76; and lack of southern

Thurmond, Strom (*continued*)
  resolve, 136–37; and race, 107; and Southern Manifesto, 163; and the Voting Rights Act of 1965, 142
Till, Emmett, 77
Times-Picayune (New Orleans), 147, 150
Tower, John, 72–73, 137–38
Transatlantic slave trade, 20, 114, 118
Trescott, William, 117
Turner, Frederick Jackson, 27
Turner, Nat, 24–25, 51, 53
Tuskegee Institute, 178

Uncle Tom's Cabin (Stowe), 49, 57
Upliftment, 82–87

Vagrancy laws, 34–35
Vesey, Denmark, 53
Vetter, C. E., 171
Virginia: and Bacon's Rebellion, 17–18; and Brown's Raid, 148; and the Colonial era, 17–18; and George Fitzhugh, 57; and Harry Byrd, 105, 135, 139, 161, 173; and integration of, 167, 175; and John Floyd, 24; and Philip Bruce, 64; and secession of, 159; and slaves in, 81; and the Turner Slave Rebellion, 24; Voting Rights Act of 1965, 46, 141–43; and William Berkeley, 18; and Willis Robertson, 134

Wagner-Van Nuys Anti-Lynching Bill, 131
War of 1812, 121
Warren, Robert Penn, 40
Washington, DC: and the Civil War, 4; and federal authority in the antebellum era, 116, 121, 154, 180; and federal Authority in the segregation era, 36, 103, 110, 133, 139, 161; and southern politicians 14, 41–42, 46, 70, 136, 138–39, 166, 171, 174–75
Webster-Hayne Debate, 118
West Virginia, 101
Westward expansion, 21, 26, 90, 127
Whig Party, 28
White flight, 47, 176, 182–83
"White supremacy," 17; in the American West, 29; in the antebellum era, 94–96; and current events, 1–2; historiography and, 2–3; Reconstruction restoration of, 37, 39, 61–62, 97; segregation and, 9–10, 43–44, 64, 70–71, 74, 102, 105, 134, 160, 166
White, Walter, 131
Wilmot, Davis, 27
Woodward, C. Vann, 5
World War I, 40–41, 128
World War II, 4, 14, 42–43, 67, 132, 134

Yeoman, 32